POOR RELIEF OR POOR DEAL?

Trevor Buck

To Barbara, Ted, Ben, Jonathan and Simon

Roger S. Smith

To Maggie, Emma, Claire and Daniel

Poor Relief or Poor Deal?

The social fund, safety nets and social security

Edited by

TREVOR BUCK and ROGER S. SMITH
University of Leicester, UK

ASHGATE

Published by
Ashgate Publishing Limited
Gower House
Croft Road
Aldershot
Hampshire GU11 3HR
England

Ashgate Publishing Company
Suite 420
101 Cherry Street
Burlington, VT 05401-4405
USA

Ashgate website: http://www.ashgate.com

British Library Cataloguing in Publication Data
Poor relief or poor deal? : the social fund, safety nets
   and social security. - (Studies in cash and care)
   1. Public welfare - Great Britain 2. Public welfare
   administration - Great Britain 3. Public welfare - Europe -
   Cross-cultural studies 4. Public welfare - Great Britain -
   Evaluation
   I. Buck, Trevor II. Smith, Roger S. 1948-
   361.6'5'0941

Library of Congress Cataloging-in-Publication Data
Poor relief or poor deal? : the social fund, safety nets, and social security / edited by
   Trevor Buck and Roger S. Smith.
       p. cm. -- (Studies in cash & care)
   Includes bibliographical references and index.
   ISBN 0-7546-3335-7
       1. Income maintenance programs. 2. Public welfare. 3. Income maintenance
   programs--Great Britain. 4. Public welfare--Great Britain. I. Buck, Trevor. II. Smith,
   Roger S. III. Cash & care.

HV51.P66 2003
362.5'82'0941--dc21   2002043956

ISBN 0 7546 3335 7

Printed and bound in Great Britain by MPG Books Ltd, Bodmin, Cornwall

Contents

PART III: THE PROSPECTS FOR REFORM

List of Tables

List of Abbreviations

ADSS	Association of Directors of Social Services
ASSEDIC	Association pour l'Emploi dans l'Industrie et le Commerce
BAS	Bureaux de l'Aide Sociale
BL	Budgeting Loan
CAB	Citizens' Advice Bureau
CASU	Commission d'Action Sociale d'Urgence
CCG	Community Care Grant
CL	Crisis Loan
CNAF	Caisse Nationale des Allocations Familiales
CPAG	Child Poverty Action Group
DWP	Department of Work and Pensions
ECA	Exceptional Circumstances Addition
ENP	Exceptional Needs Payment
FUS	Fonds d'Urgence Sociale
FWA	Family Welfare Association
HBAI	Households Below Average Earnings
IBJSA	Income Based Job Seekers Allowance
IRS	Independent Review Service
IS	Income Support
JSA	Job Seekers Allowance
NAB	National Assistance Board
NACAB	National Association of Citizens' Advice Bureaux
NGO	Non-Governmental Organisation
OECD	Organisation for Economic Cooperation and Development
PCSW	Public Centres for Social Welfare
RMI	Revenu Minimum d'Insertion
RO	Reviewing Officer
SB	Supplementary Benefit
SBC	Supplementary Benefits Commission
SFC	Social Fund Commissioner
SFI	Social Fund Inspector
SFO	Social Fund Officer
SSAC	Social Security Advisory Committee
UAB	Unemployment Assistance Board
UNP	Urgent Needs Payments
WFTC	Working Families Tax Credit

List of Contributors

Trevor Buck (co-editor)

Faculty of Law, University of Leicester. He was formerly legal adviser to the Social Fund Commissioner (1993-96) and is the author of a legal textbook on the social fund. He is the course director of a social welfare law Masters degree and a member of the executive committee of the Socio-Legal Studies Association. His teaching and research interests lie in the field of social welfare law, administrative law and socio-legal methodology. He was the co-organiser (with Roger Smith) of the conference 'Reforming the Social Fund' held in Leicester in November 2001 which prompted the production of this volume.

Sharon Collard

Research Fellow, Personal Finance Research Centre, University of Bristol. Her main research interests are: access to financial services among low-income households and the provision and quality of money advice services. Sharon is currently working on a number of projects including a study of pawnbroking and payday loans in the UK, the use of community select committees to evaluate policy initiatives and an evaluation of the government's saving gateway pilot schemes. Recent publications include: Kempson, E., Collard, S. and Taylor, S. (2002) *Exploring Social Fund use among older people*, Corporate Document Services, Leeds; Collard, S. and Burrows, B. (2002) *Good, Bad and Indifferent: the quality of money advice services in Scotland*, Monday Advice, Scotland; Collard, S., Kempson, E., and Whyley, C. (2001) *Tackling Financial Exclusion: an area based approach*, Policy Press, Bristol; and Whyley, C., Collard, S. and Kempson, E. (2000) *Saving and Borrowing: Use of the Social Fund Budgeting Loan Scheme and Community Credit Unions*, DSS Research Report Number 125, Corporate Document Services, Leeds.

Gary Craig

Professor of Social Justice at the University of Hull, UK, President of the International Association for Community Development, and an Academician of the Academy of Learned Societies in the Social Sciences. Prior to returning to academic life in 1988, he worked in a series of large-scale community development projects. His research interests include poverty and inequality, race and 'ethnicity', community development, children and young people and local governance. Recent books include *Community Empowerment* (with Marjorie Mayo, Zed Books, 1995) and *International Social Policy* (with Pete Alcock, Palgrave, 2000).

Anne Daguerre

A researcher at the University of Kent, Canterbury, School of Social Policy, Sociology and Social Research. She is currently working with Peter Taylor-Gooby on an EU funded research project, *Welfare Reform and the Management of Societal Change*. Her recent research interests include employment policies, family policy and social assistance policies in a comparative perspective (especially between Europe and the US). Her recent publications include "La protection de l'enfance en France et en Angleterre 1980-1989" l'Harmattan, Paris, 1999, "Policy Networks in England and France: The Case of Child Care Policy 1980-1989" *Journal of European Public Policy*, vol. 7 no. 2, 2000, and "La réforme de l'aide sociale aux Etats-Unis: modèle ou repoussoir?", in *La Revue Française de Droit Sanitaire et Social*, no. 3, 2001, Dalloz.

Jacqueline Davidson

Currently undertaking a PhD on the nature of exceptional need payments within social assistance schemes in Britain and the Netherlands. She is based at the Centre for Comparative Research in Social Welfare, at the University of Stirling. Her substantive areas of interest include social security, poverty, and consumption and consumer society.

Anja Declercq

A post-doctoral researcher at the University of Leuven (Belgium), Department of Sociology, Unit of Sociology of Social Policy and guest-professor at the University of Gent (Belgium), Department of Population Studies and Social Science Research Methods. She teaches both courses in the sociology of social policy and in qualitative methodology. Her current research interests are care for the elderly, with a specialisation in care for people suffering from dementia, and the sociology of social service organisations.

Koen Hermans

A research-assistant at the University of Leuven (Belgium), Department of Sociology, Unit of Sociology of Social Policy. He is preparing a PhD about the implementation of activation policies for Minimex beneficiaries in Belgium. His research interests are activation policies in Europe, social assistance in Belgium, and the experiences of young social assistance claimants.

Beth Lakhani

A welfare rights adviser based in the Citizens Rights Office of Child Poverty Action Group, London. She has been involved in work relating to the discretionary social fund since its introduction in 1988 and led a workshop on reform of the social fund at the Leicester conference on the social fund in November 2001. She gave evidence to the Social Security Select Committee examining the future of the social fund. Her other areas of particular interest are the rights to benefits of asylum seekers and others from abroad and the Government's new tax credits scheme. She trains on welfare rights and helps to lobby for policies relating to social security and tax credit law. She also contributes to CPAG handbooks.

Corinne Nativel

A researcher in the School of Earth Sciences and Geography at Kingston University. She is also a research associate at the CERVL-Pouvoir, Action Publique, Territoire of the Institut d'Etudes Politiques de Bordeaux. She was previously employed as a consultant to the Organisation for Economic Co-operation and Development in Paris, a research assistant at the University of Edinburgh, and a lecturer in European Studies at the University of Wolverhampton. Corinne gained her PhD in 2000 from the Institute for German Studies, University of Birmingham for a thesis on 'Economic Transition, Unemployment and Active Labour Market Policy: Lessons and Perspectives from the East German Bundesländer', published by the Birmingham University Press in 2002. She has written a dozen articles and book chapters on the spatial and policy dimensions of employment and welfare restructuring and is currently working on an ESRC project investigating lone parenthood and paid work in rural England.

Mike Rowe

A lecturer at Nottingham Business School, Nottingham Trent University. Mike was a civil servant in the Department of Social Security before becoming an academic. His PhD thesis, *Public Accountability: understanding through the accounts of others*, informs his contribution to this volume. His current research interests include participation in public services and the governance of regeneration and other area based initiatives.

Roger S. Smith (co-editor)

School of Social Work, University of Leicester. Dr Roger Smith has had a varied career as Computer Programmer, Residential Social Worker, Probation Officer, Youth Justice Manager, Head of Policy for a voluntary organisation, and academic. He is currently Course Director for the MA in Social Work at the University of Leicester. He has also held senior positions in local government as Chair of Social Services and Education Committees, and he has chaired the Children's Play Council. He has researched and written on the subjects of children's welfare, poverty and rights, and he has published research into the Social Fund on several occasions since its implementation. He was the co-organiser (with Trevor Buck) of the conference 'Reforming the Social Fund' held in Leicester in November 2001 which prompted the production of this volume.

Introduction

Poverty and the Social Fund

The context for this book is set for us by the continuing prevalence of poverty. It remains a widespread and debilitating phenomenon, even in advanced and wealthy societies. For those affected, the problem is compounded when unforeseen events or significant transitions impose an extra burden on their already severely limited budgets. In this book, we aim to explore the consequences for those in poverty of the mechanisms put in place by the state to deal with the hardship arising from these unpredictable circumstances.

The social fund in the UK, like its equivalents in other countries, represents a relatively small fraction of government expenditure on social assistance. Despite this, the specific position which schemes of this nature occupy is of considerable importance, precisely because they do profess to offer help in situations of extreme financial hardship and personal stress. This is so for at least two reasons. Firstly, to the extent to which they do relieve need, schemes which provide exceptional cash help have a practical impact which significantly outweighs their immediate cash value; they have the capacity to provide safeguards against disastrous outcomes for individuals and families. Their ability to provide a 'bridge' over an immediate cash shortfall, and to create the conditions for continuing security and stability, should not be underestimated. In addition, however, exceptional payment schemes like the social fund, targeted at the most disadvantaged members of society, convey strong and significant messages about how 'society' itself believes that the poor should be treated. For instance, recurrent questions about the extent to which certain categories of people in poverty are to be deemed 'deserving' or 'undeserving' are effectively decided by the manner and extent to which their needs are met when they turn to the state for help in a crisis. In short, the social fund, and comparable schemes elsewhere, demonstrate explicitly 'what we think of the poor'. This message is conveyed both in the extent to which needs are met, that is, how generous the provision is, and in the manner in which help is made available, that is how well recipients are treated by administrative systems. For these reasons, then, an exploration of the origins, development, rationale, and delivery of exceptional payments mechanisms will illustrate quite clearly some key areas of concern about the extent to which the rights of those dependent on state relief are firstly recognised, and then met.

The Structure of the Book

The book is divided into three parts in order to provide a framework for our exploration, covering first the background and ideas which inform the social fund and other social assistance measures, secondly the administration and delivery of exceptional cash help, and finally the questions of how and to what extent reforms might be needed.

Part one: the historical and political context

In Chapter 1, Craig begins by reflecting on the antecedents of the social fund, demonstrating that such schemes have been in place in the UK for at least fifty years, and that they have typically been found to be problematic for a number of reasons. These are shown to revolve around questions of sufficiency, fairness, the use of discretion, and the quality of delivery. For example, the recurrent question of the 'trade off' between guaranteed entitlements and targeted discretion in the construction and provision of single payment schemes emerges as a recurrent, and unresolved, theme.

That these are questions with an international dimension is demonstrated by Hermans and Declercq's evaluation in Chapter 2 of Belgium's highly localised resource for meeting additional needs, represented by the Public Centres for Social Welfare. It becomes clear from this Chapter that these are substantially different in character from the highly centralised and closely circumscribed exercise of discretion which characterises the UK setting. The Belgian experience also highlights a series of further dilemmas, however, such as fairness (as between localities which may operate different decision-making regimes), accountability, bias, and the role of those responsible for administering schemes, which becomes more susceptible to localised influence.

Chapter 3, which deals with the establishment and initial experience of the social fund, picks up the themes emerging from the previous Chapters, demonstrating that, as established, a number of significant defects have become evident. The overarching constraint seems to be the very limited budget made available nationally to meet exceptional needs. Within this context, and perhaps as a result of the distorting impact of resource constraints, the machinery for delivering the various elements of the discretionary social fund are shown to be both flawed and inefficient. The additional factor which represents a significant innovation here has been the introduction of loans as a means of assisting people to meet pressing financial needs. Craig questions the value of this policy development, which appears to have the effect of reducing households to living below 'the poverty line', during the period in which they are making repayments on what are, in effect, cash advances.

In Chapter 4, Smith examines the emergence of the social fund, the role of loans, and subsequent reforms, are examined for their political and ideological implications. The aim is to identify what messages can be drawn from the shape of exceptional payment schemes for wider themes in the context of state welfare such as rights and social justice. Tracing the transition from the treatment of those seeking extra help from the status of 'claimants', through being classified as 'applicants' with the introduction of the social fund, to being described as 'customers', this Chapter addresses the question as to whether the reforms introduced by New Labour can, indeed, be equated with the achievement of a 'third way' in the delivery of extra cash help to those in poverty.

Part two: meeting exceptional needs in practice

The second part of the book shifts the focus somewhat, in order to consider the direct impact of exceptional payment schemes on those who make use of them. Chapter 5 introduces the 'user perspective' by evaluating previous research and policy analyses which provide accounts of the experiences of many of those who have sought to get help from the social fund since its introduction. These accounts paint a consistently bleak picture of poor and sometimes downright hostile treatment, complexity and confusion, which have lead ultimately in a great number of cases to a manifest failure on the part of the social fund to meet needs which have been clearly demonstrated. These accounts, in themselves, pose some important challenges for those who are responsible for making and implementing policy in this area. As yet, Smith concludes, little progress has been made in this respect.

Chapter 6 explores similar territory, in the sense that it addresses the nature of transactions between those who seek help from the social fund and those who administer it. Rowe finds that this is often an uncomfortable experience for officials, who are in the position of managing demand in the context of an inadequate budget and arbitrary rules. It becomes clear that those who are often dismissed as heartless bureaucrats are revealed as experiencing very similar frustrations and sometimes anger in attempting to carry out their duties. Their 'on the job' analysis of the social fund's shortcomings complements the evidence of the previous Chapter effectively.

A comparative approach is taken by Davidson in Chapter 7, drawing on research undertaken both in the UK and the Netherlands. Certain similarities between the two administrations are observed, notably in the application of moral judgements to assess the worthiness or otherwise of those seeking exceptional cash help, and in a similar orientation towards a 'welfare to work' philosophy. However, whilst this is seen to result in a paternalistic model of supportive intervention in the Netherlands, in the UK, decisions are much more narrowly based in 'managerial' judgements about spreading limited funds as widely as possible in the form of a (minimal) safety net for the most needy. As a consequence, the social fund appears to operate rather at odds with the broader social inclusion strategy of the UK government.

In Chapter 8, the question of administrative (or process) rights is considered further, in order to explore more fully the issue of applicants' ability to seek redress when their claims are refused. Buck outlines the contribution made by the social fund review system; a unique system of legal redress in administrative law. This was a further controversial element of the social fund when first introduced in 1988 and appeared to contradict existing orthodoxies about appeal rights. The origins and current review processes and practice are examined and the Chapter concludes with reflections on the wider importance of the review mechanism and a call to develop more sophisticated forms of accessible and 'systemic' justice in the social security field.

Part three: the prospects for reform

The final part of the book seeks to build on the preceding Chapters and to consider the possibilities for reform, given the very substantial shortcomings identified, both in the substantive provision made available under the social fund, and in the way in which it is delivered.

Chapter 9 provides an account of the impact of reforms introduced under the New Labour government, notably the simplification of the Budgeting Loan element of the social fund. Collard does, indeed, find that the reforms have improved access to loans, that the service has become more 'user-friendly', and that loans do go some way to providing an acceptable form of low-cost credit which would not otherwise be available to those reliant on state benefits. The modest advances which these changes represent do perhaps suggest that there is a role for loans as part of the repertoire of options available to safeguard the interests of poor households at times of need. On the other hand, concerns persist about the impact of loan repayments on standards of living, given that repayments are taken out of weekly incomes which are already seen as inadequate.[1]

In Chapter 10 the emphasis shifts to a consideration of the policy changes required to establish the social fund as an effective tool in aiding the task of ending poverty. The specific focus here is on child poverty, which the government is committed to eradicate by 2019 (Blair, 1999), but the implications of the proposals set out are applicable to all those groups likely to have recourse to the social fund. In contrast to the apparent assumption from government that its 'welfare to work' strategy will eventually remove the need for a safety net, and it is argued that this will remain an essential weapon in any armoury of measures intended to provide a decent standard of living for those on low incomes. Lakhani advocates a number of specific new grants: a child development grant, a home establishment grant, a core items grant and an opportunity grant. Indeed, it is suggested that the longer-term goal of ending poverty could be undermined by a failure to provide effective forms of immediate relief in the meantime.

A further international perspective is introduced in Chapter 11, where Daguerre and Nativel provide an informative analysis of the French approach to providing exceptional cash help for those affected by a financial crisis. They note that a pattern of emergency intervention to meet hardship represented a break with the French tradition of social assistance and policymakers were reluctant to acknowledge the emergence of poverty in the 1970s. Again, some interesting trans-national similarities can be identified, such as the increasing reliance on NGOs or the voluntary sector, and a common concern to set limits to spending commitments in this area. On the other hand, the French emphasis on principles such as 'social solidarity' and 'insertion' indicates that exceptional assistance is accepted more readily as a communal responsibility. Some significant examples are provided of help which is provided unconditionally. Thus, there is a readiness in certain circumstances to honour claims which are not supported by additional evidence, and a generous approach to providing help through the voluntary sector. Some concerns are expressed, nevertheless, about the direction being taken in France, with a greater emphasis on setting cash limits, and, ironically, a 'distancing' effect arising out of the more central role accorded to voluntary organisations. Despite this, the relatively open approach to the provision of help in France contrasts strongly with the centralised and fettered model of discretionary assistance evident in the UK.

We conclude in Chapter 12 with a review of the evidence provided, in order to offer a forward-looking discussion of the place of exceptional payments schemes such as the social fund in the broader strategy of addressing and, hopefully, ending poverty. This will encompass a discussion of the merits and demerits of the various models and approaches adopted in the UK and elsewhere, which will provide the basis for drawing out some key principles to inform future change. The Chapter touches upon some structural issues which need to be addressed in greater detail before adequate reform proposals can emerge. We will conclude that an effective scheme must meet certain fundamental objectives and principles of reform, including the capacity to of meet need adequately in material terms, and also the requirement to treat those who seek assistance sensitively and fairly in order to promote their sense of dignity and respect.

Note

1   Both personal accounts (Beresford et al, 1999) and sophisticated calculations (Bradshaw, 2001) show a continuing shortfall between what is provided in the form of state benefits, and what people actually require to maintain a basic ('low cost but adequate') standard of living.

PART I
THE HISTORICAL AND POLITICAL CONTEXT

Chapter 1

Lump Sum and Emergency Payments:
A Brief History

Gary Craig

Historical Context

The social fund emerged in 1988 as a result of the provisions of the 1986
Social Security Act. However, prior to 1988 there had been several national
one-off payments schemes in the UK managed by government and it was
the consistently troubling issues raised by the operation of these schemes
that the social fund was intended to address. This Chapter therefore sets the
scene for the book by reviewing the experience of these earlier schemes
and identifying the key issues which government hoped to solve with the
introduction of the social fund. In particular, the Chapter will examine the
experience of the two most recently preceding schemes, the Exceptional
Needs Payments (ENP) scheme of the Supplementary Benefits
Commission (SBC) (1966-1980) and the Single Payments (SP) scheme of
1980-88.

Prior to 1934, supplementary help to those who were financially
destitute had been the responsibility of local authorities broadly under the
provisions of the 1834 Poor Law Amendment Act, which itself had been
introduced to rationalise and align a wide range of local 'parish' provision.
The 1834 Act had been intended to limit the scope of such help and to
make dependence on it as unattractive as possible, with the threat of
incarceration in the gloomy and oppressive Victorian workhouses an
ultimate threat against those who, government claimed, would not work or
support themselves. Throughout the late nineteenth century and into the
early part of the twentieth century, claimants for help were increasingly
classified, by age, gender, disability and so on but the central form of
classification was that of deserts: 'deserving' claimants such as widows
might escape the workhouse, undeserving ones (such as the unemployed)
were less likely to (Craig, 1992a). However, a major problem for the state

was the variability with which local authorities interpreted its provisions: some left-leaning local authorities manipulated its terms to provide relatively generous levels of help to the poor; and during the 1920s, at a time of considerably widespread hardship as a result of economic depression, this led to confrontation between local government and central government and to the imprisonment of some councillors. As with the introduction of the 1834 Act itself, this action was driven by government's determination to underpin the operation of its provisions with a clear ideological statement of the distinction between deserving and undeserving poor.

The introduction in 1934 of the first national scheme for social assistance, under the aegis of the Unemployment Assistance Board (UAB), was thus again driven largely by issues of central government control and rationalisation; this scheme, it was hoped, would reimpose a clear discipline, that access to the state's financial help was conditional on desert, demonstrated either by a clear incapacity to work or by frequent and manifest attempts to do so. It removed the ability of maverick local authorities to undermine this discipline by (in the view of government) unwarranted generosity. The general political pressures leading to the introduction of the UAB – an arm's length organisation supervised by government – are described in more detail elsewhere (Craig, 1992a; SBC, 1977). During the Second World War, the UAB was replaced by the Assistance Board (in 1941), an organisation noteworthy for the temporary abandonment of the strong ideology of desert. German bombs were no respecter of class and relatively wealthy people were as likely to find themselves queuing for help from the state, as were those in more obvious poverty.

Following the end of the war, and building on the publication of the Beveridge Report, the Assistance Board was replaced in 1948 by the National Assistance Board (NAB). Despite the euphoric Parliamentary rhetoric which talked of the ending of the Poor Law, the NAB's provisions were little different from those of its predecessors and only minor amendments were made in terms of the scope and eligibility of the scheme until its abolition in 1966. Demand for one-off 'exceptional needs' payments (ENPs) grew irregularly but significantly throughout the life of these schemes raising one of the key structural issues facing such schemes, that of the inadequacy of basic benefits levels. If, it was argued, more and more people had to turn to additional payments for help in managing to meet their most basic needs, did this not say something about the ability of normal benefit rates to meet those needs? By 1965, the last full year of the NAB, and in a period of considerably lower levels of unemployment than in the early 1930s, the Board paid out almost one-third million ENPs, almost twenty times as many as in the early years of the UAB. Alongside this, and despite the intention that the national scheme would reduce variability in provision across the country, its reliance on the discretionary judgement of its officers and the Board members meant that decisions might be made which were out of line with the government's dominant ideological goals.

The exceptional needs payments scheme

In 1966, the NAB was replaced by the Supplementary Benefits Commission (SBC), as part of a broader reform of social security which attempted to honour the Labour Party's pledge of an income guarantee and deal with problems of stigma and low take-up (which had persisted and led to problems of low take-up and hardship – particularly amongst older people and the unemployed – despite the abolition of the Poor Law provisions). It also was intended to respond to 'growing concern about the increasing reliance on discretion in the national assistance scheme which was not only administratively costly and inefficient but was increasingly recognised to be inequitable' (SBC, 1977, p.209). The growth in discretion was however largely identified by government as being to do with the growing number of discretionary weekly additions to benefit (which were replaced by long-term additions, called Exceptional Circumstances Additions – ECAs) rather than with one-off payments which were yet to be identified as a very serious financial or political problem (Webb, 1975).

The 1966 Supplementary Benefit Act stated that people whose resources did not meet their requirements would be entitled to benefit, a move in the direction of legal entitlement and weekly benefit was clearly marked out as for 'normal requirements'. Over and beyond this, the SBC was empowered to pay either or all of extra weekly additions for people with ongoing needs (such as for supplementary heating or dietary requirements), one-off payments (ENPs) for unusual one-off needs, and payments to people 'in urgent need' (for example as a result of fire or flood), a power which overrode all others and could be used regardless of whether applicants were eligible for weekly benefit. This immediately raised the issue of boundary problems; between what were normal requirements, ongoing needs and 'unusual one-off' needs. Arguments about these boundaries were to grow through the 1970s.

In the 1970s, the political and economic climate changed. Political interest generated by the 'rediscovery of poverty' (Townsend, 1959; Cole and Utting, 1962) and the slow but steady growth of unemployment (which reached 2.6 per cent in 1970), focused attention more sharply on the adequacy of the social assistance scale rates, and thus on the role of one-off payments. By 1970, 4 million people were wholly or partially dependent on supplementary benefit (SB), more than three times as many as when the NAB was formed. However, although the numbers of those on SB grew by 11 per cent between 1969 and 1976, in this period the number of ENP awards grew by 137 per cent. All claimant groups contributed to this growth but the number of those who were unemployed grew fastest. In 1976, the number of ENPs awarded topped one million for the first time, at a total annual cost of £25 million and growth continued until the abolition of the SBC; in 1979 1.3 million ENPs were made (a threefold increase on the 1966 levels) at a cost of £38 million, and the average value of payments rose six fold over the same period to £34 in 1979. Contemporary enquires made by the SBC showed that most expenditure went on clothing for adults and children, bedding, removal expenses, furniture, household goods and fuel. Clearly, this pattern of use provided more than adequate material for endless debate about the boundaries between normal, exceptional and urgent needs.

A report in the early 1970s (Marshall, 1972), probably the first time ENPs had had such specific attention paid to them, also analysed the receipt of ENPs by claimant group and identified several key issues. The major group in receipt of ENPs turned out perhaps surprisingly to be women with dependent children whereas Marshall's and other studies demonstrated that, despite the intention of government to make the scheme stigma-free, there was significant under-claiming by older people. Pensioners were more likely to receive weekly additions to payment but were discouraged by the discretion still inherent in the ENP scheme, as this was perceived as likely to label them as undeserving. Within the averages for ENPs, there were significant variations; although most claimants receiving ENPs got no more than one in a year, a relatively small proportion of claimants received both more than one ENP and did so at an average award level significantly higher than the average. There were also significant intra- and inter-regional variations in levels of awards and some regions accounted for as much as 50 per cent higher rates of payments than others. The SBC (1976, pp. 64-5) suggested these variations might reflect not only relatively differing levels of deprivation and, thus, need but also 'the activity of local organisations in bringing unmet needs to light', perhaps the first official recognition of the role of welfare rights take-up campaigns in placing demands upon the social security system. By 1976, the SBC noted that a range of factors might affect variations in take-up of ENPs, including the make-up of the workload, the extent of outside pressures, the attitudes of officers and the nature and situation of the area covered (SBC, 1977). By 1976, the SBC had established a wide-ranging review of the supplementary benefits system, triggered by its own analysis in the 1975 Annual Report (SBC, 1976). This highlighted the key issues which the experience of the ENP scheme had revealed and led to further proposals for reform. These issues are briefly summarised below.

Challenging decisions

Although the supplementary benefits scheme itself was based on entitlement, the ENP scheme remained firmly set within a discretionary framework. Thus, the manner in which officers interpreted its decisions was likely to vary and their decision-making was as likely to be open to challenge, either through administrative or legal processes and there is little doubt that the discretionary nature of ENPs, and the growing reliance on them, was a major driver in the growth of what became known as the 'welfare rights industry' during the 1970s. This industry became formalised in the late 1970s with the appointment of welfare rights workers, particularly within some Scottish local authorities, and has since become a common feature in the landscape of local government. One of the key debates during the 1970s was thus about the relative merits of discretion and entitlement, often conducted within the vehicle of appeals tribunals.[1] In the early 1970s, less than 0.25 per cent of all SB claims reached a formal appeal tribunal hearing but this number was to grow and the significance of ENP appeals with SB appeals more generally was to be marked. The newly-established Child Poverty Action Group had suggested that the relative lack of success of claimants attending tribunals unaided compared with those who were supported by an experienced advocate such as a solicitor or welfare rights worker, illustrated both the difficulties of obtaining justice from a discretionary scheme and the growing complexity of the scheme (CPAG, 1969). Both CPAG and others argued that appeal tribunals were less a safeguard of the legal rights of claimants than a safety valve for the system, which incorporated dissent, and that they also often degenerated into a forum for discussing the personal failings of claimants. In their view, a more legalistic system would offer better protection for the rights of claimants and be likely to meet the goals of the Franks Commission (1957), established to review the role of tribunals, of openness, fairness and impartiality. However, tribunals, like officers, continued to exercise discretion and their decision-making was frequently characterised by a lack of independence from the social security system, by bias and prejudice (Adler and Bradley, 1975) and by inequitable and inconsistent outcomes.

By 1973, the first year such figures were publicly available, the proportion of appeals involving ENPs reached 28 per cent of the total of 25,000 SB appeals heard, representing about one per cent of all ENP decisions made (a pattern which remained evident following the implementation of the social fund; see Smith, Chapter 4, this volume). Of the decisions in 1973 revised by tribunals, however, almost 50 per cent concerned ENPs; thus a high proportion of tribunals concerned ENPs and for these tribunal decisions, the chance of having an ENP refusal revised was considerably higher than for any other kind of decision. This pattern suggested that tribunals' use of discretion was indeed acting as a safety valve for dissatisfied applicants. For weekly additions to benefit, decisions revised at tribunal constituted only 16 per cent of the total of appeals heard. The SBC (1977) also noted that decisions regarding ENPs were overwhelmingly more likely to be challenged than those regarding weekly additions but its figures also suggested that the proportion of decisions reversed in the claimants' favour varied markedly between groups, again apparently reflecting perceptions of deserts. A study the SBC commissioned also pointed to the fivefold discrepancy in success rates between those who were represented (45 per cent) and those who were not (9 per cent). The operation of the tribunal system thus raised issues about discretion, fairness, bias and complexity.

Boundary issues

A scheme based on discretion and operated alongside two other schemes (the urgent needs and weekly additions payments schemes) was always likely to generate disputes about the boundaries of eligibility. Titmuss (1968), at one time a deputy chair of the SBC, had argued that discretion was more able to respond to exceptional needs and that this was a major advantage of discretionary ENPs for claimants. However, this argument was likely to be undermined where officers operated discretion narrowly and harshly, and where judgements were made between different groups on the basis of prejudice. His argument also lost force as the numbers of those on SB and claiming for ENPs grew so that the system became increasingly unable to respond sensitively to the demands of a mass constituency. During the 1970s, the tension at the boundary between the scale rates and ENPs reflected the competing pressures of, on the one hand, a growing recognition of the inadequacy of the scale rates and, on the other, an increased concern by government to contain expenditure in an area where year-by-year increases were significant and, in the view of government, becoming out of control.

Attempts to control expenditure led to other forms of boundary dispute, notably with local government social services departments (established following the Seebohm Report in 1970), which increasingly came to feel that the impact of refusals to award ENPs was being felt on their budgets. Local authorities were empowered to make cash grants to families with children felt to be at risk but a pattern was emerging which suggested that these grants were being made for items which were properly the responsibility of the SBC (Lister and Emmett, 1976). Indeed the SBC itself (1973) noted that one-third of the grants made by a voluntary organisation to SB recipients were quite within the scope of the ENP scheme. Where the SBC took a tougher line towards particular kinds of expenditure, such as fuel debts for example, a clear knock-on effect could be perceived in terms of demands made for help from local authorities. The SBC attempted to set its own boundaries by delineating four tests of exceptionality by which it hoped to contain its own responsibilities: these were that ENPs could be made to claimants living on SB 'for some time' without having made a claim, that dependent children would be involved, that chronic disease or illness requiring warm clothing might be a factor, or that 'hardship' might result if an urgent need was not met. In practice, these limits did little to stem the tide of claims for ENPs or the growing boundary disputes around the ENP scheme.

The costs of the scheme

As noted above, government became increasingly concerned throughout the 1970s at the growing cost of the scheme which, whilst insignificant compared with public expenditure as a whole or even with the social security budget, was accelerating much more rapidly than either and appeared less susceptible to central government manipulation. One aspect which appeared more open to control from the centre was the costs of administering the scheme and throughout the 1970s attempts were made to simplify the administration of supplementary benefit as a whole (also driven by the recognition that complexity was regressive in relation to claimants), and to the ENP scheme more generally. The difficulty was that standardisation of decisions led to complexity because of the need for increasingly elaborate codification and that, on the other hand, simplification led to increased costs. The operation of a more uniform approach to exceptional needs, effectively defining them as unexceptional and not open to discretionary judgement, would conflict with government's urgent desire (backed by the 1973 intervention of the International Monetary Fund which was policing the UK economy) to limit spending. The social security Minister at the time summed up this conundrum, that simplification would add to the costs of the system unless some claimants were to become poorer.

The SBC's view was that complexity was not to be dealt with by explaining complex rules but by simplification and suggested various ways to streamline the system and limit the scope of discretion. The organisation's problem was that, not only was SB an expensive benefit to deliver (costing late in the 1970s around £11 per £100 of benefit delivered compared with, for example, £1.50 for retirement pensions or £4 for another means-tested scheme, Family Income Supplement), but, within it, ENPs absorbed the most disproportionate use of time and cash and human resources. For example, ENPs were twice as costly to deliver as weekly additions to benefit on a pro rata basis. These administrative difficulties began to assume the proportions of a crisis by the late 1970s because of staff reductions (also driven by public expenditure cuts), and this in turn impacted on the quality of decision-making which became observably poorer throughout the decade. Claimants were increasingly encouraged to make postal claims, staff were discouraged from making home visits, and smaller local offices were closed or absorbed into larger, more distant ones, trends which produced the paradox of increasing failure to take up benefits (particularly amongst those less mobile claimants such as older people or those living in rural areas) at the same time as the volume of ENPs was growing. Given these growing pressures, it was hardly surprising that Marshall had concluded in 1972 that it was not possible to deduce whether ENPs were awarded to those families with the greatest need but to those who felt most able, as a result of a combination of personal and structural factors, to present those needs.

Fraud, abuse and mismanagement

A number of attempts were made at the time to explain the growth of ENPs. One basic reason was of course the growth in levels of need particularly reflected in growing levels of unemployment although this was twisted politically on occasions and described as a growth in demand, thus placing the responsibility at the door of welfare rights workers. However, a politically rather more unpleasant interpretation introduced by government and picked up by tabloid media was that of fraud and abuse. Fraud was seen as deliberately criminal activity, abuse as 'excessive' claiming, often the result of a claimant's own failure to manage their weekly benefit for the purposes for which it was intended; claimants were portrayed as living beyond their means and it was in this period that terms like 'dole-wallahs' and the 'Costa del Dole' (that part of the popular Spanish tourist destination allegedly populated by 'dole cheats' living in luxury at the expense of the British taxpayer; Golding and Middleton 1982) emerged into public discourse. The SBC was facing both ways during this period, concerned to placate government which was increasingly concerned at its performance but also recognising that its own evidence suggested that the levels of fraud and abuse were in reality very small. Lister, reporting on the Committee on Abuse of Social Security Benefits, whose establishment had been driven by a combination of right-wing popular political and public protest at the extent of abuse, observed that 'notwithstanding the Department of Health and Social Security's worst estimates of 0.1 per cent of SB being overpaid, the committee had operated as if abuse were a serious problem' (1973, p.11).

Abusive claiming was a phrase later coined by social security Ministers to describe the frequent claiming of one-off payments by a relatively limited number of claimants but analysis of the data suggests that the extent of this phenomenon was negligible during the 1970s and that, from the point of view of equity between claimants, a much more significant problem was posed in terms of the low overall take-up of payments, given that four out of five claimants were receiving no ENPs at all in an average year throughout the life of the ENP scheme.

Making sense of the ENP scheme: equity, entitlement, discretion and flexibility

The debates about ENPs were largely conducted in terms of the tensions arising from the competing objectives of equity and entitlement on the one hand, and discretion and flexibility on the other, within the context of growing governmental concern to limit the rise in expenditure. Discretion certainly would leave officials free to meet unanticipated 'exceptional circumstances', i.e. to act flexibly; however, as Hill had noted (1969) in his earlier analyses of the National Assistance Board flexibility might as easily reflect the ability of officials to yield to pressure from insistent applicants whilst otherwise operating a discriminatory system. Need was an imprecise concept and, as the SBC itself had noted, because people attach different value to differing things 'there is therefore an inescapable element of judgement as to what constitutes essential need in an individual case' (SBC, 1973, p.5). Hill's view was that need might simply represent an acceptance of such by SB officials who were particularly unwilling to take no for an answer.

The chairman of the SBC acknowledged that discretion brought with it the possibility of discrimination, moral judgements and prejudice; his personal preference was to create a scheme which would provide adequate basic scale rates without interfering with the right of claimants to spend their money as they thought best. However, in a context of tight public expenditure and increasing demands on the ENP scheme, the two advantages of discretion – flexibility and innovation – were bound to be lost and it was, instead, used increasingly as a means of rationing expenditure.

One further tension was that as demand for ENPs grew, they began to be perceived as effectively no longer exceptional payments but as a *de facto* increase in the scale rates of benefit, albeit by stealth. The Chairman of the SBC, David Donnison's response was, of course, to increase the scale rates but this proved politically unacceptable. Another was to transfer responsibility for meeting needs to the voluntary and charitable sector but few accepted that the state should abandon its responsibility for meeting needs in this way; indeed, the tendency during the 1970s was in the opposite direction, for welfare rights workers to define new 'exceptional needs' in response both to rising standards of living in the population as a whole, and to changes in the way society was organised. The growth of these new needs was later to be underpinned by consensually derived indicators of poverty constructed through, for example, the work of the Breadline Britain team (Mack and Lansley, 1992).

One of the other major points of concern in relation to the ENP scheme was that of equity, particularly equity between those who knew about the scheme and were able to take advantage of it, and those who didn't (although, it might be suggested, the answer lay in the hands of the SBC to ensure that all those entitled in principle might take advantage of it); and between those eligible for ENPs and those who, whilst in employment, might be on very low incomes thus having similar financial needs but not being eligible for ENPs. In a nutshell, there were conflicts:

> ...inherent in attempts to exercise discretionary powers for large numbers of people whilst attempting to promote equity between claimants and between claimants and non-claimants as well as, apparently, addressing how "deserving" a claimant might be. (Hodge, 1975, p.68)

The SBC review of ENPs concluded that there was a strong case for reform and put forward a number of proposals, including increasing the scale rates, introducing regular lump sum payments for all claimants, having cash limits or strongly accentuating the (then) rather marginal facility for providing loans. It argued that urgent needs payments should remain, as a scheme of last resort. There were strong differences between the SBC and what was now generally referred to as 'the poverty lobby' (the loose alliance of voluntary, community, faith-based, charitable and local government bodies campaigning around differing aspects of poverty) as to what might be an appropriate level for the scale rates and the DHSS argued that extra money was not the issue in any case but that claimants would benefit from extra help in managing their income. In the event, these debates were temporarily suspended by the election in 1979 of the first Conservative government led by Margaret Thatcher. Many of the themes emerging previously resurfaced, however, during the life of the single payments scheme which was introduced in 1980, and this is the subject of the remainder of this Chapter.

The Single Payments Scheme: Political and Economic Context

The three governments led by Margaret Thatcher can lay claim to be amongst the most radical of the 20th century in terms of their approach to social policy. This is not the place to analyse their performance in detail but a number of major initiatives, including a general programme of privatisation and specific elements within it such as the sale of council houses to sitting tenants at heavily discounted prices, were seen as marking a dramatic shift away from the consensus on the welfare state which had dominated much political thinking during the century (see Alcock and Craig, 2001 for a summary of the period). Although the actual impact of the welfare reforms was far less marked than the government rhetoric suggested was intended, there is no doubt that the position of the poor, both in work and out of it, worsened considerably throughout the 1980s and 1990s. Divisions of income and wealth widened and deepened (see e.g. Hills, 1995 and also Chapter 3 in this volume) and levels of unemployment – driven by the government's fixation with reducing inflation - reached a figure only previously recorded during the worst period of the inter-war depression. The House of Commons Select Committee on Social Services (House of Commons, 1990) noted that the poorest ten percent of the population had seen their incomes grow at half the national average rate in the first half of the 1980s.

By 1987, the numbers of families receiving Supplementary Benefit (SB) had risen by two-thirds from 1979 to 4.3 million; 1.9 million families had incomes below SB levels and one third of them were failing to take up benefits to which they were entitled. Although research at this time indicated that families with children were having the greatest difficulty in managing with the long-term effects of unemployment, both in terms of policy and by its ideological pronouncements, the government appeared far more concerned with the populist issue of fraud detection. The only planned increase in social security expenditure in 1979, following its election, was to be the appointment of 1,050 new fraud officers. The reality of fraud was revealed (and quietly buried) in a National Audit Office Report which suggested that:

> recorded recoverable overpayments of SB, including genuine error as well as fraud, amounted to £30 million or less than 0.5 per cent of SB expenditure [in 1984]. (Cited in CPAG, 1987, p.4)

Indeed, the value of overpayments was far less than the value of underpayments. In this context, the government introduced its new single payments scheme (in 1980) which it claimed would address, perhaps once and for all, the structural problems highlighted in earlier schemes.

The major aim of the new scheme was, the government stated, to reduce discretion, in order to simplify the scheme (and thus cut administrative costs) but not to increase expenditure. This would represent, it claimed, 'a great advance in fairness'. Entitlement and assessment of eligibility for SB were to be defined by legislation and regulations, with adjudication now to be carried out by SB officers within the DHSS. Rules were to be published as part of a move towards a more legalised structure (see Buck, 2000, p.16). Weekly additions (ECAs) would remain but were renamed as Additional Requirements Payments. At a broader level, the unemployed would continue to be excluded from receiving enhanced long-term SB rates. Single payment (SP) regulations would set out the range of eligible expenses and the circumstances in which payments would be allowed. In practice, eligibility for clothing and footwear, which had absorbed much of ENP expenditure, was to be severely curtailed but this was not at first publicly acknowledged. Those not receiving SB would no longer be entitled under any circumstances to SPs although they could apply for urgent needs payments, which might take the form of loans. The right to appeal to an SB tribunal against refusal of award was retained.

Although there was some initial dispute as to whether the SP entitlements had been arrived at simply by codifying the ENP scheme, it rapidly became clear that both the scope of entitlements and the manner in which they had been drafted as regulations, were intended to constrain demand for SPs. Claimants now had not only to demonstrate a need for an item and that they didn't already possess such an item, but also that they had no suitable alternative, had not unreasonably disposed of it, or failed to take care to preserve it. The notion of rights to one-off payments was thus still mediated by the requirement for claimants to define and demonstrate their 'need'. Adler and Asquith (1981) thus arrived at the view that the scheme offered greater procedural rights but fewer substantive rights i.e. less cash. Certainly, the overall effect of the scheme was to reduce considerably the scope of one-off payments both by restricting those eligible to claim and the circumstances in which claims could be made and those aspects of the SBC review tending towards a more generous scheme were summarily dismissed. The SBC, in its valedictory report (1980), noted both that it would become harder for claimants to get help for many of the items for which ENPs had been paid and that boundary disputes with local authorities were likely to grow because of the increasing constraints on the availability of one-off payments. The retention of the right to appeal was welcomed but it quickly became recognised by the poverty lobby that this was a hollow triumph as the level of activity was bound to reduce substantially.

As the single payment scheme became operational, however, and despite the hope of the government that debate about the scope and nature of one-off payments schemes, might be buried, issues began to emerge which resonated with the debates of the 1970s and earlier and these are summarised below.

Complexity or simplicity?

The government's main aim was to make the scheme simpler. However, the objectives of simplified administration and easier access for claimants immediately appeared to be in conflict. It was estimated that about one-quarter of those entitled to SB were not claiming it and CPAG took the view that the precise form of the SP regulations necessarily led to complexity.

> The Secretary of State hailed the regulations by saying "at last the public will know where they stand". The public demonstrably do not ... more importantly still, DHSS Benefit Officers [now responsible for administering the scheme in-house, the SBC having being abolished] do not seem to know where the public stand either. (CPAG, 1981, p.2)

Other commentators later confirmed this view. By 1983 the SP scheme in fact involved 12 sets of regulations and 22 sets of amended regulations as well as Commissioners' decisions and memoranda of guidance from the Chief Supplementary Benefits Officer. The price of administrative simplicity, where it had been achieved, appeared to be increasing inaccessibility for the average claimant and the major simplification of the SB scheme as a whole in any case appeared to have come about as a result of the introduction of housing benefit, now administered by local authorities.

Hill later argued that the DHSS was unlikely to have pursued the issue of rights and improving take-up enthusiastically.

> The alternative to the rights [perspective] was a view that benefits which are too easily available will be open to abuse ... there seems little doubt that a widespread view of this kind has contributed to making the system obscure and difficult. (Hill, 1990, p.93)

In fact, the DHSS response to growing administrative difficulties (apart from the introduction of the first of several major and problematic computer programmes) was:

> [U]ncompromising [to transfer] the onus for welfare promotion from the Department to the claimants; by largely ignoring its duty to determine entitlement to benefits other than the scale rates ... by often neglecting to spell out the various rights of the claimants. (Howe, 1985, p.56)

Howe's study demonstrated that the 'art' of distinguishing between 'deserving' and 'undeserving' claimants was alive and well in local offices.[2]

The complexity of the SP scheme was a strong theme also in Berthoud's detailed study of the SB scheme in the mid-1980s (Berthoud, 1984, p.4). In relation to special grants, 'the vast majority felt ignorant and fully three-quarters "had no idea at all".' Half the claimants interviewed were not aware of SPs and Howe, observing 75 interviews, found that in 23 cases where single payments might be an issue, staff volunteered relevant information on only four occasions. Complexity affected staff as much as claimants: one test question regarding furniture grants administered by Berthoud to staff resulted in more than half the staff giving the wrong answer. This finding was later confirmed by the DHSS Chief Adjudication Officer who noted that in more than half of SP decisions monitored, regulations were being interpreted incorrectly or the wrong regulation applied (Cohen and Tarpey, 1988). As the Social Security Advisory Committee, which had been established in 1980 with a right to be consulted on major social security changes had noted, 'there is no cheap route to simplicity' (SSAC, 1982, p.60). In fact the major finding of research at the time was that the new scheme had eased the difficulties of the DHSS by 'negative simplification', that is the simple removal of the power to give help to claimants in a wide variety of circumstances.

Discretion or entitlement?

Although the government at the time claimed that the SP regulations codified past ENP practice, the number of entitlements were clearly limited compared with the ENP scheme. The SSAC was quick to suggest that the balance had swung too far away from discretion and was concerned about the narrowness with which some regulations were being interpreted in practice. The evidence, reviewed in the SSAC's second report (SSAC, 1983), reflected a greater inflexibility in practice even from offices which had previously a reputation for relative generosity. However, the shift from discretion to entitlement was not as clear-cut as many believed and Beltram, a former senior social security official, noted (1984a) that the continuing use of quasi-discretionary decisions undermined the whole notion of entitlement. This was emphasised in a particularly subtle finding from Berthoud's research (1984) that, although a regulated scheme should lead to situations where there was no possibility of error or judgement affecting decisions, it was clear that in the interpretation of regulations, the preparedness of staff to ask claimants for particular kinds of information frequently had a significant effect on the outcome of applications. In effect, a disguised form of discretion was at work behind the façade of regulation, where judgement (of even the most racist kind, as one of Berthoud's collaborators observed) of a moral kind could operate freely. Although the appeals system succeeded in clarifying the meaning of the regulations in some instances, this led to increasing rigidity in the system as a whole. The appeals process, which was handling an ever-increasing number of appeals, had seemed (as a result of the 1980 changes) to push the needs of claimants to one side. Hill later concluded that:

> [the] 1980 Act did not abolish discretion ... it provided for a situation in which officers would have to have regard to statutory and publicly available rules in determining entitlement ... it still left them considerable scope for variation in the efforts they made to identify the special needs and the criteria they used to determine whether a response was appropriate. (Hill, 1990, pp.86-7)

In short, the notion of deserts was alive and well, hidden behind a smokescreen of entitlement.

The impact of narrowing eligibility

By 1981, it had already become clear that eligibility for one-off payments had been substantially narrowed. This had a number of impacts. First, as predicted, boundary problems, particularly with local authorities but also with voluntary organisations and charities, were exacerbated as demand was deflected towards other organisations. The association representing directors of local authority social services departments monitored the impact of the SP scheme and argued that they were having to cope with the consequences of maladministration and rigidity in the SB system and that there was no guarantee that the DHSS would reimburse social services departments for individual grants made in lieu of late or missing payments (Association of Directors of Social Services, 1982). Voluntary organisations such as the Family Welfare Association noted rapidly rising demand for help (see also Smith, Chapter 5, this volume): for example the number of clothing grants given by the FWA had risen from 74 in 1978-9 to 323 in 1982-3, representing a fourfold increase to 16 per cent of all expenditure (Raphael and Roll, 1984). The SSAC argued that a return to a degree of discretion would help solve many of these boundary problems.

Secondly, evidence grew of the extent of unmet need. The SSAC had already commented on this in its first report (SSAC, 1982) and this theme was picked up by the ADSS and by other commentators. For example, the ADSS report (1984) noted that to get a grant for furniture, claimants had also to be eligible for removal expenses or meet some other supplementary criterion, and that it was now much more difficult to get help for clothing. Walker, in a detailed review of the scheme (1983, p.142), pointed out that the 1980 scheme had not offered a way of dealing with the 'exceptional needs' of claimants but that 'certain categories of need, as well as groups of people, have been placed beyond the scope of the scheme ... the danger is that ... fewer demands will be made on the scheme for those expenses will fall outside its remit and governments ... will conclude that such needs no longer exist.' Berthoud's (1984) study was able to quantify the extent of unmet need, observing that only about one third to one quarter of justifiable claims were actually made for SPs. The proportion of claimants receiving SPs in any claimant group did not exceed 29 per cent and was substantially lower, at 10 per cent, for the unemployed. These difficulties for claimants were exacerbated in 1986 when the scope of eligibility was narrowed still further from the 21 'essential and exceptionally available items', specified in 1980, to eight categories.

Related to this, there were increasing arguments about definitions of eligibility. The view from outside the DHSS was that the conditions for, for example, clothing and footwear grants, were too rigid and, as a result, claimants were being sent to clothing clubs, or to seek loans, in order to acquire such 'essentials'. Organisations such as the Child Poverty Action Group took a series of test cases to the courts to challenge definitions of such clauses as 'normal wear and tear', or 'suitable alternative accommodation' but rarely succeeded in shaking the determination of the DHSS to maintain narrow definitions (see Prosser, 1983). After 1986, these arguments increased in volume as the terrain was extended, for example to furniture grants and fuel payments, over which such increasingly obscure battles (but vital to claimants) had to be joined (SSAC, 1983). All of these arguments of course had impacts on the level of resources required to administer the scheme. The costs of administering SPs were considerably larger than for any other benefit. By 1983, SPs accounted for 0.5 per cent of all social security spending, and accounted for 20 per cent of the resources absorbed by all appeals.

Patterns of single payment spending

Ironically, the further restrictions imposed in 1986 were a direct government response to the steady increase in SP expenditure year on year (see Table 1.1).

Table 1.1   Single Payments 1980-1985

Year	Number of Single Payments (millions)	Average Payment (£)
1980	1.1	£43
1983	1.9	£76
1985	4.1	£75

Source: Extracted from DHSS, *Social Security Statistics 1989*, Table 34.97, HMSO.

Total expenditure thus increased over this period more than six fold, from £48 million to £308 million. The spectre facing the Secretary of State, despite the rhetoric at the scheme's inception, was again that of expenditure out of control. Over this period, the proportion of SPs going to the unemployed had risen from 36 per cent of all payments to around 50 per cent (hardly surprising given the rapid rise in unemployment over the early 1980s). However, the 1986 restrictions were targeted in part at the unemployed, in a further attempt to restate the division between deserving and undeserving, and the proportion of SPs going to the unemployed dropped thereafter to just above 40 per cent. The unemployed were still excluded from the long-term scale rates which caused particular difficulties in budgeting for clothing and footwear for children but which were now largely excluded from the SP scheme.

Although the average payment during the life of the scheme was around £50, there was in reality considerable variation in the size of SPs, with many payments made as low as £25 and as many made for several hundreds of pounds. Some payments were so small that the administrative cost of handling them was felt to be disproportionate. What was more noticeable was that as regulations ruled out certain kinds of help, such as clothing grants, so demand for other kinds still within the scope of the scheme, such as furniture grants, correspondingly rose. Similarly, Berthoud's team noticed that claims made for items, which were now less likely to be awarded, were often accompanied with supplementary arguments such as the use of a fallback regulation which allowed payments to be made on grounds of health.[3] Essentially, constraints on certain kinds of SPs simply directed pressure elsewhere in the system.

More worrying, still, however, was the steady rise in the number of SPs being awarded. From 1982 to 1985, the rate of 'take-up' of SPs rose from 30 per 100 claimants to 87 per 100 and this certainly prompted the increased constraints introduced in 1986. This was, in the view of the Chair of the SSAC, a paradoxical approach after the introduction of a rights-based system:

> if you give people rights and then take steps to cut down when people become aware of their rights, it's a rather odd policy. (Peter Barclay, quoted in *New Statesman*, 25 July 1986)

Clearly, the government's move was associated mostly with its desire to rein in expenditure but it put another gloss on it, arguing that SPs were no longer necessary because of 'real improvements in the value of the weekly scale rates' (HMSO, 1986, p.1). In fact, DHSS figures then suggested that only one in six claimants were receiving SPs and that only ten per cent of all claimants were receiving 80 per cent of all payments and this revived the debate about the 'abuse' of the scheme by some claimants. As CPAG noted at the time, 'any "abuse" of the clothing grant regulations is probably a reflection of the absurd restrictions imposed on entitlement to clothing grants in 1980' (1986, p.2) and Beltram observed that 'it does not make sense to offer a wardrobe to a person who lacks a warm coat. Yet the regulations may prescribe the first while prohibiting the second' (1984b, p.141).

The end of single payments

Concern about the impact of the 1986 Regulations resulted in an initially heightened level of claiming until by the time the new restrictions were in force, there were 125,000 outstanding SP claims compared with a normal 16,000. This closing-down sale effect was ephemeral, however, and the Minister's aim of cutting expenditure was more than met: expected savings of £100 million per year were nearer £200 million by 1987-8, the last year of the SP scheme. By this time, however, a major new review of the social security system, the Fowler Review, initiated in 1985 and reporting in 1986, had reached a range of conclusions. Most controversial amongst them, with the possible exception of its strategy for reform of the pension scheme, were the proposals for what it called the social fund, a replacement for the single payments scheme largely based on discretion, offering predominantly loans, and operating within strict cash limits. This had swept aside a range of ideas put forward to address the criticisms of the SP scheme made from outside government, suggestions such as regular one-off payments to all claimants. This new scheme again, it was claimed, would solve the recurrent problems of one-off payments schemes, of the appropriate balance between discretion and entitlement, dealing with boundary disputes, containing expenditure, the relationship between essential needs (i.e. what should be covered by the weekly scale rates) and exceptional needs (i.e. the scope of one-off payments), and the role of tribunals in challenging decisions (see Buck, Chapter 8, this volume, for the origins of the social fund 'review' processes). As I show later in this book, (Chapter 3), the social fund might claim to have dealt with some (but certainly not all) of these issues, but at the price of generating new problems, particularly for claimants.

Notes

1   An influential official report drew an important distinction between [Supplementary Benefits] 'Commission discretion', i.e. guidance provided for staff on the exercise of discretionary powers, and a residual 'officer discretion' applied by individual officers assessing entitlement in individual cases. This report characterised the key difference between the national assistance and SB schemes as the growth of Commission discretion at the expense of officer discretion (Department of Health and Social Services, 1978).

2   This distinction between 'deserving' and 'undeserving' recipients of social assistance appears to be an assumption shared internationally (see, Hermans and Declercq, Chapter 2; Davidson, Chapter 7, this volume). French legislators, on the other hand, appear to have avoided Anglo-Saxon notions of 'workfare' precisely to prevent the distinction between 'deserving' and 'undeserving poor' arising: see Daguerre and Nativel, Chapter 11, this volume.

3   This residual discretionary power applied where a claimant had failed to satisfy any of the detailed conditions for a single payment or had claimed for an item for which the regulations made no provision: 'if, in the opinion of the adjudication officer, such a

payment is the only means by which serious damage or serious risk to the health or safety of any member of the assessment unit may be prevented'. (Supplementary Benefit (Single Payments) Regulations 1981, regulation 30). The Social Security Commissioners produced inconsistent approaches to the interpretation of this important 'longstop' provision: see Buck, 2000, p.400. Despite such interpretational difficulties, the particular wording of regulation 30 was carried over into the qualification rules for social fund crisis loans (direction 3).

Chapter 2

Social Assistance in Belgium: Public Centres for Social Welfare

Koen Hermans and Anja Declercq

Introduction: the Belgian Context

This contribution analyses the role of the local Public Centres for Social Welfare (PCSWs) in the delivering of social assistance in Belgium. International-comparative research discriminates between three types of social assistance: 'general assistance' for everybody beneath a certain income level, 'categorical assistance' for specific groups and 'tied assistance', being means-tested services or goods in cash or in kind (Eardley et al, 1996).[1] Most attention so far went to general assistance (Paugam, 1999; Guibentif & Bouget, 1997; Ditch & Oldfield, 1999) and to housing benefits as 'tied assistance'. International-comparative research of other forms of 'tied assistance' did not include Belgium (Ditch et al, 1997) or did not pay sufficient attention to the peculiarities of the Belgian system (Eardley et al, 1996). Anyhow, international-comparative research into 'tied assistance' is hindered by problems of comparability as a consequence of local and regional differences within a national system. These are all the more present in Belgium because of its decentralised system of discretionary tied social assistance delivered by PCSWs.

Belgium is a federal state with a complex constitutional structure of Regions and Communities. Although social security is, strictly speaking, a federal competence, personal matters such as education, well-being and culture are the competence of the communities and items such as the economy and housing fall under the responsibility of the regions. After the Second World War, the Belgian social security system was institutionalised due to the creation of social insurances for private and public employees, dominated by Bismarckian principles. In the 1960s, these were completed with a less extensive system for the self-employed. At the end of the sixties, means-tested categorical social assistance allowances for the disabled, for the elderly and for families and single parents not entitled to child benefits, were created.[2] In 1974, this led to the creation of a general minimum income for the active population (the 'Minimex'), implemented by the local PCSWs. These municipal centres were founded in 1976 and their main task, besides the delivering of the Minimex, is the provision of social aid to ensure a decent human existence for everybody. There is no national housing benefit.

This Chapter will consider the advantages and disadvantages of a system of discretionary tied social assistance delivered by local PCSWs. The first part consists of a legal overview of the tasks of the local PCSWs. The second part starts with a more theoretical analysis of implementation and discretion. This is complemented by empirical implementation studies, which clarify the advantages and disadvantages of a decentralised system of discretionary social aid.

The Legal Framework of General and Tied Social Assistance

In contrast to the categorical social assistance which is administered centrally, the local PCSWs implement both 'general' and 'tied' social assistance. However, their role varies between the two tasks. This section shows that, on the one hand, the act to establish the Minimex contains relatively clearly defined conditions, such as nationality, age, family situation, residence, willingness to work and need, which are checked by the local centres. On the other hand, the PCSW law is goal-oriented, as is demonstrated later. The only legal consideration is the damage to the claimant's 'human dignity'. That is, every local centre decides itself in each individual case if the claimant's human dignity is damaged and on the most suitable form of social aid to restore his/her dignity (discretionary payments, material, medical, social or psychological aid).

The Minimex

As in other European countries, two new insights, which resulted in 1974 in the creation of a guaranteed minimum income, prevailed during the sixties in Belgium. Firstly, the system of social insurance gave evidence of structural weaknesses. That is, since its benefits were based on former labour participation, those with an insufficient employment history fell through its net. Secondly, the fight against poverty and the guarantee of financial security was increasingly understood as the state's responsibility. This section deals with the general principles of the Minimex. Subsequently, more attention is paid to one specific condition governing payment, namely the willingness to work.

General principles This act guarantees a minimum income to every adult (from 18 till 65 year), who has insufficient means of existence and who shows a willingness to work (Eardley *et al*, 1996). Nonetheless, not everybody living in Belgium, can apply for the Minimex. Only Belgian citizens, EU nationals, stateless persons and authorised refugees can. Local PCSWs implement this act and consequently control the means, the willingness to work and the family situation of the applicant. People with no other resources get the full minimum income; people with other income resources get an income supplement up to the maximum level of the benefit. The guaranteed minimum income is partially financed by the local community and partially by the federal government. Since the Minimex is a residual allowance, every source of income has to be taken into account. There are nonetheless some exceptions, i.e. child benefits, other discretionary social assistance payments (see below) and study grants. The means test is part of the social investigation by the public centre's social worker in which he/she evaluates each condition: age, nationality, family situation, residence, willingness to work and need. The final decision is taken by a council consisting of representatives of the local population, who are chosen by the town council (local authority). If the applicant does not agree with the PCSW's decision, he/she can appeal to the labour court. The level of the Minimex depends on the family situation. The act distinguishes between four categories: couples, single parents, children, single persons and cohabitants. Table 2.1 shows the allowance levels for the different categories.

Table 2.1   The Level of the Minimex Allowance

Category	Monthly amount (€) euros
1 Married couple	778
2 Single-parent family	778
3 Single person	584
4 Cohabitant	389

Source: Ministry for Social Integration and Social Economy, 2002.

In 1974, the benefit rates were established to reflect the various elements of living costs. As such, it can be considered as the national poverty line. Before 1985, the levels of the allowance for the different categories increased constantly in comparison to the per capita national income (Vranken, 2000). We find the highest ratio of the Minimex to the per capita national income for category one in 1986 (53.2 per cent), for category two in 1992 (47.7 per cent), for category three in 1987 (39.3 per cent) and for category four in 1986 (26.6 per cent). After these peaks, the four ratios deteriorated. The decline in categories one, three and four is parallel. In terms of wealth, they amount to 20 per cent less than at their peaks. The trend for category two is the same, but starts only after 1992 because of its late creation in 1987. Thus, it appears that the Minimex has fallen behind in comparison to the general increase of wealth (Cantillon *et al*, 2001). Only in 2002 was there an initial reaction of the Belgian government to this deterioration of the last ten years by means of an increase of four per cent. This is still less than the ten per cent demanded by the social movements for the poor.

Willingness to work and 'activation' policies   Beneficiaries have to be available for and seeking for work, unless this is regarded as unreasonable or impossible because of health problems.[3]   The interpretation of reasonableness is left to the local PCSWs. The claimant has to provide proof of his/her willingness to work, for instance by showing application evidence. Since 1993, beneficiaries under 25 years of age, have to show their willingness to work by signing an individual integration contract. It defines the young individual's and the centre's rights and duties to avoid welfare dependency and to realise his/her social integration. If the youngster does not comply with the contract, the PCSW can decide to suspend the Minimex for one month. They are obliged to offer a contract, but there is no sanction where there is no offer.

The social integration contract was one of the first indicators of the rise of activation policies for Minimex beneficiaries in Belgium. Although Belgium was the fourth ranked country on the OECD list for the percentage of spending on active labour market policies in 1996, the actual breakthrough of activation policies happened only in 1997 because of the European Employment Strategy.[4] Before this, a number of activation measures to integrate the unemployed into the labour market were taken, but these showed less co-ordination. The European Employment Strategy forced Belgium to put activation policies on the political agenda. 'Activation' in this context means the encouragement of increasing numbers of the population to take an active role in the economy, primarily through paid employment. Even now, a co-ordinated policy remains difficult because of the Belgian constitutional system.[5]

While before 1999 activation measures had been implemented, the activation discourse became dominant only in 1999 because of the new federal government. The main purpose was to 'modernise' the so-called passive welfare state and to raise the Belgian economic participation rate, which is one of the lowest in the European Union. The concrete measures for Minimex claimants were financial incentives for the PCSWs to develop more social employment jobs (in Belgium better known as article 60 of the PCSW-act) and a new Minimex law.

Article 60 §7 has been in place since 1976, but its purpose changed during the nineties. Originally, the PCSWs could employ their clients in their own services for a period equivalent to the social insurance qualification period.[6] In that way, he/she became entitled to an unemployment benefit. During the nineties, the purpose of work experience was increasingly stressed. Instead of entitlement to unemployment insurance, the 'article 60 job' was considered as a preparation for the regular labour market. In addition, municipalities and non-market associations can have 'article 60 workers' at their disposal. The current federal government gives more financial incentives to the PCSWs to develop such jobs. At the moment, approximately ten per cent of the Minimex claimants have a social employment job. However, the employment's duration remains dependent on the reference period. Consequently, it retains a dual purpose: integration into the unemployment benefit versus work experience.

From 1st October 2002, a new general social assistance scheme came into force in which the right to the Minimex was replaced by the right to social integration. Since a job is the best way to obtain social integration, the public centres have to counsel their clients into the labour market. Priority is given to those under 25 years of age. After three months, the PCSW has to offer them a job or to draw a social integration contract with measures such as training and schooling.

Table 2.2   Amount of the Living Wage

Category	Monthly living wage (€) euros
Single-parent family	778
Single person (with maintenance costs)	681
Single person	584
Cohabitant	389

Source: Ministry of Social Integration and Social Economy, 2002.

During the first three months and during the contract, the youngster has a right to a living wage, the new term for the guaranteed minimum income, but only if no job is available, according to the PCSW. Applicants older than 25 years have the right to a living wage or a job offered by the PCSW.

Their social integration contract is optional. The main employment programme remains article 60. The categories of the living wage change slightly (Table 2.2). In conclusion, the pressure on PCSWs to activate and employ their young claimants by means of article 60 increases seriously. At the moment, it is still unclear to what extent the right to a living wage can be undermined by the obligation to participate in an employment programme.

The right to social aid

In 1976, local poor relief was modernised by the creation of the Public Centres for Social Welfare, which were assigned a very broad duty. The first article of the act on the PCSWs states: 'Every person is entitled to social aid to ensure to everybody the possibility of a living in conditions corresponding to human dignity.' In other words, they must realise the right to social aid to secure a decent human existence for everybody. These PCSWs are municipal agencies governed by representatives of the local population. They are not elected directly, but are chosen by the directly elected members of the town council. The centres are financed by the local authority. Their creation caused three major shifts in local poor relief: (1) the introduction of a legal right to social aid, (2) the broadening of traditional poor relief into the promotion of the well-being (both in material and non-material senses) of the whole population and (3) the professionalisation of the personnel as a consequence of the compulsory recruitment of social workers. Thus, the establishment of the PCSW can be considered as a Copernican turnabout: from financial poor relief to the needy within the scope of charity to social aid to everybody within the scope of the broader and less clearly defined concept of 'well-being'. The local centres also became responsible in 1976 for the implementation of the Minimex.

The concepts of 'human dignity' and 'a decent human existence' are not defined in detail in the act. That is, the PCSW-act is goal-oriented: the PCSW itself decides in each individual case if a right to social aid arises because of damage to the applicant's human dignity. Consequently, this concept can be understood differently according to the financial situation of the public centre itself, the council's preferences and the decision's point in time. Thus, the central value in the Belgian tied assistance is individualisation: each individual request has to be considered separately. The PCSWs also decide autonomously on the most suitable form of aid. Legally, they dispose of five different types; these being financial, social, material, medical or psychological aid. Financial aid consists of four types: (1) the Minimex, (2) advances to social insurance allowance or other sources of income,[7] (3) periodical social aid along with or instead of the Minimex,[8] (4) one-off financial aid, the equivalent to the social fund in the UK. The first two kinds have relatively clear legal conditions. Concerning periodical and one-off financial aid, the public centres themselves are authorised to determine the conditions and the amounts as long as the value of human dignity is realised. The public centres can also opt for aid in kind: fuel oil, food, meals, cleaning aid, home help, and childcare…

A social examination by the social worker precedes the centre's intervention. This investigation leads to a diagnosis of the situation and to a proposition about the necessary aid to actualise the value of human dignity. However, the centre's council decides and can diverge from the social worker's proposition. If the applicant does not agree with the PCSW's decision, he/she can appeal to the labour court. Apart from the interpretation by the PCSWs, the labour courts therefore play an important role in the assessment of human dignity.

Only in two specific cases, financial support can be reclaimed from the claimant: (1) when the beneficiary obtains an income by virtue of a right he had during the period of financial aid, (2) in the case of an incorrect or incomplete reporting of the beneficiaries' means of existence. However, the PCSW-law states that they decide autonomously on the most suitable form of aid to realise their task. One of those forms can be a loan. Thus, if a public centre considers a loan more sensible than a financial aid, then the public centre can give a loan to the applicant. For instance, a single parent needs a second-hand car to comply with a job. She asks the PCSW to take care of the car's costs. In this case, the PCSW can decide to lend her the money. Yet, this decision has to be sufficiently substantiated with evidence. If the beneficiary does not agree with it, he/she can always lodge an appeal with the labour court.

The Implementation of General and Tied Social Assistance

This section focuses on the implementation process in which the policy decisions made by the federal public authority are carried out by the PCSWs. Although bureaucracies do not have the constitutional power to write legislation, they translate the broad mandates of legislature into the policies citizens actually experience. Consequently, they create policy through their implementation function. However, this process is not beyond question, because it has given rise to discrepancies between the legislator's intentions and the final policy outcomes on more than one occasion. Pressman and Wildawsky emphasised this some years ago.

> There are two implementation processes. One is the initially perceived, formally defined, prospectively expected set of causal links required to result in a desired outcome; the other unexpected nexus of causality that actually evolves during implementation. (Pressman and Wildavsky, 1984, p.217)

One of the causes is the presence of intended and unintended discretion in the legislation (see also, Craig, Chapter 3, this volume, for a discussion of 'unintended consequences').

Theoretical considerations about discretion

During the implementation process, public agencies and officers translate the 'law in books' into the 'law in action'. In that way, they help determine who gets what, when and how – the central question of politics. Implementation research cannot ignore the existence of discretion. A public agency or officer has discretion whenever the effective limits on their power leave the agency or officer free to make a choice among possible courses of action or inaction (Davis, 1969). The definition shows that public agencies as well as individual officers can dispose of it. The use of discretion is especially important in human service bureaucracies, because they determine which citizens receive welfare benefits and which citizens do not (Keiser, 1999).

Discretion can be caused by several factors. Firstly, discrepancies between legal concepts and social reality are inevitable to some extent. For instance, single persons and cohabitants can be simply separated juridically, but in reality, this distinction is much more vague. As a result, every legal concept and rule has some discretion (Handler, 1979). Secondly, vague and/or conflicting goals increase the extent of discretion (Hill, 1993; Lipsky, 1981). These come into being when the legislator cannot find a political consensus, when he does not know exactly what he wants or when he reformulates the goals during the policy-making process into another direction. For instance, on the one hand, the Minimex guarantees financial security, but on the other hand, activation policies want to avoid welfare dependency. Thirdly, not only the goals but also legal notions can be sometimes vaguely defined. Belgian examples are social integration and human dignity. Fourthly, public intervention can be based upon subjective information, which can be manipulated by citizens (Stone, 1984; Keiser, 1999). In other words, some human characteristics such as willingness to work (as opposed to age and gender), can be hardly objectified.

Consequently, the implementing officials in such cases always have a certain margin of judgement. Fifthly, the legislator decides that the concrete interpretation of rules and policy decisions can only occur at lower levels of government because of their professional or technical knowledge (Lipsky, 1980; Handler, 1979; Hill, 1993). The last factor correlates with the previous: the legislator acknowledges the implementation agency's autonomy (Hill, 1993).

In general, we can distinguish between two sorts of discretion: 'intended' discretion and inevitable discretion. Discretion is intended when the legislator explicitly decides to delegate the decisions to the implementation agencies. Other forms of discretion are unintended but inevitable. This is the case with subjective information, insufficiently specified legal concepts and the unavoidable gap between rules and the social reality. Where the Belgian social assistance is concerned, both forms of discretion are present. On the one hand, the Minimex can be considered as a categorical right, which one can appeal to if one satisfies the conditions of nationality, age, family situation, residence, willingness to work and need. Nationality and the age can be easily determined. However, the inevitable element of discretion can be specifically located in the condition of willingness to work. On the other hand, the PCSW-law is goal-oriented. That is, the PCSW has to use human dignity as a criterion in each individual case and decides itself on the most suitable aid. No other conditions are specified in the act. Next to the interpretation of the PCSW itself, the judicial review by the labour courts plays a major role in the appraisal of the criterion of 'human dignity'. In other words, the legislator ascribed explicitly a substantial element of discretion in the granting of social assistance to the local public centres. Three main reasons for that decision in 1976, can be distinguished. The creation of the public centres implied the modernisation of poor relief, which was organised and financed at the local level. As such, the local level was historically the main actor in poverty relief. The Belgian legislator was also of the opinion that the local level was in the best position to assess local needs. The third reason was the dominance of the subsidiarity principle because of the Christian political party's continuous dominant position since the Second World War.[9]

Discretion has advantages as well as disadvantages. Firstly, it makes possible the narrowing of the gap between law and social reality, to adjust the general principles to individual cases and to respond better to individual circumstances. After all, rules can hardly be refined enough to cover all possible situations. Secondly, discretion facilitates the adaptation of policies to unexpected or changed conditions. Thirdly, since possibly not every problem during implementation has been taken care of, discretion cannot be restricted too much. However, legal inequality, legal insecurity and arbitrariness are the main disadvantages. If organisations at the local level vary systematically in their use of discretion (where citizens live will determine whether they receive services), then this violates our norm of an equitable public service. However, those differences can be seen as legitimate, if the legislator has explicitly decided to delegate the decision to an autonomous local body.

Applied to social assistance, local autonomy and discretionary payments are supposed to have three main advantages (OECD, 1998). Firstly, local preferences and conditions can be more accurately reflected if local governments or agencies are given the freedom to vary benefit rates (rate-setting autonomy). However, local rate setting can bring about migration of clients who search for the most advantageous payments. Secondly, efficient administration may be encouraged if local government agencies are made financially responsible for payments (financial autonomy). In addition, in a decentralised system, decisions about particular cases have a proportionally larger effect on the local budget than in a system where all comes out of a central budget. Consequently, local government has an incentive to use all possibilities for removing individuals from social assistance. Thirdly, greater policy coherence should be attained by ensuring that all relevant institutions have an incentive to co-operate with other services and service providers. However, any potential gains have to be balanced against the disadvantages when more actors are involved. In particular, it makes co-ordination more complex and it means that the information flows necessary for policy-makers to adapt policies are more complicated.

The use of discretion can be studied from two perspectives: from the level of the individual behaviour and from the organisational level (see also Rowe, Chapter 6, this volume). Within the first approach, the individual dealing of bureaucrats with rules and discretion is of central importance. The second perspective starts from the influence of the organisation on the way the members of the organisation act, assuming that organisational routines profoundly restrict the latitude of the individual actor. Both perspectives however fall short when used separately. On the one hand, certain preferences and modes of operation can be followed so often at the organisational level that they become solidified routines or hardly changeable 'standard operating procedures' that are hard to change (March and Olsen, 1989). On the other hand, the deterministic character of standard operating procedures should not be overestimated. Individual deviations and new, formalised or otherwise procedures are still possible. In this contribution, we do not want to choose between the two perspectives, but clarify that the space left by discretion can be filled in by individual officers and collective norms on the organisational level.

The implementation of the Minimex from an empirical point of view

In the light of this theoretical approach, this section will shed light on the implementation of the Minimex and the tied social assistance from an empirical point of view. Both are administered on the local level by the PCSW, but the kind of discretion in both laws diverges to a considerable extent. If available, studies of implementation as outcome – the state of having been implemented – as well as studies of implementation as output – the act of implementing will be considered (Lane, 1995, p.98; Hogwood and Gunn, 1985).

Implementation outcome Concerning the implementation outcome of the Minimex, there are chiefly static administrative data available. However, these kind of data do not allow judgements about the duration of the claims and in- and out-flows of Minimex beneficiaries. Restricted longitudinal data are only available for Flanders.[10] In short, the history of longitudinal research into poverty and social exclusion in Belgium has yet to be written for the most part (Vranken *et al*, 2000, p.50).

The available administrative data show a powerful increase of the claims on the Minimex during the nineties (Table 2.3). This trend can be observed in the whole of Europe (European Commission, 1999). The peak was in the beginning of 1999, when 83,000 persons applied for the Minimex. After ten years of increases, the number of Minimex claimants stabilised in 2000. The most recent figures, however, indicate a striking reduction (15 per cent), but it is too early to point to the causes of this recent change of direction. In general, the total number of Belgian Minimex beneficiaries is, in comparison to other European countries, relatively low because of the strong protection give by unemployment insurance (OECD, 1998).[11] Since the administrative data does not permit cross-table calculations, we can only properly assess single social characteristics of Minimex applicants. On January 31[st,] 2001, female, single and young claimants were over represented. During the nineties, most striking is the increase of youngsters, which can be explained by legal and social changes (Delathouwer *et al*, 1997). The legal changes consist of the lowering of the official adulthood age from 21 to 18 years, the removal of the study grant from the means test and the extension of the reference period in unemployment insurance. Another cause is the social changes such as increased youth unemployment, the changes in family composition and family life and the complicated relations between parents and children. During the last years, the increase of youngsters is stabilised and the amount of single-parent families and women has increased. From a longitudinal point of view, the limited available data for Flanders show that 37 per cent of Minimex beneficiaries in 1998 were already entitled for a period longer than three years. Ten per cent of them claimed a Minimex for more than ten years (Dehaes *et. al*, 2000, pp.31-35).

Table 2.3   Minimex Claimants by Gender, Category and Age, 1990-2001[12]

Percentages (%)

1990		1995	2000	2001	
Gender	Male	39.6	45.0	44.0	41.1
	Female	60.4	55.0	56.0	58.9
Category	Married couple	7.4	6.9	6.8	7.2
	Single-parent family	21.6	18.8	19.1	21.5
	Single person	47.4	52.1	56.2	52.1
	Cohabitant	23.7	22.2	17.9	19.3
Age	< 25	11.8	24.9	25.8	24.7
	25-34	23.2	21.7	21.7	18.6
	35-44	25.4	21.6	21.7	22.1
	45-54	19.5	17.3	17.3	20.3
	55-64	15.1	11.2	11.0	12.4
	> 65	5.0	3.3	3.1	2.5
Total (number)		49,479	69,740	81,905	70,364

Source: Vranken *et al*, 2001.

Implementation output There is no systematic research available about the use of the 'inevitable' discretion in the Minimex law by the PCSWs and their social workers. However, current qualitative in-depth interviewing about willingness to work in PCSWs shows differences between PCSWs, between social workers inside the same public centre and between the street-level social workers and the council, which takes the final decisions based on the reports, by the social workers.[13] This is caused by the relatively unspecific and subjective character of the concept. Although the public centres do not acknowledge their policy-making function concerning the Minimex, the research shows the existence of local differences between and in public centres, which have a decisive influence for the claimant. His/her residence determines how severe the willingness to work is evaluated and the efforts he/she has to show to be qualified for the Minimex for a longer period.

The implementation of social aid from an empirical point of view

The first article of the PCSW-law states:

> Every person is entitled to social aid to ensure to everybody the possibility of a living in conditions of human dignity.

The jurisdiction has defined this throughout the years as social aid necessary for food, clothes, housing, care, work and extra-ordinary care in case of hospitalisation. However, even this definition remains relatively vague. On the one hand, the courts stress that PCSWs decide in each individual case to what extent social aid is necessary (Cuypers *et al*, 2001). On the other hand, they permit the centres to develop their own social aid rules as long as they refer to the realisation of human dignity and as long as individual deviations remain possible. In other words, the PCSWs can develop their own standards necessary to fulfil the claimant's human dignity. The courts do not interfere with the formulation of the public centres' rules as such, but they will assess whether the applicant's 'human dignity' is damaged by the operationalisation of these rules.

There is very little known about 'tied' social assistance in Belgium. To an extent, this is caused by the strong aspect of individualisation in the act, which hinders scientific generalisations about the granting of social aid in Belgium. However, recent research by Dehaes *et al* (2001) clarifies the aggregated policy outcome of the Flemish PCSWs in the field of financial aid. Attention is especially paid to the claimant's social characteristics and to the purposes of financial aid. The study discriminates between two groups of financial aid beneficiaries: the Minimex claimants and those with another source of income. Concerning the former, four out of ten Minimex claimants receive one or more income supplements. In these cases, the Minimex is insufficient to live a decent human existence. Their proportion grows as age increases, but does not correlate with gender. An income supplement is usually meant to carry costs of medical care (21 per cent), housing costs (14 per cent), energy costs (12 per cent) and general costs (10 per cent). Concerning the latter, a large group of 21,864 people also receive income supplements from the PCSW. They mostly rely on an insufficient social security benefit (different from the Minimex). This group is characterised by an overrepresentation of women and of elderly people. The main purposes of the income supplements are costs of medical care (25 per cent), housing costs (22 per cent), general costs (22 per cent) and energy costs (14 per cent). However, the different purposes served by financial aid are formulated in very general terms. Research into the jurisdiction of the labour courts shows their divergent meanings (Cuypers *et al*, 2001). For instance, the labour courts appreciated the following medical costs[14] as necessary for the realisation of 'human dignity' in individual cases: a stomach operation to lose weight for medical reasons, a brace, traumatic stress, family therapy, kinaesthesia, etc (Cuypers *et al*, 2001). Once more, the strong individualisation in the social aid act makes generalised statements impossible.

However, this study does not discriminate between PCSWs and the amount of financial aid granted. As a result, no insight is gained into the differences between PCSWs in the granting of financial aid. Previous research can shed some light on them (Luyten, 1993; Lammertyn *et al*, 1990).[15] The description of clients' circumstances confirmed the considerable inter-municipal differences in the granting of financial aid. For some client situations, those differences amounted to €250 a month. Some PCSWs compensated (partially) for the monthly energy costs, medical care or housing costs, others not.

Half of the public centres developed their own rules for supplementary financial aid. One out of three had them formalised in written rules. The development of their own rules corresponds to municipal size: the larger the municipality, the greater the chance of formulating their own rules. Concerning their content, they can be characterised as a patchwork of diversity. Some of them use the Minimex as starting point and grant an extra percent of it for specific costs such as housing, medical care or energy. Other public centres start from the financial needs of the household (all the living costs including medical care, energy and housing costs). If the needs are larger than its income, the public centre grants the necessary amount of financial aid. Some public centres had also developed their own rules for energy and housing costs. The main reason for the development of such rules was to support the principle of equal, objective treatment for all claimants in their area and the co-ordination of the social workers' assessment. The rules are, as such, an aid to 'fine tune' the social workers' assessments. In this way, it is intended that arbitrariness and subjective judgments by social workers should be prevented.

These rules can also function for the social workers as a means to restrict the political power of the centre's council. If the centre's council has accepted the rules, then the social workers can propose financial aid without being overruled by the council. Not every social worker, though, is satisfied with these rules, because they contravene the professional norms of social work, reflected in the individualised treatment of every person.

Two main reasons for the absence of local rules can be distinguished. On the one hand, some public centres don't grant supplementary financial aid. They consider the Minimex as sufficient to live a human decent existence. On the other hand, other centres stress the value of individualisation. That is, in every individual case, the centres evaluate what is necessary to live a human decent existence, because the council does not want to restrict its own power in the process of determining eligibility for grants. However, social workers in those centres complain about arbitrariness and bias.

Virtually all types of means-tests designed for individual selective benefits and all schemes for charges with a related right to remission, involving the population of all working ages, run into these problems of moral values, incentives and equity (Titmuss, 1968, p.120). The danger of moral judgements is especially present in the Belgian system of discretionary payments. Since the decisions are taken by a council of local representatives, they can rely on their own knowledge about the claimants instead of the social investigation by the social worker. That is, subjective arguments, rumours and gossip can undermine the professional advice by the social worker. In this way, privileged treatments and judgements about the claimant can gain the upper hand of the legal nature of social aid. These are more prevalent in centres without financial aid rules, because the social workers cannot rely on them to formulate a proposal to the centre's council.

During the ten-year period to 2002, local differences in the granting of supplementary financial aid were never on the political agenda in Belgium. No policy changes concerning social aid were implemented, although the Minimex and also minimum levels of other social security benefits have fallen behind in comparison to the general increase of wealth. Consequently, current in-depth interviewing in PCSWs affirms the old considerable differences in the granting of financial aid. Thus, the discretion in social aid law gives rise to legal divergences between local centres in the granting of supplementary financial aid.

Conclusion

In Belgium, municipal PCSWs which are governed by representatives of the local population, are responsible for the implementation of general and tied social assistance. On the one hand, the act which has established the Minimex, which can be considered as the national poverty line, contains relatively well-defined conditions such as age, nationality, need and family situation. The limited and clearly defined element of discretion can be specifically located in the condition of 'willingness to work'. Local PCSWs and their social workers deal divergently with this condition. As a consequence, the applicant's residence determines how stringently 'willingness to work' is evaluated and the efforts he/she has to show to be qualified for the Minimex for a longer period.

On the other hand, the act on social aid attributes a considerable amount of 'intended' discretion to the local PCSWs. That is, they have to decide what assistance is necessary to realise a decent human existence to all. In this way, they are able to take into account the applicant's individual characteristics and offer a highly specific form of aid.

Research shows that the main purpose of social aid is to compensate for insufficient Minimex and social security benefits. However, the large amount of discretion creates at the same time considerable differences between PCSWs in the interpretation of human dignity and, as a consequence, in the granting of social aid. In other words, the same needs are treated divergently depending on the authorised local public centre. In this way, discrepancies between the national poverty line and the minimum social security benefits on the one hand and the local norm of human dignity on the other hand arise. In addition, a decentralised system in which non-professional representatives of the local population decide on the most appropriate aid, can lead to moral judgements about the 'deservingness' of the applicants. In this way, the legal nature of the right to social aid can be turned into a 'favour' as a consequence of arbitrariness and privileged treatment.

Notes

1　Tied assistance can be further divided into housing assistance and other tied assistance.
2　There are three programmes for the disabled: the income replacement allowance, the integration allowance and the attendance allowance for the elderly disabled persons. The income replacement allowance is granted to disabled adults from 21 up to 65 years with a physical or mental handicap that prevents them from earning more than one third of the amount a healthy person gains. The benefit is household-oriented and the amounts correspond to the Minimex. The integration allowance is granted to disabled adults from 21 years up to 65 with a reduced ability to live independently. Its purpose is to compensate for the additional social integration costs. The level of the allowance depends on the degree of ability to live independently. The attendance allowance for elderly is granted to the disabled aged 65 and over with a reduced ability to live independently. Concerning the elderly, every elderly person aged 62 or over can apply for this new allowance in case of insufficient resources. The basic amount, which is €4,682 per year. is increased by 50 per cent. if the applicant doesn't share his residence with others. The guaranteed family allowance ensures family benefits for families/single parents not entitled to child benefits because of an insufficient social security status. It is additional to other guaranteed minimum incomes. The amounts are of the same level as

the social insurance family benefits. The guaranteed family allowance is granted if the applicant's income does not exceed €3,200. These allowances are implemented centrally by departments of the Federal Ministry for Social Affairs.

3   Examples are care for young children and serious psychological problems.

4   Permanent employment programmes in the non-market sector, subsidized indefinitely by unemployment benefits, can explain the high ranking. Actually, those programmes restricted the flow into the regular labour market, because the unemployed got stuck in them (Nicaise, 1999).

5   Social security is a federal matter while counselling and training are regional. Employment is a federal as well as a regional competence. Consequently, the division of competences hinders the development of a coherent activation policy.

6   Public centres offer services such as cleaning, handymen, hot meals, and care for elderly, etc. The client earns a minimum wage and the state subsidises the job for an amount equivalent to the Minimex.

7   If there is an administrative delay, the public centre can give an advance to the person entitled to a social insurance benefit.

8   The public centres can give financial aid equivalent to the Minimex to those who aren't entitled to the Minimex (for instance, non-EU migrants).

9   Subsidiarity is a central characteristic of the Christian-Democrat doctrine (Van Kersbergen, 1995). From the Second World War until 1999, the Christian-Democrats were the largest political party in Belgium.

10 58 per cent of the Belgian population lives in Flanders.

11 An unique feature of the Belgian system is the unlimited duration of benefit entitlements (at least, in principle). However, it is restricted by a series of conditions: only heads of family retain their proportional benefit, other persons have a substantially reduced benefit and cohabitants lose them after an 'abnormally long duration of unemployment'.

12 As at 31st January of each year.

13 The in-depth interviews are part of the PhD project conducted by Koen Hermans, which studies the implementation of the activation policies by PCSWs. More specifically, it examines how the PCSWs and their social workers deal with the paradigm change from income security for their clients to activation and (re-)integration into the labour market.

14 By contrast, the English courts have upheld a refusal to pay expenses for incontinence pads as 'excluded' medical items under the social fund directions: see *R v Social Fund Inspector, ex parte Connick*, [1994] C.O.D 75 referred to in Buck, 2000, pp.136, 438-9.

15 It consisted of two parts: in the first part, comprehensive client descriptions were presented to the Flemish PCSWs. They had to indicate how much financial aid they would grant to the distinctive clients. If the centres had developed their own rules, then these were then subject to further qualitative analysis.

Chapter 3

Balancing the Books:
The Social Fund in Action

Gary Craig

The Origins of the Social Fund

In Chapter 1, the history of social security one-off payments was briefly outlined. This showed that some recurring policy issues emerged during the 50-plus years following the introduction of the first national scheme introduced in 1934, issues such as the balance between discretion and entitlement, the role of appeals tribunals, boundary problems with other organisations' areas of competence, and, most of all, the need to control expenditure. By 1985, it was clear that the latest one-off payments scheme, the single payments scheme, was not free from these difficulties and in 1985, as part of a wider-ranging review of the social security system, the government of the day (the second led by Margaret Thatcher), began to formulate proposals for its reform.

The social fund proposals were first published in the 1985 social security Green Paper (HMSO, 1985). Four main features were novel in comparison with earlier one-off payment schemes and all attracted considerable attention and, amongst the poverty lobby, concern and hostility. These four features were: (i) the introduction of firm cash limits; (ii) the emphasis on loans; (iii) a return to discretion as the basis for decision-making at local office level; and (iv) the replacement of the right to appeal by a review process. These proposals were, as noted, situated within the government's overarching desire for a system which was simpler and better targeted and, in line with its wider social policy goals, a reduced role for the state. The Green Paper asserted that social security spending was a burden on the economy and dismissed arguments, prompted by a rapid growth in poverty at the time, that any far-reaching reform of social security should be preceded by research into adequate living standards or the ability of the weekly scale rates to address them. The government's view was that the poor had done relatively well from the economic and social policies of the 1979-85 period – an assertion which flew in the face of mounting research evidence (see e.g. Johnson and Webb, 1990). Between 1978 and 1987, the value of the scale rates for couples on the long-term social assistance rate had fallen from 46 per cent to 38 per cent of average male earnings, a drop of almost 20 per cent and by 1987, 10.5m people were living on incomes below half national average, double the number in 1979.

The social fund was to be accompanied by a new social assistance scheme, Income Support (IS), which replaced supplementary benefit with a series of group-based premiums (weekly benefit additions) and abolished Additional Requirements Payments. Lower rates of IS were introduced for under-25s and entitlement to benefit removed for most 16-17 year-olds. The social fund itself, which replaced Single Payments (SPs), Urgent Needs Payments (UNPs) and maternity and death grants, consisted of two major parts. A regulated scheme covered funeral, maternity and cold weather payments, and a discretionary scheme (much the larger part of the new social fund scheme) offered a mixture of grants and (mainly) interest-free loans, including Crisis Loans (CLs) which replaced UNPS to a certain extent. The scheme was mainly restricted to those on IS although anyone could apply for a CL and parts of the regulated scheme were open to those on housing benefit and family credit. Community Care Grants (CCGs) were to promote further the objectives of care in the community by, for example, helping older people stay in their own homes. The aim of Budgeting Loans (BLs), the core of the social fund, was, in the government's words 'to give people a sum of money within which they manage for themselves'. In this Chapter we review the operation of the social fund in practice, focusing firstly on the early years of the fund when its difficulties emerged strongly and the fears of its critics were realised. Successive governments have taken corrective action, but generally of a marginal kind and the major structural issues inherent in the working of the fund have, in the view of its critics, yet to be addressed. The Chapter concludes by examining the longer-term trends in social fund spending patterns covering the thirteen years of operation from 1988-2001.

The Early Years

Teething problems

The social fund was established operationally in April 1988 as part of the Social Security Act 1986 reforms.[1] As noted, with the possible exception of the proposals for reforming pensions, the social fund attracted the greatest levels of public, professional and academic controversy and this controversy, though reaching a height during the fund's early years, has continued until the present day, matched only by the unwillingness of any government seriously to listen to the criticisms. This level of controversy was particularly remarkable given the fact that the fund, like its predecessor schemes, again involved a relatively minuscule proportion (considerably less than one per cent) of total social security spending. The reasons for the controversy focused on several key aspects.

- The return of the one-off payments scheme to a largely discretionary scheme (albeit with some limited regulated elements for funeral, winter and maternity payments); this led to fears that the fund would act particularly against the interests of 'unpopular' claimant groups such as unemployed young people, lone parents and members of minority ethnic groups;
- The new overwhelming emphasis on providing financial help in the form of loans – which, though interest-free, would effectively reduce claimants' weekly benefit to well below the scale rates - rather than grants; and
- The intention to cap expenditure and the likelihood that this would deflect demand onto other organisations outside the sphere of government, and/or drive need underground, and result in enhanced boundary difficulties.

The budget for the first year of the fund was set at £201 million, £140 million of which were for loans. Although this was substantially below the peak of single payments (£370 million) it was close to the level of SPs following the 1986 restrictions. In any case, expenditure during the first year consistently failed to meet anticipated levels. This was doubtless because of uncertainty about the scheme on the part of claimants and anxiety, particularly to not overspend, on the part of officials. The result was that even with a relaxation of controls towards the end of the year, final gross out-turn was only £166 million of which £41 million was on grants. Of the £125 million spent on loans, £17 million was on CLs. The budget for the following year was frozen in cash terms. However, a relatively large number of applications was carried over from the first year as a result of increased levels of activity towards the end of 1988-9 year and this 'deferred demand' began to have an impact early in 1989-90, pushing spending over the notional 'profile', the monthly proportion of local budget to which local offices were recommended to work. This profiling, together with a new dedicated computer system and intense monitoring by local managers, were all part of the array of mechanisms by which government intended that expenditure should be carefully managed. Despite this, as a result partly of this suppressed demand, by the end of 1989, extra allocations were announced by the Secretary of State to local offices but by

December 1989, some local offices were paying out no BLs at all. By the end of the financial year, the fund nationally was more or less spent up to the revised cash limits of £206 million.

Budgeted expenditure for the following year was set slightly higher at £215 million but pressure on resources continued in that and the fourth year: from 1,749,000 applications in 1998-9, demand for help rose in 1991-2 to just over three million applications, an increase of about 75 per cent. In the early part of the third year, mounting pressure on these capped resources was also accentuated by legal challenges to the Secretary of State's powers. Judicial rulings suggested that the guidance to social fund officers (a separate group of officials within each local social security office) was unlawful in relation to the ability to exceed local allocations, rulings which were then made redundant by the government introducing amending legislation in the summer of 1990.[2] By the time of this legislation, many local offices, taking a more generous view of their responsibilities (and it is worth noting that the trades union representing them was implacably opposed to the introduction of the social fund), had far exceeded their local allocations. For example, in three Glasgow offices, serving areas where there was intense poverty, after only one-third of the year, expenditures were between 71 and 91 per cent of their annual allocations. Following the amending legislation, expenditure was brought back under control and the budget for the third year, including further supplementary allocations, was £228m (of which £68m was for grants), and final total expenditure £223 million. In March 1991, the government also announced that in future, a formal net cash limit of £100 million would be implemented: thus, regardless of the actual level of expenditure, the recovery rate from loans repayments would have to be set in such a way that total net expenditure would not exceed £100 million. The final allocation for 1991-2 (the fourth year) was £277 million (£198 million on loans) and the starting budget for 1992-3 was £302 million, £211 million of which was for loans.

During the first year, the rate of recovery from loans was smaller than had been predicted at £48 million but this rate grew rapidly and by the fourth year the value of loans recovered was £148 million. Although this reflected a build-up in the value of loans awarded, there was also emerging evidence that loans were increasingly required to be repaid either at higher proportions of weekly benefit (the recommended maximum was 15 per cent but this was increasingly exceeded) or over shorter periods of time. These were further elements of the array of techniques available to local managers to contain expenditure such that, by constant surveillance and juggling, they would ensure that they ended the year close to but, preferably, slightly under budget: close to budget because they did not want to lose allocations the following year, which would have made pressure on limited resources more acute and their administrative and managerial lives more difficult, but slightly under, because they didn't want the reprimands and disfavour that would follow from senior managers or the Secretary of State. The most obvious technique however was simply to manipulate the rate of refusal of awards, and mounting evidence appeared after a year or two that refusal rates varied enormously between offices, within offices over time and between different groups of claimants or for differing types of award as the juggling process continued through the annual budgetary cycle (Craig, 1988; Stewart and Robertson, 1989; *New Statesman* 5 January 1990; National Audit Office, 1991).

In the three years from March 1989 to March 1992, refusal rates for CCGs had increased significantly, for all types of discretionary social fund payment.

Table 3.1   Social Fund Refusal Rates, 1989-1992 (March)

		Percentages (%)
Payment type	1989	1992
Crisis Loan	10	17
Budgeting Loan	39	44
Community Care Grant	49	72

Source: Secretary of State's Annual Reports on the Social Fund.

These figures masked considerable variations between local offices, it should be noted. The CL refusal rates were significant because the proportion of loans going to CLs had increased by more than 50 per cent over these four years. Each local office had the discretion to draw up its own list of priority groups for receiving awards for BLs and CCGs and these priority ratings were also used as a means of managing demand (in a similar way to the exercise of local discretion in Belgium; see Hermans and Declercq, Chapter 2, this volume). Priority lists were often narrowed to the point where even the most vulnerable families had difficulty getting help and the proportion of applicants rejected because they were deemed as of 'insufficient priority' steadily grew. Where local offices had difficulties in managing demand, they were likely to be supported by interventions from the DHSS centrally (and, from 1991, by the Benefits Agency) which frequently adjusted the formula for allocating funds between offices. The effects of these changes drove the national pattern of spending back towards the picture which had existed during the life of SPs, one of significant intra- and inter-regional imbalances (National Audit Office, 1991).

An analysis of expenditure to claimant groups (see e.g. Craig, 1992) showed that the division between receipt of CCGs and BLs increasingly reflected the long-standing divisions between 'deserving' and 'undeserving' claimant groups; CCGs increasingly went to pensioners and claimants with a disability, BLs to lone parents and the unemployed. There was also evidence that, although any claimant could in theory apply for either major award (and in law any application was treated as 'an application to the fund as a whole' until the changes introduced by the Social Security Act 1998), officers were increasingly 'directing' certain groups of claimants towards particular kinds of award. At the same time, and echoing the experience of claimants and advisers in relation to the former Supplementary Benefits Appeals Tribunals, it was clear that the intervention of advisers could make a significant difference to an applicant's chance of getting a grant rather than a loan (Clements, 1989; Cleveland County Council, 1989; Leith Rights Forum, 1989; Alcock *et al*, 1990). For both BLs and CCGs, the vast majority of expenditure (over 75 per cent in both cases) went during the first few years on furniture and household items, with only about six per cent going towards help with clothing. In this regard, the social fund showed little change from its immediate predecessor.

Familiar tensions

Once the teething problems had begun to be addressed, some very familiar problems began to emerge. First of these were the boundary difficulties with other organisations. Those who were refused loans or did not apply were, it was reported, increasingly turning to local authorities or to charities (Becker, 1989; Social Security Research Consortium, 1989; Cleveland County Council, 1989; Morley, 1990). Becker reported that:

> clients of SSDs [social services departments] were being passed backwards and forwards between the [social fund] and local social work offices as neither felt able or willing to help. (Becker, 1989, p.6)

Also, local authority cash help was being used to meet basic income maintenance needs rather than for exceptional circumstances. The National Audit Office found that 16 of the 22 local authorities it surveyed for its first major report (National Audit Office, 1991) reported increased financial and administrative pressure as a result of the introduction of the fund. Other evidence indicated that claimants were making increasing use of defective and worn second-hand goods, particularly gas and electrical appliances, borrowing from family or friends or from loan sharks and other commercial loan companies (Barnardo's, 1990; Craig, 1991).

Despite the government's hopes that the social fund would lead to a simplification of the system, administrative difficulties began to create considerable problems for staff and management alike. The novel features of the fund, especially the introduction of cash limits and the division between grants and loans required a new approach to managing demand but the contradictions which these revealed, keeping priority lists whilst responding to unpredictable demand for example, became almost unmanageable at times (particularly in light of the continual failure of the new computerised system to cope with the task involved) and led to widely varying rates of refusal across time and/or space. Neighbouring offices serving similar areas demonstrated significant but unexplained variations in refusal rates, sizes of awards, the speed at which applications were processed and the pattern of needs met. The failure of the computer to deliver robust data was underlined by the refusal of the Comptroller and Auditor General to approve the initial accounts of the social fund for each of the first three years of its operation.[3] The National Audit Office also drew attention to the high cost of administering the scheme which, in the first two years of the fund's operation, represented about 30 per cent of the value of benefits delivered, compared with 4.5 per cent for the benefit system as a whole and only 1.4 per cent for retirement pensions.

The return to discretion, which the government had argued for in terms of reversing the increasing complexity of the system (HMSO, 1985, vol. 2, para. 2.28) had been criticised as likely to lead to enhanced levels of prejudice, stigma and racism. Although the cash limits, and a panoply of guidance and directions effectively limited the scope of this discretion to the point where some took the view that the scheme was now a regulated one in disguise (a neat reversal of the SP scheme), there were still two areas where the operation of discretion was significant: whether a social fund officer (SFO) decided to make a payment at all and if so, in what form the payment should be made. The evidence from the first years showed clearly that discretion was being used to underpin the caution with which SFOs were generally approaching their task, that is to err in favour of refusal when in doubt, and that it also had an impact in terms of the refusal of SFOs to help particular groups of less deserving claimants. Individual instances of racist behaviour by SFOs were reported and these were underpinned by institutional forms of racism inherent in the social security system and within the social fund itself (Becker, 1989; SSAC, 1990; National Audit Office, 1991; Cohen *et al.*, 1992).

Finally, the shift in 1988 from an appeals system under previous one-off payments schemes to one based largely on internal reviews, had excited considerable comment, being regarded by the Council on Tribunals as the most significant loss of a right to appeal to an independent tribunal since the Council had been established in 1958 (see Buck, Chapter 8, this volume). These criticisms had led to the government introducing a second, quasi-independent tier of review overseen by an arms-length Social Fund Commissioner (SFC); claimants dissatisfied with internal reviews by SFOs would be able to make representations to the SFC. The review process was evaluated early on in the life of the fund (Dalley and Berthoud, 1992). Early use of the review process was very limited but the first reports of the SFC were critical of the evidence provided by SFOs in support of their decisions. Although, with limited demand on their time, reviews were undertaken fairly speedily in the first years, this picture deteriorated as demand grew such that by 1991, compared with the average period for a review in 1988-9 of about two weeks, it was now taking 40 days on average and less than ten per cent of reviews were cleared within 30 working days. Again, however, there was enormous variation in terms of the picture between offices; in one Bradford office, SFOs revised 21 per cent of decisions on review, in a neighbouring office also within Bradford the corresponding figure was 65 per cent. Increasingly, the High Court was being drawn in to adjudicate on the competence of those operating the system and on aspects of the system itself through judicial review but one critical insight emerging from these legal reviews was that the social fund was, quite deliberately, an inconsistent policy tool. The SFC noted that:

> the system wants it not to be consistent – it doesn't happen, there are differences in budget at different times of the year, in different offices and with different officers. In addition, inconsistency is introduced by better levels of support from better welfare rights agencies in some areas. (Social Fund Commissioner, personal communication, 27 February 1990)

Many of the issues raised by the early operation of the social fund were therefore familiar ones in the sense that they had recurred throughout the historical development of one-off payment schemes. Additionally, however, the fund presented new issues such as the role of loans and the impact of firm cash limits. The remainder of the life of the social fund to date (to 2002) provides no indication that governments of any persuasion are prepared to address them or, by addressing the failure of social security to offer an adequate weekly benefit, to render most of them redundant. One of the most dismal aspects of the fund is the way in which its most vigorous Parliamentary critics have come to accept and indeed to welcome its existence. Robin Cook M.P., Parliamentary Spokesperson on health and social security for the Labour Party in 1987 could observe of the fund that:

> [U]p and down the country, the government's new social fund will mean sweeping cuts in the help available to the poorest members of the community. (*A new assault on the poor*, December 1987, mimeo)

However, by the time New Labour came to power in 1997, the new Secretary of State could argue that:

> the regulated and discretionary parts of the social fund contribute to this goal [of tackling unjustifiable social and economic inequalities] by providing a variety of help to those in greatest need. (Harriet Harman, Secretary of State for Social Security, July 1997)

In the remainder of this Chapter, we will consider the longer-term trends of the fund over the first thirteen years of its unhappy life.

Thirteen Years of the Fund: Unlucky for Most

Regardless of government claims, the reality is that an overwhelming body of research evidence (perhaps the most substantial and consistent body of independent research evidence ever mounted in relation to a single element of government social security policy), has demonstrated that, whilst the fund may be judged a remarkable success as an instrument of financial control and of ideological discipline, in terms of providing help for the most vulnerable and needy, it is an abject failure. First of all, the fund officially sanctions the breaching of the Beveridge safety net. Social fund loans take claimants' income 15 per cent (and often more) below the official poverty line. This might be acceptable where the official poverty line was set at an adequate level. But a long tradition of rigorous research has demonstrated the inadequacy of basic social assistance benefit levels. Successive governments have long refused to countenance any official review of the adequacy of benefits. The only such review, in the 1960s, was suppressed by government itself because of its embarrassing findings (that benefit levels were inadequate for the maintenance of an acceptable standard of living). As a result, social assistance benefit levels today are not judged in terms of their objective adequacy but in relation to a series of politically expedient decisions made shortly before and after the Second World War.

The work of the Benefits Research Unit (Becker and Silburn, 1990) and the Social Security Research Consortium (1991), confirmed by later studies, showed that the social fund generated increased indebtedness amongst the poorest claimants and that it could be counted a policy success only in its (implicit) policy objective of limiting expenditure on the poorest. Even the help it gave was poorly targeted. The Social Security Consortium's (1989) review of the fund's impact on voluntary organisations demonstrated that the fund was shifting demand for help onto charities and voluntary organisations or driving it underground into the 'informal' and exploitative private loan sector. The DSS-funded official evaluation of the fund (Huby and Dix, 1992) found that 'decisions to make awards were so erratic that there was nothing to distinguish the needs of those who received them from those who did not.' Strangely, a subsequent Secretary of State, Peter Lilley M.P., apparently derived the opposing conclusion from this rigorous study and other evidence, claiming in 1993 that the 'official' evaluation, the SSAC criticisms, and those of all other research, provided 'no evidence to alter our belief that the basic principles of the discretionary scheme are right.'

Both Craig (1992) and the Social Security Advisory Committee (1992) responded to the growing chorus of intense criticism against the fund with carefully costed and detailed proposals for affordable change. Cohen *et al*, (1992) traced the impact of the fund on the day-to-day lives of families in several cities; claimants reported increased debt, enforced dependence on family and friends, and growing inability to buy essentials. A consortium of voluntary agencies, including The Children's Society, the Family Welfare Association and the Family Service Units, returned to look at the fund in 1996 (Cohen *et al*, 1996), finding yet again that 'the fund is manifestly failing to meet need and ... creating confusion and despair amongst benefit claimants' and showing, in a very detailed way, the process which drives claimants away from the social fund towards charitable help. More recent evidence from charitable bodies showed that the fund has continued to deflect demand away from government into the voluntary sector (Craig and Datta, 2000).

Early evidence, as reported above, showed that the operation of discretion was inequitable in practice and that decisions were shaped often by prejudice and discriminatory attitudes. For minority ethnic groups, the evidence suggests that structural discrimination played an important part in deterring applicants although the failure of the DSS to engage in effective ethnic monitoring has made it difficult to be conclusive about this. There is, however, some evidence that black and minority ethnic groups find the structural features of the social fund at odds with their own cultural and collective traditions for providing financial support and therefore make little use of the fund (Sadiq-Sangster, 1992). The structural discrimination built in to the social fund is also reflected in the distribution of grants and loans between different groups of claimants (see below). Although more recent changes have apparently limited even further the degree of discretion open to local officials, SFOs still have a strong influence on the way in which claimants needs are 'shaped' and (although this has not been publicly made known), on the size of loans which may be made available to them, in order to discourage claimants from applying (*Community Care*, 25 March, 1999).

The fundamental criticisms of the social fund have always been, and remain, that it is discretionary and cash-limited, elements of the scheme which have required social fund managers to juggle with budgets in the face of unpredictable demand in such a way that the notion of a lottery is inescapably built in to its workings. The description of the social fund as a lottery continues to be particularly appropriate. It remains the case that the chances of obtaining help vary significantly from area to area, from month to month, and between differing population groups in ways which can bear no fundamental relationship to logic or need. As noted above, the concern that the fund would be a means of driving expenditure into the charitable or voluntary sector, or towards local authorities (under their Section 17, Children Act 1989, powers) continues to be raised as a result of the experience of charities. For example, both national charities such as the Family Welfare Association and the RC Glasspool Trust, and small local charitable bodies such as the Dr Edwards and Bishop Kings Trust of Fulham (established to respond to local need), reported that their grant resources continue to be under considerably enhanced pressure from people refused help by the social fund. Many such charities have been forced to take defensive action by, for example, requiring evidence that claimants have approached the fund and been refused before providing help, a procedure which in itself leads to increased hardship.[4]

An analysis of the first thirteen years of the fund, seen from the perspective of a lottery, suggests that there are some safer 'bets' than others in terms of the likelihood of getting help. The fear amongst social fund managers of reprisals against them for overspending (following the near management disasters of 1990, reported above, when some SFOs had spent their whole budgets by late summer), balanced, as noted, by their desire to spend up to the prescribed limit in order to avoid loss of budget for subsequent years, has meant that February and March are always better months to get an application in: in some years almost twice as much spending has gone on *pro rata* in March as it would do on a steady spending basis. For both grants and loans, the traditional menu of exceptional items is always the best bet: cookers, beds and floor covering. Clothing scores higher with BL applications than for grant applications or CLs. This kind of statistical detail has, however, increasingly been obscured by the annual reports of the Department of Social Security (now Department for Work and Pensions) which is clearly embarrassed by the patterns it has revealed in the past.

The fear that need would also effectively be driven underground (what Craig described as the 'privatisation of human misery': Craig, 1997) by the working of the fund has also been realised in practice. Cohen et al.'s (1992) study of income support claimants of both white and Pakistani origins, and subsequent research by the Children's Society and others revealed large numbers of claimants who were unwilling to approach the social fund either because they were uncertain of their chances of getting help, because they judged that they would not be able to service even an interest-free loan from their already inadequate benefit income, or, in the case of claimants of South Asian origin (particularly those of Muslim persuasion), that the loan-based focus of the fund was alien to their own culture.

The fund's inability to meet more than a fraction of the demand placed on it has led, equally inevitably, to the fund fully justifying its sobriquet as the 'fund that likes to say no'. All that has changed in essence in relation to the social fund over the past thirteen years has been that pressure on budgets has grown and that more poor people have suffered as a result. Year on year, many of the changes introduced by the government and the DSS have essentially been attempts to manage that pressure more effectively by, for example, limiting the scope of eligibility, attempts supported, at times, by statistical distortion.

Who got what?

Community care grants budget Although gross expenditure has risen from £41 million (1988-9) to £98 million (1998-9), a fourfold rise in the rate of applications from just over 300,000 to almost 1.2 million over the same period, meant that the refusal rate rose from 48 per cent in its first year to 81 per cent in 1998-9. That represents one million people refused help in the last year of that period, and a total of about 10 million refused grants in the thirteen years since the fund began work to 1999. During this period, about 800,000 people have been refused grants not because they were ineligible but because of 'insufficient priority', that is, not because their needs were not covered by the fund but because there was not enough money in the fund to meet those needs. In 1999, the government introduced new arrangements for filtering applicants before they reached the stage of formal application. Thus significant numbers of those who might have applied for grants are now 'discouraged' (i.e. prevented) from doing so; as a result applications for CCGs in the year 1999-2000 were 45 per cent down on the previous year.

Crisis loans budget A similar pattern emerges in relation to CLs. Despite the extremely tight regime under which a CL can be made, the refusal rate climbed from 12 per cent in 1988-9 to 27 per cent in 1999-2000. Net expenditure meanwhile dropped from a peak of £11 million (in 1991-2) to only £3 million in 1998-9 but rose steeply to £9 million in 1999-2000, as a result presumably of exceptional demands. That is, the CL part of the social fund has come to be virtually self-replenishing, with income from recoveries replacing expenditure on new claims. The government might regard this as an administrative triumph and proof indeed that the virtues of careful budgeting which it champions amongst poor people by use of the fund's loans mechanisms are manifest in the fund itself. The darker side of the CLs sector however is that about 70,000 people have been refused in the life of the fund to date for one or other of two categorical reasons, the first for 'insufficient priority' again; that is, people formally acknowledged as facing a crisis in their lives because of having no money are rejected because the fund itself has not enough money to help them. The other reason is 'inability to repay', that is that people are formally adjudged to be too poor even to service an interest-free loan. This data suggests that the social fund managers are driven most of all by the need to meet financial targets and budget constraints rather than with meeting the needs identified even by their own tight criteria, of the poorest people in society.

Budgeting loans budget BLs are the operational heart and soul of the social fund: it is the largest part of the fund and the part where the disciplinary role of social security expenditure is clearest. By the end of the 2000-01 financial year, almost 17 million people had applied for BLs and roughly 6.5 million were refused help, one-third of those because of 'insufficient priority'. A total of about 3.5 million applications for help from the fund have been refused help on these grounds alone. The DSS (now Department for Work and Pensions) has also ceased publishing details of reasons for refusing help for BLs applications for reasons which are not clear. Net expenditure fell from £68 million (against gross expenditure of £108 million) in 1987-8 to £17 million in 2000-01, against gross expenditure of £435 million. To put it another way, loan recoveries have risen dramatically from £40 million in the first year of operation to over ten times that much, £418 million, in the most recent year. As a result, the BL part of the fund appears not to be under pressure and its refusal rate has dropped slightly from the initial figure of 41 per cent to 34 per cent, whilst gross expenditure has risen steadily to almost four times its original level. This apparent rise in expenditure is in reality a statistical sleight of hand which allows successive Secretaries of State to present the social fund as responding to demand and meeting the needs of the most vulnerable. Actually, it is largely the previous cohort of applicants which is meeting the needs of the next cohort, whilst the demands on social security expenditure generally fall year on year.

In the first year of operation, the net total call on the discretionary part of the fund in terms of 'awards' was £118 million; in the year 2000-01 this figure was again £118 million, some £40 million *less* than if the spend on the social fund had increased year-on-year by a (very modest) inflator of 3 per cent. This extraordinarily tight financial line is underpinned in part by the absolute refusal to help those dressed up in official language as a bad risk, the substantially more than 300,000 claimants (so far) refused because of being adjudged unable to repay even an interest-free social fund loan.

The division between the loans and grants sections also reinforces the disciplinary function of social security expenditure. The proportion of grants expenditure going to pensioners and the disabled (the traditionally 'deserving' categories of claimant) has risen since the fund opened for business, from 31 to 45 per cent, whilst the proportion going to lone parents and the unemployed has dropped from 59 to 43 per cent. The latter are the groups now even more strongly 'directed' towards the loans section of the fund where they have received between 61 and 85 per cent of the budget compared with the 10-28 per cent going to pensioners and the disabled.

The complex administration of the fund has also continued to be reflected in the public expenditure costs incurred. The real costs of the fund have not to be judged simply in terms of the net expenditure incurred every year, however, which has fallen steadily over the years. They have to be judged most of all in terms of its contribution to the hidden immiseration of literally millions of people and the social division and exclusion to which it contributes, quite at odds apparently with the New Labour government's stated policy objectives of removing poverty and social exclusion. Helen Dent, Chief Executive of the Family Welfare Association, for example, has reported that families rejected even for loans from the social fund for cookers, were told that they could buy sandwiches: 'these were families with children who were on the child protection register for failure to thrive' (*Community Care*, August 24, 2000, p.12). Additionally, the costs involved in managing the fund were substantial. Quite apart from trades' union opposition to the fund, there has been ample evidence that social fund staff broadly disliked the stress and tension generated by a scheme predicated largely on refusing help (see also, Rowe, Chapter 6; Davidson, Chapter 7, this volume). Despite the persistent defence of the fund by both Conservative and New Labour governments, the management of the fund has in reality presented enormous financial and administrative problems for the DSS, its successors, and for the relevant Minister. Formal accounts were sent back three times by the Auditor General amidst accusations of mismanagement, and other sets of accounts qualified; the reported costs of administering the fund sometimes exceeded fifty percent of actual expenditure. In 1998/9 the total cost of administering the fund was £215 million, i.e. about 35 per cent of gross expenditure, but considerably in excess of net expenditure that year of £184 million; every £1 net which reached claimants thus cost about £1.17 to deliver.

Much administrative and managerial time has been spent in coping with, initially, an ineffective computer system, then with attempting to manage underspends, then managing overspends on inadequate budgets, more recently in attempting to move money between offices in response to models of predicted demand and in order to keep the fund as a whole within national spending limits, and most recently of all in administering a complicated set of arrangements for calculating local eligibility from a complex set of criteria. These issues have continually led to a tension between consistency of policy and practice within offices and consistency between offices and have fed into the continuing image of the fund as a lottery. The process of managing reviews and complaints has itself also become extraordinarily complex and resource-consuming and public resources have additionally been committed to a series of expensive judicial reviews (see Buck, Chapter 8, this volume).

Conclusion

The existence of one-off payments schemes at all, is itself a formal, though tacit, acknowledgement that social assistance benefit levels are inadequate for even the most modest day-to-day living. The evidence summarised above and reported in greater detail elsewhere (Craig, 1992) suggests that in the social fund, government has only dealt with one of the recurring problems of one-off payments scheme–that of containing expenditure–but that the cost of doing so has been met overwhelmingly by the poorest people in the UK, those on social assistance benefits. The costs of removing the one-off payments scheme altogether–by providing social assistance recipients with a weekly income which is adequate to live on– has been beyond the political will of all governments since the first additional payments scheme was introduced in 1934.

The most detailed proposals for reform (Craig, 1992) involved a return to a scheme based primarily on grants. These original proposals were costed at about £675 million. Allowing for some modest inflation in expenditure since that date, the present gross cost of a scheme based on those proposals would be of the order of £900 million, or less than one per cent of the current social security budget. This should be set against, at least, net expenditure last year of £237 million for the whole of the existing fund, and the possibility of additional savings in administrative, review and computing expenditures. Overall, then, a reformed scheme might 'cost' not much more than one half of one percent of existing social security expenditure; the 'savings' would be a political recognition that the government of the day was indeed committed to the reduction of poverty and elimination of social exclusion. As the Social Security Advisory Committee commented some years ago:

> We make no apology for repeating our firm conviction that the poorest and most vulnerable people in our society should be protected, whatever sacrifices have to be made by the rest of the community. (SSAC, 1983)

The overwhelming conclusion of a huge range of rigorous research evidence is that the social fund exacerbates rather than ameliorates the position of the poorest in society. Governments are now alone in denying this.

Notes

1 'Regulated' social fund maternity and funeral payments, however, were introduced one year earlier in April 1987.

2 Lord Justice Woolf's landmark judgment in *R v Secretary of State for Social Services and the Social Fund Inspectors, ex parte Stitt (No.1), Sherwin and Roberts* (Divisional Court), *The Times*, February 23, 1990, was affirmed in the Court of Appeal, *The Times*, July 5, 1990. A detailed account of the operational and legislative changes prompted by these judicial review cases can be found in Buck, 2000, pp.146-151. Comprehensive research has also been conducted on the impact of judicial review on the social fund inspectors (Buck, 1998; Sunkin and Pick, 2002).

3 The Comptroller and Auditor General is under a statutory duty to examine and certify the social fund accounts and lay copies of it, together with his report, before Parliament (Social Security Administration Act 1992, section 167(4)). Two final accounts had to be delivered in 'qualified' form: see Comptroller and Auditor General (1993; 1994).

4   Equally, the priority of social fund applications is determined with regard to a number of statutory factors, including 'the possibility that some other person or body may wholly or partly meet it' (Social Security Contributions and Benefits Act 1992, section 140(1)(c)).   Applicants can consequently face a *Catch-22* dilemma: they can become squeezed between the expectations of those administering the fund that they will seek help elsewhere and of managers of charitable organisations who may require efforts to be made to obtain a social fund payment.

Chapter 4

Politics, Social Justice and the Social Fund

Roger S. Smith

The Politics of Poor Relief

As we have already observed, the social fund, and other discretionary payment schemes, have always represented a relatively small proportion of the overall budget for cash-based social assistance. In net expenditure terms, for example, the previous single payment scheme accounted for no more than 0.5 per cent of the social security budget in 1986, with the net expenditure on the social fund declining to approximately 0.1 per cent of the total in 2001 (see also Craig, Chapter 3, this volume). Despite this, the availability of emergency cash help in the form of one-off grants and loans remains of considerable importance in the overall framework of measures to address poverty. This is both because of its practical efficacy, and because of its symbolic role as a benchmark of prevailing attitudes and policies towards the poor. In particular, it appears to represent a key indicator of the extent to which and manner in which the state is prepared to support its citizens in a crisis.

Dealing with the problems associated with poverty has been accepted as a proper role for the state in the United Kingdom since the 16th century, if not before. A form of poor relief was developed, based on principles of supporting those in need in their own homes, in relatively un-coercive fashion. However, this approach was supplanted in 1834 by the much more punitive strategy based on the Poor Law (Craig, Chapter 1, this volume). This shift has usually been attributed to the emergence of capitalism and utilitarian principles which argue that people should not be dependent on the state, but should be responsible for their own upkeep. Poor relief should therefore incorporate a strong deterrent element to discourage idleness and dissipation. Certain other principles can be derived from this, including that of 'less eligibility', whereby those receiving help should not be better off than those in work. The key mechanism for enforcing this deterrent regime was the workhouse, where 'paupers' were, in effect, required to earn their poor relief. Despite this, a level of discretion was retained in the system, enabling the authorities to make judgements about the form of help to be offered, which were usually informed by:

> [A] widely held moral distinction between the 'deserving' and 'undeserving' poor. (Scott, 1994, p.8)

The consequences of receiving poor relief included losing the entitlement to vote, and this suggests that people living in poverty were not accepted as full citizens. This view has persisted in both ideology and practice in the context of social security provision, often gaining a significant degree of influence in the public arena of policy debates.

> Punitive and negative images of the poor are deeply sedimented, historically, within British society. These images reflect not only the periodic reconstruction of the poor as morally degenerate and culpable, but also a more widespread, deep-rooted and long-standing antagonism that has characterised class and social relationships in Britain. (Jones and Novak, 1999, p.5)

An alternative perspective views the establishment of a minimum level of guaranteed income as a prerequisite of citizenship. This reverses the position by arguing that people cannot be expected to meet their personal, familial and social obligations without the certainty of being able to rely on adequate means. This contrasts strongly with the view that failure to provide for themselves, or those for whom they are responsible, indicates that they have reneged on the basic duties falling to each individual citizen. Lister (1990), for example, argues for a rights-based approach to social security provision. In the specific context of the social fund, and other schemes to meet urgent needs for assistance, this might entail putting in place a system whereby:

> The social security system should enshrine clear rights to benefit. People should not have to depend on the vagaries of discretion or charity to meet their basic needs.... The social security system should be administered in a way that respects the dignity of claimants and which is more responsive to their views. Any racism in its administration must be rooted out. (Lister, 1990, p.72)

This perspective takes an 'enabling' or 'activating' (see Hermans and Declercq, Chapter 2, this volume) approach to the provision of social assistance, and single payments schemes, in particular, and seeks to avoid critical or punitive treatment of claimants.

Whilst such contrasting views of poverty and the responsibilities of citizenship have quite divergent policy implications, they are also likely to have a bearing on the way in which discretionary payment schemes are administered and experienced (see Rowe, Chapter 6; Smith, Chapter 5, this volume). The delivery mechanisms and practices of the social fund are directly related to broader perspectives on poverty, the poor and the proper role of the state in responding to their needs, or, on the other hand, promoting their rights.

The Social Fund and Ideologies of Poverty

Jones and Novak (1999) argue that the latter part of the twentieth century witnessed a process of 'redefining the poor'. As the post-war political and moral consensus crumbled, and society experienced major demographic changes, the sense of collective compassion and concern for the disadvantaged diminished, in their view. The concept of the 'underclass' emerged, to characterise particular groups of the poor, such as lone mothers and those from ethnic minorities, defining them in much the same way as the 1834 Poor Law, as irresponsible, idle and feckless:

> Behind this lies a particular view of human nature – or at least of the nature of the poor – which sees them as essentially barbaric and undisciplined, requiring the firm hand of social sanction in order to maintain respect for the law, for the institutions of marriage or the family, or for the work ethic... (Jones and Novak, 1999, p.13)

To offer excessive benefits, or even easy access to state benefits, to people in these circumstances and with these attitudes, would only be to encourage laziness, irresponsibility, and, in due course, social decay. Such views, most recently associated with successive Conservative governments in the UK from 1979-97, supported a programme of policy initiatives designed to make poverty a more uncomfortable experience. Government ministers are observed to have repeatedly made policy statements designed to conjure up a particular vision of benefit claimants.

> Secretary of State for Wales, John Redwood... argued that there was a widespread belief amongst the young that 'the illegitimate child is the passport to a council flat and a benefit income'..., while the Secretary of State for Social Security, Peter Lilley, delighted the baying audience at successive Conservative Party conferences with his equally fatuous remarks about young unmarried mothers. (Jones and Novak, 1999, p.13)

As Jones and Novak observe, it is ironic that those who suffer from the direct effects of poverty should also be subject to disparaging comments and 'insults' from those in positions of responsibility and political power.

A series of policy changes can be identified which gave substance to this strategy of first vilifying then punishing the poor, including the Social

Security Acts of 1980 and 1986 (see Craig, Chapter 1, this volume). The first of these attempted to control the growth in the number of additional payments made to recipients of means-tested social security (Supplementary Benefit, as it then was), by the introduction of a highly prescriptive scheme only allowing such payments to be made in very specific circumstances. During the Parliamentary debates leading up to these changes, leading Conservative politicians were observed to complain that the pendulum had swung too far towards providing 'rights' to social assistance. In a broader sense, these interventions might be seen as part of the project of redefining 'citizenship', at least in respect of the poor. This is associated with attempts to link the status of citizenship to paid work, such that full rights to participate in civil society should only be assigned to those in employment (Scott, 1994, p.148). Ironically, however, the attempt by government to restrict the number of additional payments coincided with a period of increasing unemployment in the early to mid 1980s, so that the 1980 legislation provided only a temporary expedient. Following an initial fall from 1.2 million single payments in 1978 to 0.8 million in 1984, this figure increased sharply to 3 million in 1984 (Jones and Novak, 1999, p.60). As Craig (Chapter 1, this volume) points out, this also represented a massive increase in expenditure. Whilst the cause of this increase may appear to have been obvious, that is, the equally dramatic parallel increase in the numbers out of work, which in turn was linked to wider government economic policy, the official response was the imposition of further pressure on those making use of the available provision for emergency cash help. By 1985, the government was ready to act again, in ways which further emphasised its own ideological preconceptions about the causes of poverty and the responsibilities off the poor.

'A Reasonable Level of Help'

The Green Paper issued in 1985, and the subsequent White Paper (Department of Health and Social Security, 1985a; 1985b; 1985c) set out the government's aims for reform. These were clearly inspired in part at least by a desire to control social security expenditure (Craig, Chapter 3, this volume), but they also incorporated measures which were consistent with the political project of redefining the nature of citizenship and the rights and responsibilities of those seeking assistance from the state in the form of benefits.

The starting point for the Green Paper (Department of Health and Social Security, 1985a) was the argument that the single payment scheme then in existence was both expensive and inefficient, requiring as it did the work of 2,500 officials and constituting 21 per cent of the cost of all social security appeals (Jones and Novak, 1999, p.60); at the same time, the Green Paper argued that the help on offer was poorly targeted, in that only a 'minority' of benefit recipients genuinely required extra help, and then only in 'exceptional circumstances', or at times of crisis.

> The Government argued that the existing system, based on statutory entitlements, was complex, inefficient to administer, and unfair. It was suggested that single payments were unreasonably concentrated on a small number of claimants, and that non-recipients of benefits on similarly low incomes were not entitled to help by way of single payments. (Smith, 1990, p.4)

The implications of these arguments were that the provision available was over-generous, and that people who did not need help were benefiting at the expense of both the taxpayer, and others, particularly those on low incomes who were not entitled to additional help. This led the government to conclude that cutbacks were necessary.

> The rapid growth in single payments in the last few years has raised considerable questions of fairness with those not on benefit.... The Government considers that routine provision of one-off payments in principle open to all claimants, is no longer appropriate. (Department of Health and Social Security, 1985c, p.22)

This clearly raised echoes of the kind of argument advanced in favour of the Poor Law in the 19th century, that perverse incentives to decline or avoid paid work should not be incorporated in the mechanism for providing social assistance. Thus, benefit recipients should be expected 'to manage their own income' (Bennett, 1989, p.2), and live within their means, rather than expect to be 'bailed out' when things go wrong.

The changes envisaged by the government in these proposals were intended to be radical, and it was explicitly argued that 'tinkering' with the existing regime would not solve the fundamental problems identified (Smith, 1990, p.3). In a statement of intent which appeared to envisage social security provision as a vehicle for promoting freedom and enterprise, as opposed to dependency, the government argued that:

> No system of Social Security should either stifle personal responsibility or discourage voluntary action. Social Security should be built on twin pillars – a partnership between the individual and the State. (Department of Health and Social Security, 1985a; quoted in Smith, 1990, p.3)

In fact, this rather vague aspirational pronouncement could be interpreted in a number of ways, although the emphasis on personal obligations and self-help in this context again conjures up echoes of the Victorian era, where coercive measures to discourage failure to provide for oneself would be backed up by the offer of voluntary or charitable help, from bodies such as the Charity Organisation Society (Jones and Novak, 1999).

The principles established by the Green Paper were shortly followed by detailed implementation proposals in the White Paper (Department of Health and Social Security, 1985c), which gave substance to the government's aspirations. It was at this point that it became clear that the government was serious about requiring people to live within their means, and that at least part of the provision for payments to meet urgent needs would be in the form of loans. This represented a new departure for the UK at this time, although it is clearly also an established principle elsewhere (e.g., in Belgium, Hermans and Declercq, Chapter 2; and in the Netherlands, Davidson, Chapter 7, this volume). In addition to this, a fixed annual ceiling would be put in place, capping the budget, with no facility for spending above this figure. In publishing the White Paper:

> The Government announced its intention to set a fixed budget for the social fund, and to ensure that spending would be monitored and decisions taken on priorities within available resources. (Smith, 1990, p.5)

In terms of reshaping the regime for making one-off payments in cases of urgent need, these two changes are probably the most fundamental in their impact on subsequent practice.

Despite substantial criticism of the proposals from opposition politicians, the voluntary sector (which did not want to reassume the role of the Charity Organisation Society; see Cohen *et al*, 1996), and claimants' organisations (Bennett, 1989), the government remained committed to its plans. The principle of 'less eligibility' was clearly re-emphasised. Social security should provide only a 'reasonable level of help', which should be determined in the light of the returns and 'rewards' available to the general population. Those on benefits were thus characterised both as a threat to the assets of the community as a whole, and also as undeserving of more favourable treatment than others on low earned incomes. Such a state of affairs, the government stressed, was unacceptable.

> The availability of payments for those on benefits stands in sharp contrast to the position faced by many others, on what may not be very different levels of disposable income, who have to budget for such items. (Department of Health and Social Security, 1985c, p.22)

The unfairness of this situation was also held to be compounded by the evidence of a concentration of single payments amongst a relatively small number of claimants, who were, if anything, those least deserving of help in the government's view, that is, lone parents and the unemployed (Craig, Chapter 3, this volume).

In this sense, the package of social security reforms proposed by the Conservative government were intended to deal with problems of equity and fairness by concentrating help more directly on those who were less able to help themselves. For example, premiums would be payable on top of weekly benefit rates to specific groups of claimants, such as the disabled, pensioners and families. Surprisingly, perhaps, too, economic arguments about additional costs outweighed the Tory ideology of the family, with the result that a premium would also be available to lone parents. Others, however, such as the unemployed, representing the 'able-bodied' poor, would not be given additional help, and would lose entitlement to the higher long-term benefit rates previously payable (Jones and Novak, 1999, p.61).

The social fund would complement these changes by introducing four types of 'targeted' help: Maternity and Funeral Grants, Budgeting Loans (BLs), Crisis Loans (CLs) and Community Care Grants (CCGs). These would be directed to specific groups, in specific circumstances, with the aim of concentrating and containing the amount of additional cash help provided. Entitlement would be replaced by discretion for most of these payments (all except Maternity and Funeral Grants[1]). The aims of the social fund would be achieved by:

- Focusing on individual needs rather than detailed regulatory frameworks;
- Offering flexibility in adapting to changing needs;
- Encouraging 'local decision-making based on local circumstances'; and
- Being subject to local management review rather than formal appeals.
  (Smith, 1990, p.4)

This clearly set the tone for the establishment of a scheme based on assessment and professional judgement, with payments to be based on evidence of 'need' properly presented and evaluated, rather than on pre-determined 'rights' to assistance. We have seen already (Hermans and Declercq, Chapter 2, this volume) that this kind of approach is not unique to the UK, but it does appear to establish a different kind of relationship between the provider and recipient of help. This change of focus was emphasised, in turn, by the highly symbolic change of terminology, which transformed 'claimants' (with clearly defined rights), to 'applicants' (whose entitlement would depend on the quality of their case), seeking help at the discretion of officials, whose decisions, in turn, would be based on individualised assessments, *and* the level of available resources. This clearly has significant implications for the way in which those relying on benefits are perceived, and the way in which their needs, however pressing, are considered and addressed – to qualify, it would seem, one must demonstrate a sufficient level of inadequacy or social incompetence. One consequence of this may well have been that, on implementation, it was reported that:

> Many of the people [applicants] we saw felt very demeaned and humiliated by the process. (Davies, 1989, p.55)

As we have seen, the social fund was duly introduced as part of the Social Security Act 1986, coming into operation in April 1988, with only a few significant changes from the original proposals of the White Paper. Firstly, it was recognised that there should be two categories of social fund; a discretionary and a regulated scheme.

> Funeral and maternity expenses were thought to be more predictable and certain, and therefore their inclusion in a discretionary scheme, it was argued, would cause difficulties. In effect, the Government conceded that these types of payment, although called social fund payments, would be governed in the same way as the regular benefits by means of statutory instrument and the normal adjudication arrangements. (Buck, 2000, p.31)

Secondly, the government made some concessions to the review system envisaged and added an external element (the social fund inspectors) with a Social Fund Commissioner as their administrative head (see Buck, Chapter 8, this volume). However, the government had not responded to criticism, for example that a discretionary scheme would enhance the risk of discrimination and racism (Bennett, 1989, p.7); and ministers continued to reiterate the view that its purpose was to reinforce the responsibilities of those dependent on state benefits, in a way that explicitly did not give them any undue advantages. The principle of repayable loans was, by now, central to this objective.

> In his letter to the chair of SSAC [Social Security Advisory Committee] on 25 August 1987, Nicholas Scott [Minister of State for Social Security] wrote of the government's aim of 'reducing dependence on the "benefit culture" for extras' by providing them with a 'sum of money within which they manage for themselves'. (Bennett, 1989, p.9)

At the end of this intensive period of policy development, debate and legislative change, it was concluded that the government had indeed been successful in transforming views about poverty and the role of social security and single payments in addressing people's needs.

> One commentator has stated that 'the most remarkable feature of Norman Fowler's social security review... is that it successfully redefined the terms of the debate.

Priorities, not poverty should be our concern today, he argued.... More recently, John Moore MP, then Social Security Secretary, talked of the need to move away from an over-emphasis, as he saw it, on 'rights'. The government's plans for the social fund – the 'safety valve of the safety net' – were criticised so vehemently precisely because they seemed to embody these shifts in perspective. The social fund was – and is – seen as a sorry symbol of the treatment a relatively wealthy country was prepared to see meted out to some of the poorest and most powerless in the community to meet their basic needs. (Bennett, 1989, p.9)

The concepts of entitlement and rights had been replaced with notions of self-reliance, personal responsibility and special pleading.

Social Security and New Labour: Rights and Responsibility Together

In opposition, Labour spokespeople and Shadow Ministers had criticised the Conservative attitudes and policies on social security as harsh and uncaring towards those living in poverty (Craig, Chapter 3, this volume). The specific inadequacies of the social fund, for example, by compounding the effects of 'social exclusion', also appeared to be of concern to them (Field, 1990). However, subsequent tensions emerged between those who held to Labour's historical position, and those who were concerned to modernise and present an acceptable (electable) face to the public. For example, Jones and Novak (1999) draw attention to a dispute between Shadow Ministers about whether or not Labour should oppose the 'Jobseekers' Allowance', which would make benefit payments conditional on seeking paid work.

The *Commission on Social Justice*, established by the former leader of the Labour Party, John Smith M.P., represented a short-lived attempt to bridge these differences; and in producing a comprehensive report on the future of the welfare state, it advanced specific recommendations for the reform of the social fund.

We would support... a three-tiered system to replace the single discretionary payments and loans which now exist. Regular one-off payments should be made to claimants, including one at Christmas, to provide help with larger costs. Special payments should be available for defined crises, such as a cooker or washing machine breaking down. And officials should have a wider discretion than at present to help meet special needs. (Commission for Social Justice, 1994, p.252)

However, the death of John Smith signalled a change of leadership, and the emergence of a rather different approach to policy development, encapsulated in the elaboration of a strand of thinking about government and social welfare depicted as 'the third way' (Newman, 2001). According to this vision, the establishment of a new 'social contract' between state, economic and other interests and citizens can achieve positive and progressive change.

> The emergence of a Third Way was used to mark out Labour's departure from the politics of a social democratic state, signifying a reconfiguration of relationships between economy and state, public and private, government and people. (Newman, 2001, p.40)

These changes had specific implications for the restructuring of the welfare state, with an increased emphasis on achieving a balance between rights and responsibilities. The residual role of the state in providing for those who could not provide for themselves was replaced by a more active conception of its purpose, which would be to ensure that people *would* be able to provide for themselves. The state would create the opportunity to do so, and its citizens would be responsible for taking it up. The state would commit itself to a programme of social investment to provide 'equality of access', rather than equality of outcomes.

Such aspirations were set out more fully in the government's agenda for social security reform, published shortly after it came to power (Department of Social Security, 1998). According to the Prime Minister's foreword, the task was to tackle the failings of an outmoded welfare regime which was failing the people, not because insufficient money was being invested in it, but because it was inefficient in addressing needs, and created, as opposed to removing, barriers to enterprise and employment:

> We must return to first principles and ask what we want the welfare state to achieve. This is the question this Green Paper seeks to answer. In essence, it describes a third way: not dismantling welfare, leaving it simply as a low-grade safety net for the destitute; nor keeping it unreformed and underperforming; but reforming it on the basis of a new contract between citizen and state, where we keep a welfare state from which we all benefit, but on terms which are fair and clear. (Department of Social Security, 1998, p.v)

The vision set out here has clear implications for reform of social security in general, and in its references to improving on the existing 'safety net', for the social fund in particular. The options set out in the Green Paper *A New Contract for Welfare* offered a choice between privatised welfare, increased spending (and increased costs), or the government's preferred alternative, 'promoting opportunity instead of dependence' (Department of Social Security, 1998, p.2). The aim would be to improve the support and incentives for people to move from benefits into work. Support should specifically be directed towards groups such as the disabled and families, and there should be concerted action to tackle the factors leading to social exclusion.

For those out of work, investment should be directed at specific job creation programmes, and in matching people to these opportunities through individualised 'packages of help' (Department of Social Security, 1998, p.3). At the same time, perverse incentives, such as the 'benefit trap', which discourage people from seeking work should be removed – the social fund, of course, might be seen in this light, as we have already observed.

For specific groups in receipt of benefits, such as families and the disabled, the same broad principles should apply. It should not simply be assumed that the members of these groups would be unwilling or unable to work, given the right forms of support. Financial incentives should be created which would leave people better off in work, and tax allowances improved for the low-paid to enable them to retain paid jobs. With the implicit assumption that all those on benefits can be provided with a route into employment, there appears to be only a very limited role for continuing measures to help those not in work, such as the social fund. Whilst the government clearly did not envisage an enhanced role for single payments schemes, it did, like its predecessor, set out its aspirations for a strong role for the voluntary sector:

> Today, government and the voluntary sector act in unison to maximise help for those in need. (Department of Social Security, 1998, p.16)

In expressing its belief in partnership in this context, the government also seems to have been arguing for a less central role for the state in relieving need, and showing a degree of consistency with its predecessor in challenging the assumption that the state will always be the provider of last resort. Even where people 'are not in a position to help themselves', the aim of the government would be to create partnerships to tackle social exclusion which would directly engage those affected. Existing state provision could be seen to be part of the problem in many cases.

> Many of the individuals and communities affected by social exclusion are on the receiving end of many separate public programmes and professional services. The poor rarely have the chance of helping to determine the programme of action for themselves. (Department of Social Security, 1998, p.63)

The essential aim of intervention should be to provide opportunities for people to help themselves, to prevent social exclusion and dependency, and to become less reliant on state provision. The emphasis on self-help and 'welfare to work' left little room for proposals to boost spending on a system of support such as the social fund which appeared to represent all the drawbacks of previous thinking. It appeared to focus on repairing damage rather than preventing it; it delivered financial aid exclusively provided by the state; it appeared to promote dependency; and was believed to be acting as a disincentive to paid work.

Despite this, limited reforms of the social fund were put in place subsequently by the government, as we shall see. These changes were significant in that they appeared to represent the beginnings of a redefinition of the role of the social fund by the government in the light of its wider aspirations for welfare reform. Whilst on the one hand, these changes could be seen as minor and largely cosmetic, on the other hand, they may be taken as representative of a more fundamental shift in the role of the government in providing help for those in situations of urgent financial need. Indeed, whether or not this was explicitly intended, there are signs of a degree of consistency with the wider New Labour project, as will become clear.

Reforming the Social Fund: a New Vision?

Within six months of taking office in 1997, the Labour government had commissioned and published research into the experiences of those making use of the benefits system, its 'customers'. This revealed a high degree of inefficiency of administration and significant levels of frustration amongst those turning to the Benefits Agency for help, which the government quickly acknowledged.

> Complicated paperwork, misleading information and lack of understanding are all highlighted as causes of frustration for some people using the benefit system. (Department of Social Security Press Release, 21 October 1997)

In particular, the social fund was highlighted as being the source of the highest number of 'contacts' and the highest number of 'unnecessary contacts' along with Income Support 'customers' in general, specifically in relation to making appeals, reporting lost payments and chasing payments not received (Stafford et al, 1997).

In common with many other aspects of New Labour's reform programme, and consistent with its overview of social security (see above), the primary focus seemed to be on the inefficiencies and poor delivery of the service, rather than the fundamental question as to the nature and scope of provision overall. Speaking in response to the research findings, the then Minister of State for Social Security emphasised the government's commitment to providing an 'efficient' and 'modern' social security service, better able to meet people's needs. Insufficient resources did not appear to be an issue.

> We will reform the Welfare State around the work ethic. What people will get from us is not just a bureaucratic system that administers handouts of benefits. (Keith Bradley M.P., Department of Social Security Press Release, 27 October 1997)

Subsequent government announcements addressed specifically to the social fund, appeared to pick up these themes. In December of that year, a second Minister of State for Social Security announced.

> The modern social fund will be simple to understand, cost-effective to administer and will produce clear and comprehensible decisions. (John Denham M.P., Department of Social Security Press Release, 2 December 1997)

The focus on better management and simplicity of operation once again appears to support earlier evidence of government priorities. Notwithstanding this, however, a number of other significant changes in emphasis were beginning to emerge. Firstly, the BL element of the social fund would no longer be discretionary, or based on arbitrary judgements about the merits of applicants' specific circumstances:

> Applications for budgeting loans from the social fund will be based on a common set of factual circumstances for everyone, replacing the current discretionary system. (John Denham M.P., Department of Social Security Press Release, 2 December 1997)

This decision-making framework would take the place of the time-consuming and intrusive 20-page application form currently in use. Applications would be dealt with on the facts of the case, and would be processed quickly by computer. The new system would be cheaper to run.

Two other changes were also signalled at this time. Firstly, by implication, the common application process for BLs and CCGs would no longer operate; and, secondly, the purpose of BLs would also be extended to incorporate preparation for work;[2] a development which was clearly consistent with the government's broader 'welfare to work' agenda.

> Budgeting loans will also be available for someone looking to start work again. The money could be used, for example, to buy clothes to attend a job interview.
>
> The Government has removed the previous restriction against getting loans for this purpose. (Department of Social Security Press Release, 2 December 1997)

This linking of assistance to efforts to get back to work is not restricted to the UK (see Davidson, Chapter 7, this volume), but these relatively small changes do appear to amount to an attempt to reposition the social fund (or, at least, BLs) to act as a form of accessible interest-free credit, available to people on low incomes with limited borrowing options, to help them manage cash flow problems, or important transitions, such as a move of house, or more importantly (in the government's view), the start of a new job. In this sense, then, these early tentative steps might be seen as the beginning of a project to redesign the social fund to reflect New Labour's aspirations to create a different, more active, kind of partnership between the state and those reliant on its services.

Changes to the CCG scheme were also announced at around this time (late 1997), and these, again, helped to cement in place a much sharper distinction between grants and loans.[3] The remaining strand in common between the two was the purposive nature of cash help, which should be targeted at meeting specific objectives, rather than simply maintaining people on the breadline. Thus, in March 1998, the government announced amendments to rules relating to CCGs. In response to concerns about the lack of help available to homeless people seeking accommodation, changes were proposed to ensure that they would be eligible for grants, but only within a specific context.

> Homelessness is a major cause of poverty and social exclusion. The Government wants to take all possible steps to prevent people falling through the net.... That is why we are extending the rules to include specific help for people setting up home as part of a planned resettlement programme. (Department of Social Security, Press Release, 3 March 1998)

This amendment to direction 4(a) would, it was suggested, provide for such needs to be given consideration, although additional funding did not support the amendment. We can see evidence here that the grants element of the social fund was being refocused to deal more explicitly with the task of social inclusion for clearly identifiable groups and individuals, such as the homeless, who had fallen outside the normal networks of support. This approach is consistent with a broader shift on the part of New Labour towards 'targeted help' (Hewitt, 1999). However, with no new money being provided for such specific aims, the implication would clearly be that other, less well-focused, forms of grant expenditure would be diminished (see also, Craig, Chapter 3, this volume).

The reforms of the social fund promised by the Labour government were incorporated into the Social Security Act 1998, and implemented on 5th April 1999. Announcing this, the Minister of State for Social Security reiterated the arguments of her predecessors, stressing, too, the anticipated improvements in administrative efficiency.

> Applications for Social Fund loans will be decided according to a few simple set factual criteria.... In keeping with the Government's aims for an active modern Social Security service, these changes will make the applications process much simpler, and the decisions process quicker, fairer, less intrusive and easier to understand, while

administration of the scheme will be more cost-effective. (Angela Eagle M.P., Department of Social Security Press Release, 4 March 1999)

In addition, however, the Minister also announced a substantial increase in the (gross) social fund budget (seven per cent), most of which would be allocated to BL expenditure. This achieved two things: an apparently generous increase at very little cost (assuming, as is the case, that most loans are repaid); and a further step towards establishing the loans service as a widely available source of interest-free credit.

Further government announcements and official reports on the social fund appear to have refined and reinforced these developments. The budget was increased further in 2000/2001 to £596 million, an 11 per cent increase on the previous year. Of this rise, again, the great majority went to provide further loans, with only £2 million allocated to the CCG pot, taking that element of the overall budget to £100 million. The increase in the increased gross loans budget, however, could only be supported through 'improved loan recovery performance', that is, quicker and more intensive recycling of loans. Once again, the managerial ethos of government policy is evident.

A fuller account of the government's reforms, and their intended impact, is set out in the *Secretary of State's Annual Report on the Social Fund for 1999/2000* (Department of Social Security, 2000). The separation of the elements of the social fund is made more explicit, as is the emphasis on better management and improved efficiency:

Before 5 April 1999, each application was considered for all three types of social fund payment [BLs, CCGs and CLs], making the scheme confusing for applicants and time consuming for staff to administer. This cumbersome procedure has been abolished. Social fund leaflets have been revised and now contain information focusing separately on each of the three payments in order to help applicants decide which payment best suits their needs. (Department of Social Security, 2000, p.18)

For most people, it must be observed, this 'decision' would not be a difficult one! However, the important point is that the emerging conceptual distinction between the different payments is now also being reflected in specific information and advice, and the establishment of different processes and routes towards payment. There are also differences in the review processes for BLs, and CCGs/CLs (Buck, Chapter 8, this volume).

Much of the emphasis in the *Annual Report* is on the new approach to BLs, and further support is given to the argument that government has begun to consider them primarily as a credit facility for people on low incomes to help facilitate income management, rather than as a form of emergency payment.

> The aim of the budgeting loan scheme is to help as broad a spread of people as possible. (Department of Social Security, p.19)

The rules would accordingly be adjusted to prevent people continually 'topping up' loans to meet 'one-off lump sum expenses'.

In addition to this revised aspiration on the part of government for the usage of BLs, there is also a subtle change in its characterisation of the relationship between the state and those who seek to access the social fund. Whilst the previous government had deliberately and purposively replaced the term 'claimant' with 'applicant', New Labour favoured the term 'customer', claiming, too, that the revised scheme presented a more acceptable face to those who used it.

> The consensus of views provided is that the scheme is quicker and easier to access and administer.... Both customers and staff consider the fact-based approach to decision making to be fairer. (Department of Social Security, 2000, p.20)

Indeed, it might seem that BLs are being recast as a kind of banking facility.

> The revised scheme also takes a more flexible customer focused approach to budgeting loan repayments by providing... a choice of loan offers and repayment rates.... It is the responsibility of the applicant to decide which of the loan offers best suits their needs and financial circumstances. (Department of Social Security, 2000, p.19)

This even extends to the option of having loan repayments deducted from weekly benefits 'at source', which 'customers' are claimed to consider as an 'advantage', enabling them to manage budgets more effectively (Department of Social Security, 2000, p.21).

These claims were partly based on more detailed research carried out on behalf of the government into the relationship between BLs and other credit sources, such as credit unions (Whyley *et al*, 2000). This research provides some endorsement for the government's revised approach to the administration of loans. Respondents to the study were broadly positive about their experiences of seeking loans, which were seen as an acceptable alternative when other forms of credit were not accessible or appropriate. The quality of service and the treatment of applicants also seemed to be viewed favourably. This contrasted with rather more negative views of the previous arrangements (pre-1999). However, most received less than the full amount requested, and some felt that repayment rates were too high (Whyley *et al*, 2000, p.4).

In the main, this research demonstrated a high degree of 'customer satisfaction' with the new arrangements for providing BLs, and the implied parallel with credit unions is also of interest. BLs could be seen to meet needs which were not provided for by credit unions, and they also seemed to be accessed by a rather different constituency – BL recipients were generally younger, poorer and more 'disadvantaged' than those with access to credit unions (Whyley *et al*, 2000, p.50). In this sense, it might be argued that the social fund was beginning to fill an important gap, contributing to the government's broader strategy of promoting social inclusion, simply by improving people's ability to meet their own responsibilities with their dignity intact.

Despite these developments, subsequent changes to the social fund since 1999 tended to concentrate on improving provision in relation to grants. These appear to have followed the emerging trend of enhancing help for specific groups at risk of exclusion. Interestingly, in this context, improved payments under the discretionary part of the social fund have been accompanied by a very substantial (in percentage terms) increase in the amount of money available in the form of (Sure Start) Maternity Grants under the regulated social fund, from £100 to £300 in 2000, and £500 in 2002. Alongside this increase, additional money was injected into the discretionary CCG budget, with specific needs again being highlighted, in an attempt to change the profile of recipients. Firstly, in April 2001, an additional £3 million was announced, which was intended to:

> Help ease exceptional pressures on the most vulnerable families.... The extra money will provide help for those most in need, especially for disabled people and families with children. (Department for Work and Pensions, Press Release, 2 April 2001)

As Hewitt (1999) notes, this can be seen as part of a broader programme of new government measures to improve help for those who 'cannot work', intensifying distinctions between those who are entitled to help for special reasons, and those who should be 'helped to help themselves'.

> For both groups, those in- and out-of-work, social security provisions are becoming more individualised and diversified and less reliant on the broad distinctions associated with the classic welfare state. (Hewitt, 1999, p.170)

Cash help in the form of grants is increasingly tied to evidence of a clear and quantifiable risk of social exclusion, determined by the characteristics of those concerned. In announcing this additional help, the Minister of State for Social Security re-emphasised the twin themes of improving the quality of management and administration, and meeting needs which could be closely defined.

> We have already introduced major reforms and we will continue to look at ways of improving the Social Fund to ensure it provides a focused, sensitive and efficient

service – helping families and individuals at the most difficult moments of their lives. (Angela Eagle M.P., Department for Work and Pensions Press Release, 2 April 2001)

It is, of course, one of the questions consistently raised in the present volume, as to the extent to which the package of reforms introduced by New Labour can genuinely be classed as 'major'. However, there is no doubt that the government could be observed to pursue a consistent agenda in restructuring the social fund, and presenting these changes as a new and improved strategy to tackle some of the problems arising from poverty, and thereby to promote social inclusion. On the other hand, the extent and nature of the reform programme might be construed more as a fairly limited and superficial attempt to address some of the more extreme effects of poverty, rather than a significant contribution to its elimination. In other words, the presentation of the reform programme as radical and fundamental can be contrasted with the rather modest series of practical changes actually delivered.

By 2002, a further cash injection into the Community Care Grants budget was announced, and once again, it was introduced as a means of addressing highly specific needs facing particular vulnerable groups. The Minister of State responsible explicitly pinpointed the anticipated recipients of the new funding.

People who have suffered domestic violence may get essential help for items like clothing or household appliances, helping them through difficult times. Families with disabled children, for example, may use the money to buy a washing machine to ease their domestic burden. Or an elderly person may buy carpets for a new home closer to their relatives, enabling them to keep their independence. (Malcolm Wicks M.P., Department for Work and Pensions, Press Release, 25 March 2002)

An additional £5 million was to be injected into the grants budget, coming 'on top of' previous above inflation increases. The Minister stressed, however, that the extra cash was intended to support and enable 'vulnerable' people to cope through difficult times, with the aim of achieving and maintaining personal independence. The social fund should not be seen as a way of perpetuating dependence, but of reinforcing people's ability to provide for themselves, whatever their circumstances. In many ways, the language of self-help, and the targeting of support on the 'most deserving', are reminiscent of much older and more deeply entrenched discourses on poverty and meeting need (Brundage, 2002).

New Labour has clearly acted coherently and consistently both to reform the social fund, and also to 'rebrand' it as part of a wider project of establishing a new social contract with those reliant on benefits. These reforms can be seen as part of a wider 'welfare to work' strategy, which balances 'rights' and 'responsibilities' and promotes personal achievement and independence (Hewitt, 1999). On the other hand, the re-emergence of traditional and well-established notions of 'desert' and extreme need also suggest a degree of continuity with long-standing ideas about the relief of poverty.

The Social Fund and New Labour – a New Deal?

This section examines whether New Labour's reforms in relation to the social fund can shed any light on the meaning of the government's wider change agenda. As already noted, previous characterisations of single payment schemes have tended to take opposing views of their role and function. On the one hand, they have been seen as a necessary evil, acting to bail people out financially in extreme circumstances. Payments should not be provided readily, or without due scrutiny, and they should in no way encourage indolence or dependence. In addition, cash help of this kind should only be made available to those who are 'deserving' of it. On the other hand, single payments should be made more readily available to citizens at times of hardship, and they should be provided as of right. In seeking help of this kind, claimants should not be made to feel inadequate, or required to undergo intrusive or humiliating investigative procedures. Elements of these two positions can be identified in earlier manifestations of single payment schemes, as already observed (Craig, Chapter 1, this volume), and there is also some evidence of international divergence in the way that schemes are thought about, constructed and delivered.

Attempting to chart a course between extremes, New Labour has instead emphasised principles of 'rights and responsibility', 'purposive help', 'partnership' and 'positive targeting'. The emphasis is on mutual obligations between the state and its citizenry, and the expectations which one is entitled to place on the other, for example, to seek work in return for cash help. Within this framework, the moves by the government to refine and redefine the role of BLs as a source of credit for those in difficult financial circumstances would appear to be both attractive and logical. The notion that loans could become a resource to help with cash flow management, or to provide a sound basis for moving into work, seems to fit well with the overall aim of establishing a sense of mutuality.

By contrast, CCGs (and, indeed, CLs) can be seen only to serve a limited purpose, meeting highly specific needs for individuals who are clearly identified as facing extreme and urgent problems, such as women experiencing domestic violence. However, the aim of such payments should still be to promote independence and personal responsibility. Thus, help for the homeless should be provided on the basis that they participate in a resettlement programme, and help for the elderly so that they are either able to leave, or do not enter, (costly) residential care.

In addition to this clear differentiation between the types of help on offer and their intended purposes, there is also evidence that the Labour government has sought to change the relationship between those seeking help (especially loans), and providers (the Benefits Agency). The way in which assistance is provided appears to be almost as important to New Labour as the amount of help available through the social fund. It is notable that government research appears to have focused more on the experience of using the fund, and the social security system generally, rather than the more fundamental question as to whether it is able to meet identified needs (e.g., Stafford *et al*, 1997; Snape *et al*, 1999; Whyley *et al*, 2000).

How, then, do these reforms to the social fund relate to other aspects of the New Labour project? To what extent are they consistent with wider attempts to develop a 'Third Way' in state welfare provision? The response to this question depends at least in part on how the 'project' itself is understood. It is possible to construct alternative interpretations.

> One view of the Labour government sees it as continuing [the] neo-liberal agenda, for example in its focus on equipping the UK workforce for the global economy and in its attempt to 'modernise' the welfare state. (Newman, 2001, p.1)

According to this reading of events, the new language adopted by New Labour, such as the substitution of the word 'customer' for 'applicant', and the associated administrative changes to the social fund represent nothing more than a refinement of a market philosophy in which the only role for social security is as a residual and disciplinary mechanism. Its primary purpose, on this view, is to prepare recipients for a productive role in the economy, and to deter them from relying on state help. However, in Newman's (2001) view the changes evident are not merely ones of style and presentation. The initiatives of the Labour government represent more an attempt to complement pre-existing welfare policies, than simply to perpetuate them. Thus:

> The Third Way was an attempt to blend the legacies of neo-liberalism with a focus on social cohesion. (Newman, 2001, p.170)

According to this view, New Labour saw itself within a political terrain in which it was clearly understood that there could be no going back on the economic restructuring of the Thatcher years, and the reframing of social welfare associated with this. Thus, the task would be to develop and modify provisions such as the social fund, in order to make them more acceptable, rather than to replace them. Despite its attempts to create a new political consensus and construct a more modern social contract, New Labour appeared to be constrained by a powerful sense of the 'limits of the possible'. Thus, rather than being seen as an exercise in cynical manipulation, it may make more sense to think of Third Way policies as a pragmatic attempt to bring market forces and principles of social inclusion together, so that their strengths and values could complement each other in pursuit of both economic and social well-being.

In this sense, too, it may be possible to portray the reformed social fund as reflecting this aspiration to create synergy between ostensibly opposing goals. Thus, improved management and better customer relations, allied to a new role for the social fund in providing a route (back) into paid employment and social inclusion, can be seen to be directed towards this end. At the same time, the absence of fundamental change, and the promotion of personal responsibility through increased use of loans, together suggest an accommodation with market principles of independence and self-sufficiency.

Of course, this rather benign view of the New Labour strategy and its achievements is not shared by all. The process of gradual reform and accommodation with the market must also be set against what is known about the consequences for those who make use of provision such as the social fund. This, ultimately, is the test of whether or not the reforms introduced can be seen as one aspect of the development of a new and mutually beneficial social settlement. As will be seen from other chapters in this volume, the available evidence is not hugely encouraging on this score. There are those who would argue that the evidence of the impact on individuals, or indeed the aggregated evidence from social fund reports and other sources, offers confirmation of the fact that what has been achieved is little more than a gloss on deeply entrenched and long-standing practices of punishing the poor.

> New Labour appeals to notions of community, to social responsibility, social inclusion and the need to overcome divisions. But in terms of policy and practice the trajectory remains largely the same. (Jones and Novak, 1999, p.176)

The dynamics of poverty and disadvantage are, according to this analysis, too deeply embedded in structural causes and fundamental imbalances of power to be changed to any significant degree by minor and essentially superficial administrative reforms. For these commentators, the only difference between New Labour and the 'new right' is their respective views of the state. Whilst the new right is more suspicious of and antagonistic to the state, even whilst in power, New Labour strategists accept and promote a more thoroughly interventionist role for the state. Hence, the social fund is recast from being an unwelcome drain on resources to become a useful lever by which households and families are reincorporated as economically active units. If this is the case, we should expect to see welfare reforms as both relatively limited and modest, and as revealing a consistency of focus which is primarily concerned with delivering economic goals rather than social benefits. As a result, it is suggested, there may well be quite damaging consequences of reform. In the view of one commentator, it may be difficult to assess the numbers:

> Of lone parents, unemployed and disabled, whose needs could be passed over by Labour's twofold approach...who will remain dependent on Tory policies that Labour has so far no plans to scrap, principally means-tested Income Support and the Social Fund. The worst scenario would be for Labour inadvertently to create from its rhetoric about the poor who can and the poor who can't work, a third welfare division of those left behind. (Hewitt, 1999, p.170)

The failure, for example, of the Labour government to deliver substantial additions to the CCG budget suggests a reluctance to acknowledge arguments based on rights and entitlements for those in urgent need; and, the increasing degree of differentiation between grants and loans, almost seems to confirm the residual nature of any unconditional help that may be on offer. Divisions between the 'deserving' and 'undeserving' are, if anything, intensified by these developments. The rhetoric of New Labour may, indeed, be little more than a variation on a very old theme in the representation and (rather shabby) treatment of the poor.

Notes

1   The government's original intention was to include maternity and funeral grants within the discretionary legal structure. It was only later during the passage of the Social Security Bill 1986 that it conceded maternity and funeral needs should be governed by ordinary 'regulations' and subject to the ordinary appeal arrangements. See Buck, 2000, p.31.

2   'Work related expenses' were expressly included in the list of *excluded* items and services applying to BLs, CCGs and CLs from 1988 to 1999. With the introduction of the revised BL scheme in 1999, direction 12 (exclusions relating to BLs) was deleted. At the same time the qualification conditions for BLs were changed to include seven categories of 'generic' intermittent expenses (see direction 2(a) to (g)). One of these categories (direction 2(f)) is: 'expenses associated with seeking or re-entering work'. However, such work related expenses remained excluded items for the purpose of CL and CCG payment: see directions 23(1)(a)(xi) and 29 respectively.

3   This distinction had, however, clearly been in the minds of some social fund officers from the early days of implementation; loans were felt to promote a greater sense of 'personal responsibility' (Walker *et al*, 1992, p.42).

PART II
MEETING EXCEPTIONAL NEEDS IN PRACTICE

Chapter 5

Claimants, Applicants, Customers or Supplicants?

Roger S. Smith

Poverty and the Social Fund

It would be wrong to carry out a detailed inquiry into the organisation and administration of the social fund and other discretionary payment schemes without taking account of the direct experiences of those whom such schemes are intended to help, collectively some of the most disadvantaged members of society. In order to address this specific task, it is important, first, to remind ourselves of the context of social exclusion and poverty, and their impact (see Lakhani, Chapter 10, this volume). We will consider poverty as the prevailing backdrop for those who are likely to come into contact with the social fund as 'consumers' of its services. This, in turn, will allow us to relate the delivery of the social fund to the question of whether or not it meets the needs of those whom it is intended to benefit. Their experiences and views offer a crucial insight into its value as an instrument of welfare policy. In a very real sense, these are the most important indicators of its effectiveness.

Low Incomes: Prevalence and Persistence

Poverty and inequality have been long-standing features of most societies, and they have not been eliminated by social and economic progress. Even advanced industrial economies are characterised by substantial numbers of people experiencing inadequate incomes, and being forced to depend on one form or another of social assistance. For example, despite the acknowledged time lag in much data collected on a European basis, the available evidence suggests that poverty is a persistent feature of most countries in the EU. Indeed, poverty was found to increase in all members of the European Community during the 1980s, and by 1995, 62 million individuals were identified as 'poor' (Howard et al, 2001). Whilst the trends varied between countries, the percentages of national populations in poverty (household incomes below 50 per cent of that country's mean average) by this date were quite similar for most of those dealt with in this volume (19 per cent in the UK, 17 per cent in Belgium, 16 per cent in France, but only12 per cent in the Netherlands).

In addition, it has been observed that, across Europe, certain groups within the population are more susceptible to poverty, including lone parents and their children (three times the proportion in the general population), disabled people, unemployed people, and pensioners. In addition to estimates of poverty based on income, it has been demonstrated that degrees of inequality between different sectors of the population are quite dramatic. This is reflected in the sense that many people have, of being 'socially excluded' in specific and concrete ways. For example, many households cannot afford new clothes, and have to rely on second-hand sources: 9 per cent in France; 12 per cent in Belgium; 13 per cent in the Netherlands; 16 per cent in the UK (Howard *et al*, 2001).

Considering the available UK figures in more detail, we can see that the extent of poverty (those living below 50 per cent of mean income) has increased significantly over the past twenty years or so, from 5 million in 1979 to 14 million by 1999/2000. Within this overall trend, there are wide variations in the risk of experiencing low income between different sectors of the population. Older people (31 per cent) and the unemployed (77 per cent) are significantly more likely to be poor, as are children (34 per cent), and especially, children in lone parent families (61 per cent), according to the Child Poverty Action Group (Howard *et al*, 2001), findings which are supported by government statistics (Department for Work and Pensions, 2002b).

This very brief overview provides us with fairly strong evidence that low or insufficient incomes affect populations unevenly, with certain groups being particularly susceptible to experiencing disadvantage. To an extent, this appears to be a feature of different points in the lifecycle, with the young and the old being noticeably more at risk of being poor, but we should also be aware that people who are vulnerable for other reasons appear disproportionately in the poverty statistics, such as the disabled, and those from particular minority ethnic groups. In 1999/2000 in the UK, 64 per cent of children from Pakistani/Bangladeshi origins were in the lowest fifth of the income distribution, three times as many as found amongst the majority white population. Other Black ethnic groups are also likely to be relatively disadvantaged (Department for Work and Pensions, 2002b).

The evidence of the prevalence of poverty at particular points in time should also be supplemented by recognition that, for some, being poor is a persistent experience, affecting them over a period of some years. As the government observes, there is some evidence that those at the extremes of the income distribution (the richest and the poorest) tend to remain in that position for prolonged periods. The majority of people in the bottom and top 'quintiles' in 1991 went on to spend five or more years in that income band over the next eight years (Department for Work and Pensions, 2002b, p.131). Again, it is particular groups who are more susceptible to persistent low income.

> Certain groups are systematically more at risk of falling into poverty and being in it for longer. These include: large families, lone parents, single people, households with a very young or old family head, those with low levels of educational attainment, people from minority ethnic groups, those living in areas of high unemployment or who are themselves unemployed, retired, disabled or on maternity leave. (Howard *et al*, 2001, p.47)

It is noted, for example, that 'persistent child poverty' stood at 16 per cent of all children for the period 1996-9.

For those who consistently have to survive on insufficient means for extended periods, it is almost inevitable that they will have difficulty in obtaining or replacing major household items, such as cookers, essential furniture, or curtains and carpets. Those who remain in poverty for some time have no opportunity to save, so exceptional costs cannot be met easily. When these are incurred, the quality of everyday life will suffer as a result.

The consequences of this kind of continuing deprivation are both direct and indirect. For young people living in poor households, for instance, both immediate opportunities and longer-term aspirations are diminished. Roker's study of adolescents growing up in low-income families found a sense of frustration and depressed ambitions as consistent themes.

> I feel bored with my life. I just want to get money and a job.... Get my own room. (14 year-old female, Roker, 1998, p.48)

> No, I'm not optimistic. I mean you just don't know what's going to happen to you... it could totally backfire. (15 year-old female, Roker, 1998, p.49)

Immediate concerns about having insufficient money can also be related to wider 'quality of life' issues, such as peer status, health, leisure and participation in social activities. An early study of the impact of the social fund found evidence of the gradual diminution of both living standards and expectations over time.

> I've got mortgage arrears of £500, and the wallpaper's hanging off the walls. I can't decorate... (Lone mother, Smith, 1990, p.71)

The consequences may be that people feel 'trapped' in an impoverished and inferior lifestyle, and that they fail to achieve socially expected norms.

> I don't like having to say 'no'. It did bother them [the children]. Next door were going to the pictures and I couldn't afford it. They felt left out. (Lone mother, Smith, 1990, p.73)

Studies consistently report a sense of inadequacy and unease about having to claim benefits, with recipients 'feeling like scroungers', and showing a real aversion to making claims, particularly among minority ethnic groups (Snape *et al*, 1999).

Associated problems, such as poor health, are also evident amongst people in low-income households. Not only are these a cause for concern in themselves, but they are likely to lead to greater expenditure, for instance on recurrent items such as asthma treatment, or extra heating requirements, which are not covered by standard benefit payments.

> Socio-economic inequalities have the effect of producing health inequalities among children, and likewise, health inequalities that can be observed among adults can have a knock-on effect on the health of children. (Shaw *et al*, 2001, p.65)

Across a range of health indicators, poverty is associated with increased levels of risk. Illness is more prevalent in poorer households, as are rates of injuries and accidents. Where ill-health is long term, extra costs are inevitable, but it is also highly likely that they will not be met in full by regular social assistance payments or subsidies.

> They need shoes and costs, especially my son, he's got splayed feet and there's nothing allowed by Income Support for it. (Lone mother, Smith, 1990, p.64)

> I have to keep the heating on.... The bills are very high. (Lone mother, Smith, 1990, p.65)

So, we have observed that certain groups are more susceptible to poverty in general, they are more likely to experience low incomes for extended periods of time, and they are also disproportionately likely to experience other associated problems, which, in themselves, can be a source of increased expenditure commitments.

The impact of poverty is experienced not just by individuals or households, as official statistics tend to suggest, but in a collective sense. We have already seen how particular ethnic groups are more likely to be living on low incomes; in addition, there is a geographical dimension to poverty, whereby inadequate standards of living are concentrated in particular neighbourhoods, or areas of the country. This has been particularly well documented for the UK by the government's Social Exclusion Unit (2000). The Social Exclusion Unit's report on neighbourhood renewal found that deprivation was most heavily concentrated in 44 local authority districts in England, and that collectively, these districts could be characterised, in comparison to other areas, by:

- two-thirds more unemployment
- one and a half times more lone-parent households
- 30 per cent higher death rates
- significantly higher levels of poor housing (Social Exclusion Unit, 2000).

This overview supports more detailed evidence gathered from specific area studies, including an earlier study of the use and effectiveness of the social fund, which concentrated on the community of Greater Pilton, near Edinburgh (Cohen *et al*, 1996). In this area, in the early to mid-1990s, it was estimated that 70-80 per cent of the local population was in receipt of state benefits of one kind or another. Linked to this was evidence of a higher than average incidence of lone parenthood, high levels of 'long term or limiting illness', and very low levels of car ownership (as low as 20 per cent in some parts of the district).

This is further evidence of the cumulative impact of continuing dependence on low incomes, not just for individuals and families, but also for whole communities, not least because of the absence of significant sources of material help elsewhere in the area. This is not to suggest that those living in disadvantaged communities lack any sort of sense of responsibility or mutual commitment, nor that they do not do what they can to help each other. However, their ability to do so is limited, and may, in some circumstances amount merely to 'recycling' poverty.

> Credit unions are great. [But there] is a kind of creaming off of the poor from the very poor.... The people who are not making use of them are those who are already in debt and particularly lone parents because they cannot save. (Holman, Memorandum of Evidence to the Social Security Committee, 2001, p.55)

Indeed, there is a sense in which those who are in the most precarious situations are placed under pressure to support each other,[1] even at great personal cost.

> Social security want you to borrow from your family. They're all unemployed.... I have to borrow from my sister at the end of the week. I owe me mam a tenner, and me sister's lending me a fiver. I'll pay everybody back and then I'll be short again. They can't afford it either. Sometimes I just have to go without. Nobody can live on the amount they [Benefits Agency] give... (Lone mother, Smith, 1990, p.61)

Debt and Survival

As we have noted, the experience of living on low incomes for a sustained period has a destructive and demeaning effect on the lives of those affected. It is important now to consider the options available to people in such circumstances to deal with the inevitable consequences and the occurrence of costs which cannot be met out of weekly benefits; weekly benefit rates, themselves, have been judged to be inadequate to maintain accepted levels of decency (Bradshaw, 2001).

For people on benefits, the options are inevitably limited, when the unforeseen occurs, or even when anticipated heavy demands on expenditure arise, such as at Christmas time. The kind of urgent financial needs which face those on low incomes are perhaps not dissimilar to those which affect most households. The problem is that they have a disproportionate and destabilising impact, often resulting in people having to 'go without' basic items for unreasonable periods of time. Indeed whilst there is common agreement about what constitutes essential items, many people report that they are simply unable to afford these (Gordon *et al*, 2000). Studies have repeatedly shown that low income and benefit dependency have a profound impact on households' ability to afford essential items, including food and clothing (Millar and Ridge, 2001; Lakhani, Chapter 10, this volume). The consequence for those trying to make up this kind of shortfall is almost inevitably debt, in some form or another.

Debts can originate from a number of sources, including, for example, fuel debt, which is identified as commonplace by Citizens Advice Bureaux (Howard *et al*, 2001), and housing debt (in the form of rent or mortgage payments outstanding), with unemployed households, in particular, being ten times as likely to be in mortgage arrears than those where the head of the household is in paid work. For many people on low incomes, their indebtedness leads to them having to live below the accepted minimum benefit level. This is, effectively, officially sanctioned in a large number of cases.

> Some claimants can be living below the basic income support level because their benefit is reduced at source. Benefit deductions can be made for social fund loans, overpayment of benefit, debt or fines. (Howard *et al*, 2001, p.110)

Additional items for which deductions can be made from benefits at source include child support, council tax arrears, rent, and fuel and water charges. In May 2001, 1.22 million Income Support claimants were having money withheld from their weekly payments (Millar and Ridge, 2001), and it has been pointed out that the proportion of those subject to such deductions increases with the length of time people are on benefit. As a result, less than half of those interviewed for one study could say that they were 'keeping their heads above water' (Kempson *et al*, 1994); whilst others have indicated that deductions can have a destabilising effect on tight budgetary management (Whyley *et al*, 2000). The social fund itself is reported to have accounted for significant deductions from weekly benefits for nearly 800,000 claimants (Millar and Ridge, 2001).

Erosion of benefit levels of this kind can have a further damaging consequence, in that people in these circumstances are forced to an even greater extent to budget *ad hoc* for their daily needs. They are forced:

> To shop on a day-to-day basis in order to eke out their very limited resources. The result of this, of course, [is] that they [are] less able to shop economically and to make the savings associated with buying larger quantities. (Smith, 1990, p.56)

In addition to their 'official' debts, those that are recognised, imposed and taken into account by the benefits system, low income households very often have debts of other kinds, often to lenders who offer expensive unsecured loans, high interest credit, or the services of 'loan sharks' (Whyley *et al*, 2000). Holman, for example, observes that there may indeed be a place for this kind of option.

> You might argue that there is a role for the illegal loan shark.... I am saying this because he does provide a loan for a person who could not get a loan anywhere else, although it comes with strings. In Easterhouse [Glasgow] there is no main line bank so where do people turn for credit? They have got to go to high interest bodies. (Holman, Memorandum of Evidence to the Social Security Committee, 2001)

The impact of continuing indebtedness can be experienced in a number of ways, including: restricted lifestyles, feelings of guilt and shame, ill-health (both physical and psychological), fear of the consequences of failing to meet debts, and fear of family disruption (Howard *et al*, 2001).

People living in such circumstances, surviving on low incomes and having to make decisions about the extent to which to go into debt, appear to have one of two choices: either, deciding what to do without in order to limit their commitments and remain within budget, or juggling (or ignoring) debts in the desperate attempt to maintain a decent standard of living, often for the sake of their families (Kempson *et al*, 1994), but it is commented that neither 'juggling' nor 'cutting back' can be seen as effective long term solutions. Personal accounts of the kind of choices to be made are highly revealing.

I stick to sandwiches... I'm OK at the beginning of the week... but come the end of the week...! (Lone mother, Smith, 1990, p.63)

I don't have a dinner. I only have my evening meal, so the kids can have a decent meal during the day. (Lone mother, Smith, 1990, p.63)

These hard choices are not restricted to parents, however, and for older people too, difficult decisions have to be taken.

I have to put up with this dangerous cooker. I use it to cook for my friend, who can't get about very well, but I may not be able to carry on. (Pensioner, Smith, 1990, p.75)

On the other hand, previous research has provided us with evidence of the incredible feats of dexterity undertaken by those in poverty in balancing the demands of multiple creditors. People who are often criticised for fecklessness and irresponsibility demonstrate formidable management and negotiating skills in these circumstances.

I can't buy everything at once. When the electricity bill is paid off, I'll buy shoes, for the one who needs them most. In the meantime, they might have to wear ones that are a bit tight. (Lone mother, Smith, 1990, p.63)

I just have to ignore some of the things I owe, like the bank overdraft. (Lone mother, Smith, 1990, p.57)

Sometimes, too, the experience of being in debt gives rise to impressive demonstrations of loyalty and mutual support within families. The burden is willingly shared.

Sometimes I give my mum a bit every week in case she's a bit short, and I buy stuff for us. (13 year-old male, Roker, 1998, p.18)

Often mum's just not got anything, so I get whatever I can, use any money I've got saved up to get her stuff. (16 year-old male, Roker, 1998, p.18)

Despite this, shortage of money is clearly also a source of family conflict. Whereas in more affluent settings, it is sometimes possible to spend one's way out of a problem, this is clearly not an option for the poorest households.

Money is our biggest problem, it's the thing we argue about. (17 year-old male, Roker, 1998, p.29)

I've stormed out of the house but I would never chuck anything in my house because it would just break things and cost money at the end of the day, and we just can't afford it. (15 year-old male, Roker, 1998, p.29)

Indebtedness can be seen to be a persistent feature of the lives of people on low incomes for any length of time, and despite their best attempts to manage the problem, it can be seen that its consequences are manifold. In effect, the need to borrow money or go into debt compounds the experience of poverty in a number of ways.

- It reduces the flexibility of very limited budgets even further – people often speak of 'robbing Peter to pay Paul'.
- It adds to the cost of living, through interest payments, and the increased need to make short-term purchases.
- It curtails lifestyles, and creates a feeling of shame and inadequacy.
- It creates a climate of stress and sometimes fear.

These inherent features of indebtedness are further compounded by the options available to those on low incomes, which leave them open to exploitation. Indeed, the social fund itself may be partly responsible for curtailing the choices of those who need immediate cash help.

> Debt on our Doorstep believes that the move away from single payments and towards loans as opposed to grants has left many people with no option but to turn to the alternative credit market in order to raise money to meet essential needs. (Debt on our Doorstep, Memorandum of Evidence to the Social Security Committee, 2001)

Whilst it might appear that the social fund should have a central role in providing for the difficulties encountered by those in a state of financial crisis, for large numbers of people it does not serve this purpose. As the organisation Debt on our Doorstep observes, there is clear evidence of an increase in the activity levels of door to door loan companies, with a steady increase in both the customer base and levels of loans provided, paralleled by a decline in the numbers receiving Community Care Grants (CCGs) (Debt on our Doorstep, 2001). Profits have risen, too, for the loan companies. High rates of interest ensure that:

> [One] consequence of the failing social Fund is that money is leaving the poorest communities as profit for door to door lenders and other 'alternative' credit providers who routinely charge excessive rates of interest. (Debt on our Doorstep, Memorandum of Evidence to the Social Security Committee, 2001)

During the lifetime of the social fund, increasing levels of demand for financial help have also been noted in the charity sector (Cohen *et al*, 1996; Howard, 2002). The Family Welfare Association (FWA) is one of the largest grant-giving charities in the UK, and it provides direct financial help to families and individuals in meeting many of the urgent needs that are also provided for by the social fund (Howard, 2002). Applicants to the FWA are explicitly:

Asked to apply for any statutory funds available, particularly the social fund, before sending an application to FWA. (Cohen *et al*, 1996, p.41)

Despite this requirement, the FWA very often finds itself responding to applications from people who have been rejected by the social fund on grounds of ineligibility, or 'insufficient priority' (Department for Work and Pensions, 2001a), or other rather more spurious reasons, such as 'not providing money for children'. Indeed, people are reported by the FWA as being routinely deterred from applying to the social fund, even in quite extreme circumstances. Examples have been given, for instance, of families where children have extensive health needs being refused help with the cost of a washing machine because this is seen as a 'luxury item', or 'not a priority' (Cohen *et al*, 1996, p.48).

The FWA also reports that, in some cases, the social fund fails to alleviate debt, and may in fact exacerbate it. The question of the level of repayment rates, and the basis on which applicants are judged to be able to afford to repay a loan remain persistent problems for those trying to get help (Whyley *et al*, 2000; Howard, 2002). One survey of FWA applicants (100 cases) showed that:

In some cases, people in great need of specific items are being denied them because they are unable to pay back additional loans; almost a quarter of the applicants to FWA... have felt obliged to turn down a social fund loan because they recognise that they cannot afford repayments. Together with the applicants turned down by the social fund on similar grounds, this makes a total of over one-third of applicants to FWA who reject or are rejected for a loan on the grounds that they cannot afford it. (Cohen *et al*, 1996, p.48)

Despite its increasing role as an alternative to the social fund, the FWA itself is only able to respond favourably to a limited number of requests for help (25 per cent of applications received positive answers in 1994, for example), with a total grants budget of less than one per cent of the CCG element of the social fund. For many of those struggling with financial hardship and continuing debt, then, the alternatives are bleak, and exploitative sources of credit may be the only realistic option (Whyley *et al*, 2000, p.65).

Seeking Help from the Social Fund

Whilst it has already been observed that the social fund is not always well suited to addressing urgent needs, it is the source of cash help to which people on benefits expect to turn in a crisis (Smith, 1990). For people who are in receipt of benefits for any length of time, it is almost inevitable that a financial emergency of one kind or another will arise. As we have seen, it is almost a fact of life that they will routinely forego basic items, cutting back on food or heating, or managing without important items of furniture or clothing. When the pressure becomes too great, however, they may well turn to the state for help, for example, to replace a broken washing machine (Whyley *et al*, 2000). However, it is important to bear in mind the context. This is not simply a routine financial transaction. People on benefits may already feel a sense of guilt and inadequacy, for instance, at being unable to provide properly for their families. It is sometimes a matter of having to swallow your pride.

> I don't want to put in a claim. I put in for a bed before, but it was turned down. The bed is held together with a piece of wood. (Lone mother, Smith, 1990, p.59)

Such responses, incidentally, help to dispel the assumption that people in receipt of benefits are simply 'scroungers'. Potential applicants may also feel that they are not treated fairly or with respect by commercial and public organisations. People living in certain geographical areas may find it impossible to get credit from banks or 'respectable' lenders; they may not be able to get insurance cover; and they may be discriminated against in terms of employment. For those from ethnic minorities, these experiences will be compounded by a more specific sense of discriminatory treatment (Craig, 2001).

In addition, the experience of those dependent on statutory agencies may well have been one of inadequate services, brusque and officious treatment, and regular experience of rejection. To contemplate approaching the social fund in these circumstances may represent quite a challenge.

> It feels like begging. (Lone mother, Smith, 1990, p.68)

> The simple answer is... no you are not told. When you go to an office to make a claim, you are under a lot of stress. You are worried about where the next penny is coming from, how you are going to feed your kids. You are so panicky about getting the money. (Mackenzie, Oral Evidence to the Social Security Committee, 2001, p.51, para.176)

For some people, their personal circumstances, too, can add to the difficulty of making an application. They may be concerned for their own or their children's safety, they may have caring responsibilities, or they may simply be unable to devote the hours of time sometimes needed to negotiate an unpredictable and unresponsive system. Not only are people reluctant to seek help, but they are also deterred by their experiences when they do make an approach.

> There's always a queue a mile long. Being stuck there all day is a waste of time. (Lone mother, Smith, 1990, p.66)

Arbitrary and apparently hostile responses, such as those reported to the House of Commons Social Security Committee are likely to intensify feelings of worthlessness.

> You feel you are always in the wrong. You are very intimidated. They [agency staff] do not come across as real people. They do not accept that your situation is probably the most distressing thing in your life.... They are very hard-hearted. (Forest, Oral Evidence to the Social Security Committee, 2001, p.51, para.178)

In this context, the rejection rates reported for the social fund act as a clear reminder of the futility of the application process for very many of its 'customers'. Nearly two-thirds (61.7 per cent) of CCG applications, and one-third (33.6 per cent) of Budgeting Loan applications were turned down in the year 2000/01, for example (Department for Work and Pensions, 2001). Others claim of being 'fobbed off', harassed with accusations of fraud, being misled into believing they are not entitled to help, and simply of doing everything they can to avoid the 'hassle' of the entire process.

> With our nearest Benefits agency about 10 miles away it is no joke for a young person to walk all that way because they have to apply in person only to be told 'no, you are not entitled to a crisis loan.' They then have to face the walk back, often not having eaten or drunk anything for several hours if not since the day before because they have no money. (CPAG, Memorandum of Evidence to the Social Security Committee, 2001)

However, the difficulties of negotiating the system do not end at the initial point of contact. Applicants' experience of the decision-making process is also confusing and frustrating (mirroring the evidence presented elsewhere in this volume; see Rowe, Chapter 6). Sometimes, for example, the advice given is simply wrong.

> In North London, a CAB [Citizens' Advice Bureau] referred a disabled woman to the BA [Benefits Agency] to apply for a CCG for a carpet (ruined by flooding), cooker (leaking), fridge and clothes. The BA counter officer told the woman that these items were not eligible for a CCG, which is not correct. As a result, the woman completed a BL [Budgeting Loan] application instead. A BL was awarded, but this left her with a big debt which she might have been spared if she had been allowed to apply for a CCG. (National Association of Citizens' Advice Bureaux, Memorandum of Evidence to the Social Security Committee, 2001, p.96)

Applicants also receive misleading or unhelpful information about the options open to them, which appears to be directed towards controlling expenditure rather than addressing their needs.

In the South West, a man with cancer of the throat, who has to feed himself with warm food through a tube to his stomach urgently needed a cooker to heat his food. He was receiving Income support and applied for a CL [Crisis Loan], but was advised by staff to apply for a BL, which would be processed speedily. The local CAB thought he should have been advised to apply for a CCG. (National Association of Citizens' Advice Bureaux, Memorandum of Evidence to the Social Security Committee, 2001, p.97)

As NACAB points out, there is a responsibility for Benefit Agency staff to consider whether another option than the one applied for would be more suitable for the claimant. However, there appears to be little evidence of such a proactive approach being taken in their view. Rather the contrary, they report a 'disturbingly high number of cases' where staff appear to have given bad advice or have actively put people off making applications. Time and again, it seems, the concern appears to be not the well-being of those seeking help, but the perceived need to operate according to organisational priorities, such as the requirement to limit public expenditure. The House of Commons Social Security Committee reports a case of an applicant to the regulated social fund[2] for a funeral payment. She was:

A woman on Income Support whose mother had recently died. Her father, who was aged 90 and registered blind, was rendered incapable of doing so or signing anything due to the shock of his wife's death. The client therefore filled in the form for him and signed as his appointee. The claim was turned down as she had not filled in form AP1, necessary in such circumstances. (Citizens Advice Bureaux – Scotland, Memorandum of Evidence to the Social Security Committee, 2001, p.166)

Whilst this example relates to the specific provisions under the social fund for funeral payments, those seeking help under the discretionary element of the fund encounter similar problems.

In North West London a lone carer and her son, both suffering from mental health problems, were re-housed by the council after discharge from hospital. The client applied for a CL to buy essential items for the unfurnished home but was refused on the grounds that there was no serious risk to their health and safety. A review was unsuccessful. The BA could have treated the CL application as a CCG application but did not do so. After refusal of the CL, no application for a CCG is possible for 26 week. (National Association of Citizens' Advice Bureaux, Memorandum of Evidence to the Social Security Committee, 2001, p.97)

These examples appear to demonstrate two inherent problems in the operation of the process for responding to social fund applications. Inaccurate information is provided on the one hand, but there is also an unwillingness to take positive action to provide advice and assistance to people who have real needs, but simply do not comply with the administrative rules.

In the West Midlands a woman with children, aged two and six, left her partner and was given a council flat. She had no money to buy furniture and was – wrongly – told by BA staff that she would not be eligible for a CCG until she had been receiving IS for 26 weeks. As a result, the client was sleeping on an airbed and her children were sleeping on blankets on the floor. They had no cooking facilities. The local CAB advised the client to insist on applying for a CCG on grounds of exceptional family stress. (*Ibid*, 2001, p.97)

These experiences of the process of seeking help from the social fund can be observed to have two distinct effects. The first is that many of those in dire circumstances are further placed under stress and demoralised by their treatment. Rather than receiving help and support, they are left isolated and victimised by the 'safety net' which often appears to be their last resort. By contrast, Holman (2001) describes how a small, local hardship fund that is more accessible, amenable and sympathetic, can sometimes compensate for the failings of the social fund. Family Action in Rogerfield and Easterhouse (FARE) established a small fund to help people in financial crises in 1999, which has been able to respond flexibly and creatively to some of the problems which the social fund has failed to address.

A lone parent with an income of £113 after deductions for a social fund loan for a cooker applied for an additional loan when the bed of one of her children collapsed. Her request was refused and the girl slept downstairs on the sofa. The Hardship Fund made a grant of £200 for a bed and bedding. (Holman, Memorandum of Evidence to the Social Security Committee, 2001, p.55)

This highlights a further problem which seems to be inherent in the social fund's operation, and that is simply that many people are arbitrarily disqualified from getting the cash help they need at times of crisis.

In the LGA's [Local Government Association] view, it is the cash-limited nature of the discretionary social fund that is its most significant flaw and has produced some of its worst characteristics – a high refusal rate; refusal to allow claims; a lack of clear advice and guidance for potential claimants, which has had the effect of limiting demand; excluded items and greater indebtedness by those already suffering severe hardship. This has meant that the process of helping the most vulnerable groups in society is inevitably inadequate... (Local Government Association, Memorandum of Evidence to the Social Security Committee, 2001, p.66)

In personal terms, the consequences of this failure of the state to help in picking up the pieces when things go wrong can be quite dramatic.

My husband had lost his job to start off with.... Then the marriage broke down.... We had a mortgage. We had allsorts of debt. We had bank loans; we had Provident cheques; we had everything, money lenders. We had to go to these people because we had to wait 26 weeks to access the social fund.... My husband was quite violent...he got a jail sentence.... I was left with all the debts, all the worry. Again, I had to go back into the system, make a new claim and start afresh, wait 26 weeks before I got any more help.... I had to go back to the money lenders and ask for more money. The people that I did go to were not very helpful, putting on a lot of pressure.... It got so bad that my house was repossessed at Christmas time. (MacKenzie, Oral Evidence to Social Security Committee, 2001, p.48)

Getting Help from the Social Fund?

So far, we have concentrated on the difficulties of those who have problems accessing the social fund, but it is also important to consider the experiences of those who do get help in one form or another, whether in the form of grants or loans. Of course, the picture is not entirely negative, as we are reminded elsewhere in this volume (Collard, Chapter 9, this volume). For some people, the experience of seeking help from the social fund is both straightforward and positive (Smith, 1990; Huby and Dix, 1992).

In the midst of the continuing evidence of the social fund's failure to address wider needs effectively, we should not overlook the fact that some people do benefit from it, and are satisfied with the help they get.[3] From the early days of the social fund, there have been reports that it does provide a lifeline. For example, neighbourhood projects providing support for families have found that the service provided is efficient, in the sense of reducing bureaucracy and providing a quick and understandable response to claimants (Smith, 1990, p.46). This observation may partly be accounted for by the evidence that help from an independent source such as a welfare rights service appears to improve significantly the chances of success (see, for example, Sunderland Welfare Rights Service, 2001). Nevertheless, for some, the process of seeking and then securing help from the social fund is relatively painless and leads to a positive outcome, in that their requirements are met. The government has argued that this can be attributed to the personal attention accorded to each claim.

> The Community Care Grant scheme is one in which the priority accorded to an application depends on all the circumstances of each *individual* case, which helps ensure that the available funds are disbursed to the most needy applicants. (Secretary of State for Work and Pensions, 2001, p.5)

This has been echoed in the comments of some recipients, for whom the process of applying is problem free, and represents a distinct improvement on previous arrangements.

> You get dealt with more quickly, it's a better service. (Lone mother, Smith, 1990, p.69)

Despite this, however, there is also a less encouraging body of evidence which suggests that, for many of those who are 'successful' in securing help from the social fund, this needs to be qualified by the observation that there are also significant drawbacks associated with these apparently beneficial outcomes.

For some, it is simply a matter of not getting all the help that is needed, with relatively small cash payments being provided in respect of costly items that are needed urgently. It appears that there are some quite unrealistic views held by those administering the social fund about the cost of basic household items of a reasonable quality.

> The cooker you get is always a second-hand cooker 'cause they only give you £100 to get a cooker, so my cookers have all went within two years of having them. (Social fund applicant, Cohen *et al*, 1996, p.36)

This observation is supported by organisations whose task is to provide independent advice and advocacy for claimants.

> The payments from the social fund are based on the purchase price of cheap appliances (eg cookers and refrigerators). This is a false economy for public finances. The cheaper cookers and refrigerators become obsolete more quickly. (Sunderland Welfare Rights Service, Memorandum of Evidence to the Social Security Committee, 2001)

Thus, for many of those receiving grants, the problem of inadequate provision is a source of recurrent problems, with cheap and unreliable goods needing constant replacement.

For many other applicants, however, being forced to settle for Budgeting Loans (which are more likely to be awarded; Department for Work and Pensions, 2001), rather than CCGs, is very much a second best option, forcing them to make economies elsewhere. For example, one study reports a case of a family with three children.

> Who had been living on Income Support for five years [and] were refused a grant when they were rehoused for a second time, because they had been given a grant on the first occasion. Instead they were awarded a loan of £200. One of the children had health problems, and the mother is disabled. She has to pay £10 per week for gas and a similar amount for electricity (in the winter months), and has a commercial loan of £25 per week. She described how she was forced to cut back on food in order to make ends meet... (Cohen *et al*, 1996, p.37)

Although this could be classified as a successful outcome, in that a loan was awarded, for people in these circumstances help that is offered in this form, requiring repayment over an extended period, even when it is interest free, merely compounds their indebtedness, reducing daily living standards yet further. Even where repayment rates are relatively low, they reduce the margin for error in very limited weekly budgets. The same study reports another example.

> A lone parent with three children was repaying a social fund loan at £3 per week (for beds and bedding) from her Income support of £103. In addition, she pays £10 per week for a Provident loan and between £17 and £20 per week on fuel. (Cohen *et al*, 1996, p.38)

In other cases, however, the repayment rates for Budgeting Loans themselves can be too high.

> A lone parent with 3 children, one of whom has a kidney complaint, receives a total of £110 per week and has been offered a loan of £260 to be repaid at £12.39 per week. (Cohen *et al*, 1996, p.38)

This problem persists, and has not been resolved by subsequent reforms, according to a number of those who gave evidence to the House of Commons Social Security Select Committee in 2001.

> CABx [Citizens Advice Bureaux] clients report great difficulty in affording the high weekly repayments which are demanded for BLs, which can be over £40 per week and are often £10 to £20. These are very large amounts to lose from levels of benefit which barely provide a decent basic standard of living. It is also of concern that the arrangements for considering a reduction in the repayment rate are so inflexible. (National Association of Citizens Advice Bureaux, Memorandum of Evidence to the Social Security Committee, 2001, p.104)

To illustrate this concern, NACAB provides a number of examples.

> A single mother in Cheshire, with 2 children [who] needed to replace her washing machine. She was refused CCG and offered a BL to be repaid at £40 per week. It was not possible to get this reduced before accepting the loan, so the client accepted although she could not afford the repayments because of catalogue debts for clothes. When the client sought a reduction in the repayment rate, BA [the Benefits Agency] refused to agree. (National Association of Citizens Advice Bureaux, Memorandum of Evidence to the Social Security Committee, 2001)

The lobbying group Debt on our Doorstep confirms that this problem of substantial repayment rates is not confined to specific cases, but is a matter of general concern.

> In February 2000 it was reported that 709,000 claimants had an average of £9.41 deducted from their benefits each week to repay social fund loans. Deductions of this size lead to increasing pressure on the weekly budget. (Debt on our Doorstep, Memorandum of Evidence to the Social Security Committee, 2001)

By February 2001, it is to be noted, these figures had risen to 771,000 recipients of Income Support, paying back an average of £9.90 per week (Department for Work and Pensions, 2001).

Success is also a somewhat devalued notion for those who find themselves having to make repeated applications to the social fund, a situation which is to be expected for those who remain dependent on benefits for any length of time; a common experience, as we have already observed. The achievement of a relatively satisfactory outcome in response to an initial application may not mean much for those who have to seek help on a second or subsequent occasion. Indeed, the inadequacy of the initial payment itself may contribute to continuing difficulties.

> The idea that you can furnish a house for £200 is nonsense, and yet at the same time it breeds this dependency... the stuff is low quality that you buy, so therefore you will be back again in 2 or 3 months' time. (Advice worker, Cohen *et al*, 1996, p.36)

In other cases, a 'successful' outcome conceals a continuing failure to provide an adequate level of resources, and fails to alleviate almost impossible budgetary pressures on vulnerable households.

> In Bedfordshire, a lone mother, with a child aged six, was relocating from an institution to private unfurnished accommodation. She applied for a CCG for furnishings and equipment but received only £300, which did not meet even her basic needs... the client was not informed that she could seek a review of the amount awarded. Under the rules she was prevented from claiming a further CCG for 26 weeks. (National Association of Citizens Advice Bureaux, Memorandum of Evidence to the Social Security Committee, 2001)

So, the suggestion that the social fund meets applicants' needs consistently or adequately must be treated with some scepticism in the light of these widespread accounts of its limitations, even where it is providing payments in response to applications. There appears to be a clear and strong dichotomy between the evidence of very many people's direct experiences, and the official view, which has been consistently restated.

> The Government does not accept that the operation of the social fund works against its wider social policies such as the eradication of child poverty. The social fund provides a considerable amount of help in the form of grants, loans and payments to millions of the most vulnerable people in our society. The Government has made a number of improvements to the social fund since it came to office. (Secretary of State for Work and Pensions, 2001, p.13)

Despite this, the accounts offered by applicants, the evidence gathered by voluntary organisations, and the substantial body of research carried out into the social fund do not support these claims. It has major shortcomings according to these sources, and far from meeting need and promoting social inclusion, its administration and delivery work to compound feelings of dependency and inadequacy amongst those who seek help from the state when they are in difficulty. From the perspective of those who are forced to rely on it as a safety net, the social fund is far from adequate to serve this purpose. The government itself has acknowledged that:

> The social fund alone cannot lift people from poverty. (Department for Work and Pensions, 2001b, p.2)

On the basis of the accounts reported here, this is undoubtedly true. The question is rather one of whether the social fund has made any real contribution to alleviating poverty at all.

Notes

1 One of the particular statutory factors which decision-makers must have regard to in determining a social fund award is 'the possibility that some other person or body may wholly or partly meet [the need]' (Social Security Contributions and Benefits Act 1992, section 140(1)(c), annotated in Buck, 2000, pp.328-9).
2 The regulated social fund is that part of the scheme which provides for payments 'as of right' to benefit recipients, in certain clearly defined circumstances, such as the birth of a child (Sure Start Maternity Grant) or the death of a family member (Funeral Grant), and cold weather payments. See Buck, 2000, chapter 6 ('The Regulated Social Fund') for an account of the origins of these payments and the current regulations.
3 It should perhaps be noted, however, that researchers have found little to justify the pattern of outcomes whereby some applicants are successful and others are not. For example, it is reported: 'We cannot say that people who receive social fund awards are in greater general need than those who are refused....' (Huby and Dix, 1992, p.127).

Chapter 6

Decision-making Processes

Mike Rowe

Introduction

At the conference entitled 'Reforming the Social Fund' held in Leicester in November 2001, the junior minister in the Department of Work and Pensions, Malcolm Wicks M.P., outlined the government's extensive package of measures to address poverty and social exclusion. In front of an audience of welfare advisers and advocates, he suggested we could not possibly be interested in the minutiae of one of the many mechanisms, the social fund, given the progress being made on so many fronts. However, it is precisely with the minutiae that this piece is concerned since the experience of operating and applying to the fund is fundamental to understanding the nature of that fund. This study illuminates a number of features of the social fund that suggest that, even were there no concerns about its effectiveness in addressing exceptional needs, there are serious arguments for its reform.

The social fund appears to operate within a clear framework. Discretion is clearly defined, constrained and subject to oversight. However, the variations that can be expected within these confines are also substantially affected by the circumstances and practices of the offices and officers involved. Research conducted by various academics and independent agencies has questioned the consistency of the application of directions and guidance (e.g. Becker and Silburn, 1990; Craig, 1990; Huby and Dix, 1992; National Audit Office, 1991; Rowe, 1999 and forthcoming). The research, on which this Chapter is based, was part of a study of the changing nature of public accountability on behalf of the National Audit Office. Drawing upon the social fund as a case study, the work contrasted the statements and accounts presented of the social fund with the experience of applicants and their advocates.[1] The work was conducted in 1998, that is before the introduction of the revised Budgeting Loan (BL) scheme in 1999 (see Collard, Chapter 9, this volume). However, the work indicates the continuing differences in the actual operation of the social fund from one district to the next ten years after its implementation.

Drawing on interviews in three district offices, this Chapter will first demonstrate the problems posed by the particular levers used to influence the decisions and the complex array of outcomes that might be possible in any given case. The outcomes were frequently dependent upon the timing of the application and the location of the applicant. Using the narratives recounted by welfare rights workers, the Chapter will develop this insight to illustrate the way in which decisions are actually made and the experience of applicants to the fund.

Office A

The district budget allowed high and medium priorities to be met for loan applications, and high priority for grants. Medium priorities were not met for grants, and low priorities were not met for either grants or loans. Circumstances, while not too tight, meant that claims were carefully, and critically, examined.

> So we are looking initially at eligibility where we are bound by law and directions; we are then looking at qualification where again we are bounded by law and directions; we then look at priority for which again we are guided by law and directions, and which we are guided on by our area social fund officer; and then we use all the information, evidence, facts, circumstances available to establish the level of priority that we attribute to a particular item or service that the customer requests, and that's where we use our discretion. (Social fund officer)

In law, social fund officers are bound to accept as evidence the information provided, unless the evidence is inherently improbable. However, in examining the circumstances of an application, the problems of verification and of applicants 'playing the game' were emphasised in discussion.

> I get these telephone calls, before an application form has been sent out. They say to me 'what can I claim, what should I claim?' That's the strangest question you can get when they ring up and say 'I've got this application form, but what should I claim?' They do, don't they? They will ask you that. 'You tell me what I should claim.' Now, if there were a genuine need, you wouldn't be asking that when you ring up for an application form. You apply for a clearly defined need, but not 'what should I claim?' And again the genuine people, who do need, suffer. Especially at certain times of the year. (Social fund officer)

The impression of applicants using the rules to their own advantage is a recurrent theme suggesting that, with an understanding of these rules, claimants can secure outcomes not intended. Ignorance of these rules places an applicant at a distinct disadvantage, to which we will return.

Having established a level of priority, and bearing in mind the budgetary situation and directions from the area social fund officer, an award is made. The officers discussed at length the means of managing the budget.

> The law says that we should pay the customer the amount that they request as long as it falls within a range of average local market prices. We know what things cost locally. Therefore, if it's not too excessive, then we are obliged to pay it. But we've had cases whereby we've been strapped for cash and we've reduced award amount to, well not the very minimum, but certainly sufficient to purchase the item new at the likes of *Argos*. (Social fund review officer)

At certain times, when financial constraints are greatest, decisions will differ from those made at other times. A frequent observation made of the social fund is that decisions might vary from day to day and from month to month. The officers suggested that the level of review activity in their office was high. The number of decisions altered at the review stage (see Buck, Chapter 8, this volume) was a consequence of the lack of information available when the initial application was considered.

> At the initial stage you use the evidence that's available and in a lot of cases that's when you can get away with using quite a bit of discretion. That's up to the customer really. If the customer disagrees with that then it's reviewed, in which case you are then in the evidence gathering stage. The more evidence you have, effectively, the less discretion you have because there is only one decision you can make in accordance with the law when all the evidence is there in front of you. (Social fund review officer)

The targets for processing claims require completion within five working days. It is generally not possible to seek more evidence from an applicant within this period, and this works against them receiving proper consideration at the initial application stage. With knowledge of this 'rule of the game', an applicant might either present more information at the initial stage or persist to seek a review of the initial decision. Without information, discretion might again be exercised in ways not intended.

Office B

The district loans budget was not under pressure, while pressure on grants was extremely high. Applications for loans were, consequently, not submitted to rigorous scrutiny so long as they qualified under the directions and were not applying for items that it would be unacceptable to meet.

If they've got no debt, because we've got the underspend at the moment, I'll award and it'll go. If I have to juggle, that's when I start to cut back. We are in the fortunate ... fortunate, unfortunate, whichever way you look at it ... financial scenario at the moment, that we can do that, but that is really the process that should be applied at the beginning ... We used to ask for reports – on evidence. 'Oh, my cooker has broken'. 'Can we have an engineer's report that it is irreparable?' So we'd get this stamp from Mick, who's an engineer, saying the cooker is irreparable. And he has taken a week to do it. If that's the level of evidence I am working to... they want the money, what is the point? If the level of evidence is they want a pram, they're a couple, give them the pram. (Social fund officer)

The state of the budget for loans meant that discretion was scarcely exercised at all. Only where budget constraints were severe, such as on grant funds, was supporting evidence sought. Even then, as this account indicates, reliable evidence was not readily available.

The problem of confirming the information presented in applications was raised on a number of occasions. Management targets also affected the manner in which this takes place, as the following discussion about handling grant applications illustrates.

I would write out to possibly less than 1 per cent of my claims. The management targets are just as important [as Secretary of State targets] because obviously they are performance. It's one of the problems with management by target. You concentrate on certain areas to the exclusion of others, so it leads to a lop-sided service. The concentration on those means we are often brutal in our decisions. One of my beliefs is you can ask for a review and it keeps [name of a social fund review officer] in a job. If I've got a dubious decision, which is 50:50, I will give them a loan and [name] can sort it out. Because, otherwise, I start writing correspondence. Second class post, which we have to use. It takes three days to get there, three days to get back. (Social fund officer)

Sometimes when I ask for confirmation, they don't give the information for three or four weeks. (Social fund review officer)

A range of targets affects the manner in which decisions are made. Pressures on the social fund grants budget mean that there is a tendency to offer a loan instead. Targets for clearance times mean that a letter might jeopardise its achievement. Finally, pressures on administrative budgets, requiring the control of costs on postage, aggravate this concern for speed. It has already been noted that the more information is available, the less discretion an officer is able to exercise. However, rather than resolve a case properly, this exchange depicts officers making partial decisions. Because there was no clearance time target at the review stage, there was less constraint upon seeking information to support an application. It also introduces a theme that will emerge from other discussions. Rather than make thorough decisions, and in order to protect scarce funds, discretion is used to put up barriers to applicants for assistance, requiring persistence to overcome them. And yet, an officer described another extreme.

> We know that things go on. For example at Christmas, it's normally like downtown Beirut, isn't it? Everybody's cooker explodes. It would be easier if people could apply for Christmas money of £250. They don't have to go through the farce of concocting a disaster. We don't have to go through the farce of listening to it. 'Oh, you've got the ability to repay. Here's £250, off you go.' Other times are September for school uniforms, May and June for summer holidays. They know. We know. They know they are lying. We know they are lying. We don't care. (Social fund officer)

Office B, in managing its loans budget, was faced with a different imperative to that faced by Office A; the imperative to spend the budget. Refusals and reduced awards were more likely to be the result of the financial constraints upon applicants. Problems particularly arose with the level of debts accumulated by the applicants. In many cases, applicants were already in debt to the social fund to the maximum allowed, in addition to other debts.

> In the end, if they get into debt, one of the problems you might say with the scheme with our budget status at the moment, it is intended to provide such and such a need. But if we are giving them as much as we can at the start, then for other needs that arise, we are not able to do so. The political imperative to spend the budget, the consideration of Direction 42 which allows that - you can't overspend. At the moment we are underspending by about two per cent, which in real terms is £80,000. That's a lot of money of an underspend. Give it to them. Then the next time something happens, say in three weeks time, 'I am sorry. You are up to £1,000. I can't lend it to you.' It is not anywhere near in the spirit of the scheme. But, on the other hand, that's their problem. They want £1,000, give them £1,000 and they can sort it out. (Social fund officer)

These two accounts together suggest that the processes undermine the policy intentions that lie behind them. The 'rules of the game' can be manipulated by those knowing the rules to produce unintended outcomes. At the same time, the combination of high levels of debt and genuine needs place greater pressure on the grants budget. Office B operated in similar fashion to the first example, so far as grants were concerned, tightly controlling applications and awards.

> So you can get a cooker on a grant for £200. But on a loan you can have £400. Which is ridiculous isn't it? That's Direction 42, which underpins everything. You must have regard to zeroing the budget at the end of the year. (Social fund officer)

Financial constraints on the grants budget necessitated tight control over each application while the same financial imperative operated differently on loan applications. These consequences appear perverse, even to those delivering the social fund.

Office C

The interview conducted in the third office became particularly forthright in discussing discretion. One person who had been working on the social fund for many years dominated the interview. She described a number of instances in which the system failed to respond effectively to individual needs.

> The worst cases to decide on are the ones where you sit there and think 'why didn't this person ask me for a cooker?' I would've given them £300 for a cooker, but I ain't going to give them £300 for ... Because he's asked for that item, I can't pay him. That's the worst sort of decision to make because you've seen all those other people who you know play the game. You are paying money out to them. Some poor soul who ain't been on benefit very long, doesn't know what's going on and he asks for what he wants, and we say 'no way'. (Social fund officer)

Again, the image of a game is used in this account, with rules that can be learnt and used to advantage. What emerged from the interview was a process of deception and attrition, one in which the genuine applicant might lose out and in which the attitude of the social fund officer is central.

> You can tell the ones that are really weird, and if you're not happy with it you have got the power, if you like, as the officer making the decision, to ask them to prove as much of the claim as you think appropriate to your decision. So, if you think it's dodgy or strange, you look into it. You don't have to take what they've said. But you wouldn't do that on the majority of claims, because the majority of claims, there is no need to do that. (Social fund officer)

How the social fund officer exercises discretion, 'plays the rules', might also affect the outcome. But, again, this process of writing out to applicants for further evidence can only be taken so far.

> You have got to concentrate on the targets, but sometimes you try. Sometimes you try and you still have to do it [refuse the applicant], because they don't write back to your letter or haven't given you permission to contact or haven't given you any social services contact, or anything like that. You might write out and say ring me up, or answer these questions. You've got to make a decision. You can't just say 'well, I can't make a decision', can you? In the end you've got to do it on what you've got. The thing is, if you haven't got the information to support a decision to pay, and you've tried everything, you've got to not pay. It might be wrong not to pay, but it's even more wrong in those circumstances to pay. If they ask for a review, you get more information. If they don't, well ... (Social fund officer)

In this account, the officer describes trying to use the rules to assist someone deemed worthy of assistance but cannot. As with any rules, both sides need to be using them to get the intended outcome. This same officer was, at times, open about the role that prejudice might play in decisions.

> I think the hardest ones to do, personally, are the ones where I think 'am I doing this because I hate this person?' Not that I know them, you know what I mean? There are circumstances you come across continually and you are thinking 'this can't happen to them all.' But you have to live with the fact that you can't always get the evidence to say no, because you can't prove that what they are saying is not true. If you can, I think that's fair enough. But if you can't ... You've just got to go with the fact that this person has to have this amount of money because their statement comes in front of your statement. You haven't got anything to dispute it. I know, in some cases, you can do 'this is inherently improbable', but it doesn't work. (Social fund officer)

This officer appeared highly judgmental, using the rules both to try to assist those she perceived to be genuinely in need and also to hinder those she deemed not worthy of assistance. This is the essence of discretionary decision-making. Yet, behind it all, lies the need for adequate information with which to make proper determinations. Reflecting on the problems of evidence, and supported by a rare interjection from a colleague, she described a process that failed in its basic approach.

> The thing is, it's all down to reason. You know that there's more to this than meets the eye. The forms are really ... well, I don't know if it's the format ... part of it's the format of the form. Instead of directly asking them what's the matter with them ... Instead of saying 'what are your health problems?'; 'how does it affect you?', it doesn't say that. It says 'do you think you might enter care if you don't get help?' That's a really dumb question. That's putting our directions into English to ask them how they feel about it. It's not evidence. It's not evidence of the right sort. For that one, they should say not whether they feel they should go into care – because that's our decision to make, really, in a way – but 'what's the matter with you?'; 'how does it affect you?'; 'can you look after yourself?'; 'do you need help feeding yourself?'; 'do you need help cleaning yourself?' or whatever. That's actually more relevant to us than ... People who come in for interview, like ... They will not say 'I think I might go into care if you don't help me', because they don't want to admit that. We can say 'Cor, look at the state of disability there'. They won't say that, because they live in the community and that's how they are. They don't want to go into a hostel, do they? So they say 'I won't go into care if you don't help me.' They tend to put in the other one [question box], 'are you having difficult problems?' 'Yes.' But you still don't always get the full facts. The questions are stupid. You want more about 'what are your difficult problems?'; 'what are your health problems?'; 'how does it affect you?' (Social fund officer 1)

> The ones who lay it on thickest, if you like, straight out front, I tend to disbelieve rather than the people who give slight hints. Because no one likes to tell all their problems to strangers for no reason. We are strangers. (Social fund officer 2)

Without knowing a person's circumstances, properly considered decisions are not possible. Yet, according to these accounts, the forms do not appear to support this process of information gathering. In eliciting highly personal information, it is not clear that forms could suffice in any case. In other services, such as social services, trained professionals conduct face-to-face interviews, during which a relationship and understanding can be developed. Yet the administration of the social fund has degraded any such element to a sterile documentation trail. Without understanding what lies behind some of these questions, and without knowing with whom they are communicating, applicants in genuine need may not receive the assistance intended.

The Advocate's Perspective

This image, of being intrusive strangers, is particularly illuminating when discussing a service intended to respond flexibly to individual circumstances and needs. It was something remarked upon by a number of welfare advisers.

> The other aspect of social fund decision-making that's always intrigued me is the totally impersonal nature, because most customers never really get to have any contact with an actual social fund officer, even verbally. (Senior welfare rights adviser)

For a scheme meant to be flexible, the social fund appears hostile and unresponsive to applicants. Only at review is there some sign that an individual's evidence will play a proper role in the decision. Talking about the review process, two welfare advisers discussed the experience of reviews.

> They [applicants for review] don't like to argue really, do they? They are worn out by the process of being there in the first place. Sometimes waiting an hour, sometimes an hour and a half. They sit in a very hostile environment often, and they are completely worn down by the time they get to see somebody. (Welfare adviser A)
>   They sit in a tiny little room on rock solid benches at a very awkward angle with a glass screen in front of them, to go through this appeal. The rooms are filthy, fag ash everywhere. (Welfare adviser B)
>   And we are, both of us, talking about people who are sick. The levels of anxiety among my clients are very high anyway, so the sooner they can get out the better. They aren't going to argue about what's written down. But sometimes they [social fund review officers] come to the home on a visit. (Welfare adviser A)
>   Yes, you can get them to do a home visit for a review. It can take a bit of forceful pushing to get that to happen, but when they do that the reviews generally go quite smoothly and you get the award. I find, with the reviews done at home, the social fund officer goes away saying well, you should perhaps make another application for that

and that and that, because they are actually seeing the conditions someone is living in and it does, in some cases, shock people. (Welfare adviser B)

Breaking from the impersonal nature of forms and understanding an individual in context allows for a more rounded consideration of the applicant's needs. Other opportunities to obtain a more personalised view of applicants, it was suggested by advocates and welfare advisers, were not taken. Application forms ask for a contact person who might provide supporting evidence, such as a social worker or GP, yet these references are rarely contacted in the experience of welfare advocates. As a consequence, at the final tier, the social fund inspector's review, new information is still emerging in many cases.

> And then it comes to us. And the letter we send out actually says things like 'if you need bedding, tell us what bedding stocks you've got and what condition it's in.' Nobody might have ever asked them that. Our covering letter along with the papers says 'information our inspector may need to know'. For example, 'tell us what bedding you've got' if you want bedding. 'Tell us what happened to your clothes and what stocks of clothes you've got', if you've asked for clothes. (Social fund inspector)

This echoes the points already made by social fund officers. For a system intended to respond to individuals, this is a surprising situation. At the first review, with the social fund review officer, applicants are given an opportunity to verbally present their case, but formal questions, designed to obtain useful information, are only asked at the second review stage. This suggests a system that is not genuinely striving to respond to applicants.

Indeed, the picture presented during the course of these interviews was of a system that can respond, but this is very much dependent upon the attitude of the social fund officer and the persistence of the applicant. Each is playing a part in a game, though there is an asymmetry in information, particularly about the rules of the game. These rules can be used to achieve the results that might have been envisaged by policy-makers. Equally, the outcome might be to provide assistance to people who have played the game and misrepresented their circumstances. Some of the rules and questions on application forms, in the opinion of social fund officers, actually encourage perverse decisions. Yet the social fund 'directions' have scarcely been amended since the social fund was introduced, even though they are a legal innovation intended to be capable of flexibility.[2] At the same time, some of the targets imposed upon social fund officers aggravate this rigidity. Constrained by targets and rules, the image presented of discretion in these discussions is not the one presented in government publications. What was intended to be flexible, appears perverse. Rules that allow room for discretion at times limit that discretion.

Instead of responding to the specific needs and circumstances of individuals, the handling of initial applications appears almost routine. Only if an applicant persists to the review stage might they have an opportunity to present a clear description of their case for assistance and gain some understanding of the rules within which the game is being played.

In effect, social fund officers act as gatekeepers to the limited funds available. Two types of gatekeeping have been identified in recent studies. managerial, involving the formal local rules; and bureaucratic, that is informal systems that frustrate or prevent access (Rummery and Glendinning, 1999). While not always so easily separated, both varieties were clearly in evidence. Perhaps the most blatant example of bureaucratic gatekeeping was described in a discussion between two homelessness workers.

> The prevention of access to the social fund, in terms of Crisis Loans, is quite systematic. Because it starts at the initial reception when the client will ask, inquire about the possibility of applying for a Crisis Loan and they get told by the receptionist, well, you've got no chance, you're wasting your time. The reception may or may not inquire about some brief details. That would deter most clients.
>
> And then, if a client does get past that stage, we try to encourage the client to insist on seeing the social fund officer who is the only one empowered to make the decision. But the social fund officer will also, very often, take the same approach, that you're not going to get one. And the clients, by this time, will have waited for some time to see the social fund officer.
>
> Then the client may ... we've tried to forewarn them ... they may insist on making the claim anyway, and they're told, well, you're wasting your time. You can make one if you want to, but you are wasting your time. That will maybe take to some time mid-afternoon, after the client's been there all the morning... (Homelessness advice worker E)

> Heaven help you if you go in at 4 o'clock in the afternoon. (Homelessness advice worker F)

> Then the social fund officer fills in the form, and the clients that have got that far will often report that the social fund officers are reluctant to show them what's on the form. They're asked to sign it, but they're not ... The client's asked to sign it, but the social fund officer doesn't really want them to look at it. And then of course the client will look at it and will not be happy with what's in there. There's a lot of questions on there that they just haven't ... the answer's been assumed or abbreviated. And then, finally ... because we do recommend that the client insists on a written decision, because the verbal decisions that are given are atrocious, are unbelievable. They're told that, for example, because they're using the day centre that they can get food on a credit system and they are not entitled to a Crisis Loan. They're never told that, obviously, in writing, but they're told that frequently. Or they're told things like, if your Jobseeker's Allowance has not been processed yet, we can't pay you until you are

on computer, which of course defeats the point of applying for a Crisis Loan. (Homeless advice worker E)

In a discussion conducted off-tape at the request of the official concerned, one policy official spoke of the case of an office refusing to accept social fund applications after 3.30pm on Friday afternoons. The requirement to complete the assessment process might eat into the weekend of social fund officers. Informally alerted by a welfare rights organisation, the official resolved the problem, but other interviewees remarked on the same phenomenon.

Failure to issue forms and stories of verbal decisions and of similar barriers were recounted by a number of interviewees. That these barriers represent a deliberate policy, albeit at a local and informal level, was suggested by a number of interviewees. Echoing remarks made by social fund officers, clear motives are attributed to perceived policies.

> One issue is that we've ... there've been periods of time when we've strongly suspected that DSS take advantage of people's reluctance to appeal, and not all of the people we try to persuade to appeal agree to do so. And that would mean they would calculate that only 50 per cent of people turned down will in fact bother to appeal. The reality is that very high proportions of appeals [i.e. 'reviews'] are successful, and we often wonder whether DSS do this as a kind of way of automatically bringing down the amounts they have to pay out. (Homeless advice worker)

While this represents suspicion, other welfare rights advisers had presented evidence of similar barriers to the Department of Social Security on a number of occasions only for it to be rejected as unsupported.

Perceived Irrationality

The complexities described raise questions about the experience of users. If the processes are not readily understood, how is the service received to be understood? Researching the social fund, two official reports suggest the difficulty in understanding the patterns of decisions that emerge (National Audit Office, 1991; Huby and Dix, 1992). The first, a value for money study conducted by the National Audit Office, examined cases in a number of offices and concluded.

> This [demand leading to budgetary pressures] meant that, during 1989-90, although these offices met the requirement that the funds available should always be concentrated on those whose needs they had identified as having greatest priority, they were unable to treat similar applications consistently throughout the year. (National Audit Office, 1991, paragraph 2.14) and,

The Department told the National Audit Office that these variations [in the priority level given to the same groups of applications] reflect the discretionary nature of the scheme and the requirement for local offices to establish their priorities in the light of local circumstances. In addition there were evident variations between different parts of the country under the schemes which preceded the Fund. In response to changes in the local level of demand and the consequences for their budget local offices are required to review and revise their priority lists, so as to meet the overriding policy requirement that the funds available should always be concentrated on those with needs of greatest priority. (*ibid.*, paragraph 2.17)

The response of the Department of Social Security was to await the findings of a further research project it had commissioned. This was undertaken by the Social Policy Research Unit at York University. It reached similar conclusions, identifying apparent irrationalities in the decisions of social fund officers, consequent failures to meet real needs and hardship caused by loan repayment. Commenting that there was no clear way to understand the difference between applications refused and those awarded, they observed.

Social fund officers are the repository of the administrative definition of needs and their decisions have a major impact on the extent to which the social fund can be said to be meeting need. Yet officers can reach different decisions about the same applications. They sometimes make identical decisions but for very different reasons. (Huby and Dix, 1992, p.86)

Evidence suggests irrationality remains a key characteristic of the social fund. Discussing with colleagues the experience of exercising discretion in a consistent fashion, one social fund officer observed.

That's the hardest thing about decision-making, isn't it? It's discretionary, and no two cases are the same. But on our shoulders is the fact that we're supposed to be consistent. There's ten of them, and we're supposed to be consistent. I don't know what's going on inside your [colleagues] heads. We communicate with one another, and we discuss cases, but you don't know what's going on in someone else's brain all the time. So I think it's really difficult being discretionary and consistent. (Social fund officer)

A social fund inspector, commenting on the differences she had observed in the cases she dealt with, commented thus.

The system isn't fair because different parts of the country have more or less demands on their budget. It may well be that people in North Worcestershire can have anything they ask for at the moment, providing they can afford to repay the money and their debt isn't over £1,000. Whereas, parts of Scotland, you can barely get a cooker. When we look at things like exceptional pressure, if you are dealing with a case like a Scottish case where maybe 60 per cent of families are lone parents with lots of children living in poor accommodation, you do sometimes see a social fund review officer will say, 'oh well their situation is no worse than every other family in this area.' So they tend to say they are not under exceptional pressure. Rather than saying everybody living here is under exceptional pressure, or anybody in this situation, overcrowded, six children, lone parent, health problems, damp accommodation. They would say that's the norm, instead of saying that's exceptional pressure, now we are going to look at the priority of it. They think it's easier to say nobody qualifies rather than saying, ok they do qualify but we just don't have the money, so we can't pay these.

Effectively, this is a form of gatekeeping. Commenting on the nature of discretion, an academic with a substantial record of research on the social fund remarked:

The unpredictability relates to all sorts of things, like the time of year, the time of the month and, of course, issues of personal prejudice and all the rest of it. Did they have a bad night last night? Is the claimant black? I have seen people have their social fund applications torn up in their face by officers in [location] as it happens. (Social policy academic)

Similar views were expressed much more explicitly by user advocates.

There's another thing. If you've got a foreign sounding name you are less likely to get an award. We all know that. (Welfare rights advocate)

Whether this is true is difficult to know. But what it does illustrate is the consequence of apparently irrational decision-making. In one sense, the key question is not whether discretion is tainted by racism and prejudice. As important is the fact that it is hard to demonstrate that decisions are not affected by the individual biases and preferences of decision-makers. Referring to studies undertaken by the Commission for Racial Equality, in conjunction with the Benefits Agency, one lobbyist commented.

They found a considerable degree of discrimination, just generally across the board in the delivery of benefits, whether you were likely to be ... there was a delay, whether or not you were likely to have fraud brought up in association with your claim, and whether or not you were likely to succeed in the area of discretionary benefits. (Social policy campaigner)

The Department of Social Security and the Benefits Agency, however, would not undertake ethnic monitoring.

Reflections

Given that discretion is part of the social fund, some variation can be expected. The problem arises when trying to account for the variations, to expose them to external scrutiny and to explain differences to users, whether they have been awarded or refused assistance. It will be fruitful, at this stage, to dwell on an account of one couple's experience of discretion.

> One I've got, which is ongoing, which is someone paying his hospital fare to go and visit their daughter. This has been going on for eighteen months now, and they have to apply every three months. I think I've done five reviews so far. I think only two of the awards were all right. Each person makes a different award and decides for this three months it's all right for mum and dad to go four nights a week. Then the next person decides, no, only dad needs to go one night a week, or mum two nights a week. Same case. Nothing's changed, and you never know what decision you are going to get out of it. The last time, they refused it on the grounds that they're asking for an excessive amount of money, that it wasn't reasonable. And they were asking for the amount of a weekly travel card. I can't really work out how that would be unreasonable, because that's the cheapest way of getting there. It's just one example. (Welfare rights advocate)

There are a number of illuminating elements about this one story. From the perspective of the claimant, and of the advocate, the variations appear irrational. Indeed, the advocate believes that there was one 'right' award. The problem is that different social fund officers fail to come to that answer. The review process becomes a means of getting that 'right' award. This perspective on the social fund argues that, because the circumstances of the applicant have not changed, the decision reached should be the same. However, other factors may have changed, particularly the state of the budget and the priorities being met on each occasion. It is quite conceivable that, from the perspective of social fund officers, each of the different decisions appear to be 'right' in light of this changing context.

The nature of discretion is exposed in this one account. The potential for variation in the treatment of even the same case is clear because we are able to compare a number of applications for the same item from the same couple. An applicant, making just one approach to the social fund, would receive one decision. Without any form of comparator, how is that applicant to understand the decision made? Publicly available information provides no basis on which to understand any single decision. If the couple, in the account presented above, made just one application, would they be in a position to understand whether the decision was 'right'? The response of individuals refused assistance for items can be incomprehension. The sum of the complexities that underlie the exercise of discretion is not easily communicated to individuals. Rather, the impression is of a service that simply fails to meet that individual's needs and, thus, fails in its very purpose.

Reflecting on this problem, a number of respondents remarked that, while applicants and their advocates may see irrationality as failure, the Department of Social Security (now the Department of Work and Pensions) viewed the social fund differently.   The Department's priority was to contain costs within the set budget and, in recent years, to increase the rate of loan recovery.   Essentially, a system exists to meet unforeseen needs, but the key determinant of its success or failure is, from the Department's perspective, financial.   This is a very limited conception of success given the aims formally stated for the social fund.   Underneath this success lies a system of discretionary decision-making that does not clearly respond to needs and appears irrational to all but those who know the intricate rules of the game.   Indeed, social psychologists would suggest that the situation is worse than this.   If the outcome of an application can be so apparently random, it contributes to 'learned helplessness' in applicants, the impression that, regardless of our actions, there is nothing we can do to affect the outcome from a system or process.   The features of learned helplessness are motivational problems, difficulty in learning and understanding and a depressed affect (Abramson *et al.*, 1980).   In effect, the social fund may not simply fail to address the needs of some of the most vulnerable but might also aggravate the experience of exclusion and of powerlessness.   In this sense, regardless of the way in which success is judged, there are serious arguments for reform.

Notes

1   This Chapter draws on interviews with eight Social fund officers, five staff from the Independent Review Service, two academics with a research interest in the social fund, ten officers from national pressure groups and sixteen local welfare rights advocates with experience of the social fund. Social fund officers were asked to describe how they handled applications, balanced evidence and reached decisions. Advocates were asked to describe the experience of applying to the social fund and of seeking reviews of decisions.

2   Unlike Statutory Instruments, the most common form of delegated legislation, the social fund directions are not laid before Parliament. They are simply issued by the Secretary of State and appear in the *Social Fund Guide*. The original intention was that a change of policy could be reflected quickly by issuing new directions rather than incurring the delays of normal Parliamentary procedure. A certain amount of judicial unease was shown in the early judicial review challenges to the *vires* of the directions, though in the event the courts would not strike down the Secretary of State's powers to issue them. In the Court of Appeal, Purchas L.J., stated: 'It may be that in this case in the execution of the legislative process that "Homer nodded" with the result that wholly exceptional and, it might be thought by some objectionable, powers without any Parliamentary fetter or supervision other than the annual report...was achieved by the Secretary of State. On the other hand it may be an unwelcome feature of a dominating executive in a basically two-party democracy.' *R v Secretary of State for Social Services and the Social Fund Inspector, ex parte Stitt (No.1) Times*, July 5, 1999 (CA).

Chapter 7

Safety Nets and Trampolines: The Implementation of Exceptional Need Provision in Britain and the Netherlands

Jacqueline Davidson[1]

Introduction

There are few better ways of testing the limits and the content of social citizenship it is argued, than by concentrating on 'the margins of the welfare state' (Leibfried, 2000, p.191). This Chapter draws on an in-depth comparative analysis[2] of what might be conceptualised as the line at which these margins, in the form of exceptional need payments provided on a discretionary[3] basis within social assistance schemes are drawn in Britain (the social fund), and the Netherlands (*Bijzondere Bijstand*). The value of cross-national research in social policy has been recognised for increasing our understanding of social policies (Clasen, 1999). This Chapter aims to add to the existing research which compares either the relative nature, and/or the government systems and structures in place to meet the exceptional needs of social assistance beneficiaries in European countries (Craig, 1992; Ditch, 1995; Eardley et al, 1996).

Broadly speaking, both the UK and the Netherlands may be described as having exceptional need schemes which are implemented on a discretionary basis to meet the one off needs of social assistance claimants (and in some cases others in immediate need) requiring help to purchase items such as washing machines, cookers or clothes, which people may find increasingly hard to meet either after long periods on benefit, or in an emergency. Similarly, both schemes from a general viewpoint are budget limited, decentralised, and function as a system of loans and grants. As this Chapter illustrates however, these broadly similar schemes 'acquire substantive meaning' (Heclo, 1974, p.17) through different political and administrative social assistance structures in the two countries, which influence and affect the principles and aims of these payments, as well as the politically defined needs which can be met by them.

One of the clearest observations to be drawn from the development of European social assistance schemes in recent years has been that political conceptions of social citizenship are not static. Along with many other European countries, the goals and aims of social assistance in Britain and the Netherlands have altered in response to changing social, economic and political contexts. Specifically, in an attempt to encourage beneficiaries reliant on this last resort form of income maintenance to become self-sufficient, both Britain and the Netherlands have increased levels of compulsion and benefits now have a tighter degree of conditionality (for some groups) on work seeking behaviour. The state structures through which provision is implemented in the two countries however, currently position those charged with making discretionary decisions about exceptional need within divergent configurations of social assistance.

In the Netherlands, the municipal administrator is charged with all income needs of the beneficiary and may also be responsible for overseeing the claimants' obligations or work seeking behaviour. In the UK, the social fund is administered by civil servants in local (formerly Department of Social Security (DSS)), now Department of Work and Pensions (DWP) offices. The social fund decision-maker is separated from the administration of social assistance and welfare to work,[4] and deals only with exceptional need payments. Relatively speaking, the social fund decision-maker's discretion is constrained by the (national) directions and guidance for awarding payment of Community Care Grants (CCGs) and Crisis Loans (contained in the social fund decision-makers guide). They must negotiate and work within very narrow and nationally defined policy aims and objectives to provide a safety net for the most vulnerable.

Whilst highlighting central points of comparison with the UK the first part of the Chapter outlines the wider context of financial provision to those on a low income in which *Bijzondere Bijstand* is provided in the Netherlands, and for which the administrator may be responsible. It illustrates that the central-local government structures of provision in the Netherlands influence what is provided to those on a low income.

The Chapter then moves on to compare the principles on which administrators in both countries award these discretionary payments. It highlights that the policy aims underlying the two exceptional need schemes, and the organisational contexts from which they are implemented, condition the way that the administrators in both countries 'perceive a problem and frame a solution to it' (Lipsky, 1981, p.27). The social fund decision makers' main concerns are to negotiate the constraints generated by their aims to meet the needs of those most in need in their 'managerial' context of inadequate budgets and targets for clearing work (Clarke and

Newman, 1997). This in effect leads to a concern to ration the social fund through deterring and excluding applications. On the other hand, the Dutch municipal administrators are charged with meeting exceptional need whilst trying to activate social assistance beneficiaries, either socially and/or to the labour market. *Bijzondere Bijstand* is therefore used as a complex tool of 'paternalistic' (Mead, 1997) implementation in an attempt to persuade, or discipline beneficiaries into 'working with them'. There are therefore, differences in the degree that the administrators in the two countries are concerned to administer exceptional payments as a safety net: to stop people falling any further, and/or as a trampoline, to lift beneficiaries out of social assistance.

The Context of Social Assistance Provision

The Netherlands, along with many other European countries, has social assistance structures and delivery systems that operate at a sub-national level (Ditch *et al*, 1997; Eardley, 1996). The constitutional and legal position of municipalities within the Dutch state is characterised by autonomy and co-government, and national legislation in the field of social assistance provision depends upon the Dutch municipalities for its implementation (Hupe, 1990). Provision is thus the concern of both national and municipal tiers of government, (and has been since the establishment of a national social assistance safety net in 1965), with each level having its own responsibilities.[5]

Currently, as is the case in the UK, central government in the Netherlands defines and provides for the national social minimum via social assistance rates, which are currently linked to the Dutch minimum wage.[6] There has always been some ambiguity in the UK as to what needs the social assistance scale rates should cover, and commentators (Eardley *et al*, 1996) have argued that the Income Support system has no principled relation to any minimum standard or conception of a minimum level of living. Rather, the benefit level in the UK is said to be determined by the principle of 'less-eligibility', in that benefit levels should not exceed the rate of the lowest paid worker, and public expenditure constraints (Veit-Wilson, 1998). Conversely, the Dutch social assistance Act (Ministry for Social Affairs, 1990, p.95) refers expressly to meeting what are constructed and referred to as the beneficiaries' essential needs. The term covers the cost of food and drink, clothing, housing, heating, furniture and recreation, these needs being regarded as essential costs 'necessary to enable the individual to live a life worthy of a human being'.

The general principle for social assistance is that it be given as a last resort, and its primary stated objective is to provide a guaranteed income to all Dutch citizens in need. Its subsidiary aims are to prevent long-term dependency on benefits and to promote social integration (Eardley et al, 1996), presently couched, in the context of a social assistance 'activity fare', in terms of enabling social assistance 'recipients to provide for themselves' (Spies and Van Berkel, 2001, p.108) through, where possible, paid work. Social assistance and labour market activation measures are administered by the municipalities[7] (often in conjunction with private agencies), who must measure the social assistance beneficiary's distance to the labour market and devise an individual re-insertion plan (Spies and Van Berkel, 2001; Van Oorschot, 2002). Clients are encouraged and compelled to participate in the activity fare, i.e. education, training and voluntary work, which will eventually lead them to the labour market. The opportunities provided for social assistance beneficiaries have, as Spies & Van Berkel (2001, p.114) point out, been complemented with firmer surveillance and tougher benefit sanctions for beneficiaries, emphasising the obligations of unemployed citizens, and an implicit assumption that unemployed people are at least partly to blame for their status.

Under the national social assistance Act, municipalities are also obliged to offer *Bijzondere Bijstand*, which can be used to tailor or individualise social assistance to the needs of the individual and family. However, within this national framework, *Bijzondere Bijstand* is to a large extent the concern of local or municipal policy makers. In keeping with the principle of subsidiarity,[8] found in a number of European countries, central government devolves a yearly budget for *Bijzondere Bijstand* to the *Gemeentefonds* (or municipal funds, which constitute the main instrument in central-local finances). From the *Gemeentefonds*, the municipalities are obliged to formulate a local anti-poverty policy based on what they perceive the needs of their inhabitants to be. Municipalities thus design and implement an assistance policy comprising the rules under which beneficiaries can claim supplements to their basic benefits, subsidies for education and training, costs related to part time work, and special needs costs (Van Oorschot, 1998). Since the devolution of a block grant in 1991, which in keeping with the drive to activate social assistance beneficiaries, was in part to enable municipalities to help 'people with special obstacles to the labour market' (Legislative Notes, 1989/90) the Dutch municipalities have had a degree of autonomy in determining the eligibility criteria and circumstances that warrant the granting of *Bijzondere Bijstand*. In effect therefore, the municipal eligibility criteria and definitions of special circumstances that warrant support may encompass other low-income groups, and not only those reliant on social assistance.

Subsequently, diversities in this form of provision exist within the Netherlands, as well as between the Netherlands and the UK. The form and detail of municipal anti-poverty measures therefore can and, the present research suggests, does vary from one municipality to the next, depending on what they perceive the needs of their inhabitants to be. For instance, in one municipality, the policy was to award payment by way of a grant for a washing machine to beneficiaries who had been reliant on social assistance for a set number of years, whilst in the other, the decision to award a loan or a grant for this item remained at the discretion of the administrator. The latter municipality however, in effect administered a blanket income subsidy, over and above social assistance benefit, to their low-income inhabitants, whilst the former did not. At the time of research (2001) this was a few hundred guilders per year and was intended for social and cultural activities and the prevention of social isolation (see for examples of such local initiatives, Van Oorschot and Smolenaars, 1993).

It seems that geographical diversity and the resultant inequality in the position of Dutch citizens reliant on the social minimum will remain a continuing feature of this form of social protection. Not all municipalities for instance will have large numbers of people reliant on social assistance, and 'complexities in the political and religious compositions' (Ditch et al 1997) of municipalities exerts some influence on what is provided. It is thus argued that such an extensively decentralised system lacks a 'collective character' (Van Oorschot 1998, p.14) in a social security system often characterised as social democratic and all encompassing.

However, from a comparative perspective *Bijzondere Bijstand* appears a relatively integrated and flexible system for meeting the exceptional needs of social assistance beneficiaries.[9] The present research suggests that *Bijzondere Bijstand* is not administered in isolation from other forms of municipal provision for those on a low income. For example, social assistance beneficiaries, who requested payments for a household item, would often be referred on by the administrator to the Municipal social lending bank for people on a low income, if considered able to bear the debt (Tester, 1987). In comparison with the UK's social fund, *Bijzondere Bijstand* is administered according to the principle of individualisation i.e. whether the individual in their social circumstances needs the item requested, rather than the social fund's narrow emphasis on groups and categories of individuals and needs. *Bijzondere Bijstand* can further be given to meet a one-off or an on-going need (for example monthly payments for people who have exceptionally high washing/heating costs).

However, those who implemented the provision outlined above, (especially in the main municipality of the research study) [10] did so in the context of an 'activity fare' and therefore perceived that their overall function was to oversee the balance between the social assistance beneficiary's rights and obligations. In addition to providing clients with an income, administrators were therefore also concerned with supervising their (re)integration: changing the client's attitude and/or behaviour (Hasenfeld & Weaver, 1996) and thus of meeting exceptional need within a context of activating beneficiaries as near to the labour market as possible.

Implementing Safety Nets and Trampolines

Those charged with discretionary decision making on exceptional need and thus by definition, as Handler and Hollingsworth (1971) imply, the separation of the 'deserving and undeserving poor' in the two countries are essentially asked to do so in divergent configurations of social assistance. The following part of the Chapter highlights that the policy aims underlying these exceptional payments, generate different administrative constraints that inform and influence the degree to which administrators in the two countries regard 'changes in a client's behaviour (in a desired direction) important' (Lipsky 1980, p.59) when reasoning an exceptional need application. In a comparative perspective, this directly affects 'who gets what and why' (Van Oorschot, 2000).

In the Dutch system, with its concern with activation, the division between impotent and able-bodied social assistance clients is of paramount importance for the administrator when determining any given applicant's exceptional need request. A clear administrative distinction was therefore made between those clients who were thought (at some future point) able, and those who were not expected, or had been categorised by the administrator, as unable to work.

> Some people couldn't help if they are not working, because there are a lot of situations, em, some people are not capable for to work. So, uh, like their living must be, as, we must try to give them a life as good as we can. (Respondent Neth 1)

Whilst the non-able bodied or the 'morally pure' (Handler & Hasenfeld 1991) thought to have little control over their poverty, should be socially activated with exceptional payments, those not 'morally excused from work' (Handler & Hasenfeld 1991) the able-bodied, were not automatically considered as 'undeserving'. The administrative perception was that the client could almost always do something about his or her problem and in the frame of social assistance obligations and rights, should be doing something about it in an attempt to become self-sufficient and leave the municipal welfare roll. In the Dutch configuration of exceptional need, a major criterion of deservingness for a discretionary payment was the work seeking behaviour and/or reciprocal attitude (Van Oorschot, 2000) of able-bodied beneficiaries thought to have some control over their poverty.

As well as a consideration of whether or not the items for which payment was requested might get the applicant closer to self-sufficiency, the administrative decision for such able-bodied clients entailed an explicit moral evaluation of the clients perceived ability and willingness to work and whether or not they were perceived to be fulfilling their obligation to look for work or participate in a reinsertion program. The following administrator's quote highlights that for an applicant (in this case a hypothetical male) requesting an exceptional payment for travelling expenses and clothing to attend interviews for employment, the concern centres on how well the beneficiary might have co-operated in his re-insertion plan, and therefore how deserving of payment he might be.

> First I will see how hard he worked about education, experience in work eh? Maybe volunteers work, or whatever he was doing. When he really can show me that he was really active and, yeah, really already working on it. When he was really active in it, I would consider (granting payment for a suit and a pair of shoes to attend interviews). (Respondent Neth 2)

Given the relatively flexible nature of this form of exceptional provision, as outlined earlier, municipal administrators often voiced that they had removed a variety of barriers to the labour market that motivated beneficiaries had faced.

> I had a client, a former addict to drugs, and I found him a job and he wanted to go to the job, he was motivated. But it started at 6am in the morning, very early, and there were no buses at that time, and he needed a motorbike, not just a bicycle. So he said 'yes I want to go to the job, but I don't have any money'. And so he asked could we pay for the motorbike and a helmet and insurance from *Bijzondere Bijstand* and I did. ... those kinds of ideas are more and more nowadays. (Respondent Neth 3)

Conversely, in the UK, the hypothetical applicant was extremely unlikely to be granted a discretionary payment from the social fund for clothes and travelling expenses to attend interviews for employment because staff either considered such items excluded by law (the national Directions) and/or not a high enough priority. However, such beneficiaries seeking work-related items might be eligible for a social fund Budgeting Loan (BL) if their outstanding debt could stand it and if they had been on a qualifying benefit for long enough.

> We don't actually offer people, who we should be offering help, enough of a help. Hopefully Jobcentre Plus will change that to some extent. ... for example, you've got to be on (a qualifying benefit) six months to get a Budgeting Loan, which has no restrictions now. But a Community Care Grant and a Crisis Loan are actually excluded by legislation for any help with work related expenses. ... we have friction with clients, because they're sort of palmed off by our colleagues at the Jobcentre: 'yes go to the social fund' ... and then the client comes in and thinks 'everybody else is telling me "get a job, get a job", I'm asking for a loan'. And we're saying 'sorry, can't even consider you'. (Respondent UK 1)

Whilst there are other options available for those seeking clothes to attend interviews in the UK's fragmented system (for instance from New Deal Personal Adviser's or local authority initiatives) what this research suggests is that not all beneficiaries, or social fund staff were actually aware of these options; and could not therefore relay the information on to such customers.[11]

Social fund staff often resented the relatively tight constraints on their discretion. Unlike the Dutch administrators, they considered that the narrow policy aims for CCGs and immediate Crisis Loans effectively worked against the government's wider welfare to work policy, and prevented them awarding payment to (who they defined as) responsible applicants seeking work. For such applicants, the social fund was therefore considered:

> Very harsh. Uh, it seems silly that we're here to try and help people, so why wouldn't we be trying to help them into work, *and* a benefit saving at the end of the day. It's a dual thing, um, but no. (Respondent UK 2)

In the Dutch system, as well as helping motivated people who were perceived as wanting to work back to the labour market, exceptional payments were also used to discipline, encourage or chastise those who were considered by the 'activity fare' administrator as not wanting to, rather than not able to work. Essentially, the Dutch administrators perceived that 'enforcing mandatory welfare to work programmes' was a 'major difficulty with those clients perceived not to want to work': they could not physically force, what they termed as an unmotivated, or non-reciprocal social assistance beneficiary to the labour market (Hasenfeld & Weaver, 1996, p.235). Generally, the relief of misery by way of an exceptional payment (especially as a grant) was contradicted by the administrator's need to try and enforce and 'uphold the work ethic' (Handler and Hasenfeld 1991, p.37), because this would only encourage such clients' reliance on social assistance and would not provide a spur on to the labour market. Therefore, for clients categorised as unmotivated (and asking for a washing machine for example), the administrator would be more inclined to award *Bijzondere Bijstand* as a loan (if their debt could stand it) and/or send the applicant to a second hand shop for the items requested. However, under an intensive case-management system one set of municipal administrators would have been more inclined to award payment as a grant to unmotivated beneficiaries: if they considered that it might act as a 'lever to ensure compliance' for getting the beneficiary to the labour market (Mead 1997, p.5). In such instances, the client's reciprocal obligations were made explicit, and the expected behavioural conditions for the receipt of aid firmly laid down by the administrator:

> In six months you have to find a job, and out! And you are not coming back to this office within two years. (Respondent Neth 4)

Comparatively speaking, situated in their paternalistic 'activity fare' context, the Dutch administrators were concerned to exert relatively high levels of control over social assistance beneficiaries. Therefore, not only were exceptional payments explicitly tied to the work seeking attitude/behaviour of the able bodied applicant, the administrators were also concerned that those beneficiaries not thought able, or not expected to work, displayed and conformed to responsible spending patterns. In contrast to what we might perhaps expect from what has been described as a social democratic welfare state (Muffels et al, 2000), impotent clients, i.e. those thought to have little control over their poverty and/or exceptional need, should ideally be 'visibly poor' by administrative standards. The Dutch administrators had the time and opportunity to engage in house visits to applicants requesting relatively expensive items of furniture. House visits could in effect encompass the administrator identifying other items that the beneficiary needed, but had not asked for. However, in order to be constructed by the administrator as deserving of *Bijzondere Bijstand* by way of a grant, the impotent applicant's home should display no signs of what administrators considered to be improper or imprudent money management, or having squandered money on what administrators considered to be luxury items like 'big televisions, nice carpets' and 'lots of stereo equipment'.

> I need to know what's happening there, if there's a big television and that kind of thing. That's not, uh (laughs). No. That's not the necessary things ... you need a washing machine with two children, three children. But if you have a television and a stereo and all kinds of debts and no washing machine, I think, ok. (Laughs) you must learn the people also to get responsibility for their own actions huh? So um, ok you have money, you buy a television and you come here to get a washing machine? If (the client) says 'yeah, I bought the television a month ago', huh? Then I say, 'ok, well you can't get a washing machine from me (by way of a grant). (Respondent Neth 5)

Such moral evaluations of clients are made explicit in this exceptional need scheme (for example, one municipality's guidelines for awarding payment as a grant or a loan asks the administrator to consider the client's 'understanding of their responsibility'). Whilst such evaluations of customers were not absent from the frame of reference of those who administered the social fund, the efforts of Welfare Rights services, the Citizens Advice Bureaux and the Independent Review Service for the social fund, were all thought to work against social fund decision-makers being prescriptive or carrying out house visits.[12]

In comparison with their Dutch counterparts, the social fund decision-makers' discretionary decisions were more informed and constrained by their managerial obligations to, 'look after the budget', as they described it, and their targets set by central government for clearing work. Whilst, from a broad overview, both exceptional needs systems may be described as budget limited, a striking finding in a comparative perspective was that controlling a budget hardly permeated the decision-making framework of the Dutch administrators. Indeed, at the time of research, the Dutch administrators voiced that they were more likely to be told by municipal policy makers who monitored *Bijzondere Bijstand* spending to be more lenient, or to give payment as a grant rather than a loan to certain groups of beneficiaries, for instance families with teenage children.

Social fund decision-makers however faced a daily struggle in trying to manage what they perceived to be a very inadequate budget for CCGs. In effect, staff perceived that they could not manage the budget and meet all of the need presented to them. Therefore, in an attempt to ration scarce resources over a large number of applicants, decision-makers in all of the offices of research were concerned to award only the highest of the high priority items in keeping people out of care, to those applicants that fitted the directions

> It's a nightmare sometimes. It's very difficult, knowing that these are people's lives and that's ... .*All* the items they're applying for are important, but you've got to try and prioritise them. It is very difficult. (Respondent UK 3)

Comparatively, this led to a lack of discretion for the items and circumstances the UK administrators could award payment for. Social fund decision-makers in each office of research had informally agreed on the most essential of human needs which could be met by way of a CCG, which in all cases were entirely in keeping with 'liberal' conceptions of welfare (Ignatieff 1990). Essential needs for the 'fit and healthy' CCG applicant for example, mostly translated to those for sleeping and eating.

We work on the premiss of the most essential items, for anybody is: cooker, beds, bedding, pots, pans, crockery and cutlery. Now if they had no health problems: young and fit, um, those would be the items that would be the most essential. Every other item, if they're fit and healthy as I've said, and they're in walking distance of supermarkets, or there's shops around: they can shop daily. So that: no fridge. Washing machine, things like that: if there's a launderette (nearby) or they're perfectly fit and can wash by hand and there's a drying area, then. As long as ... we can say 'well, no, you're fit and healthy'. No. (Respondent UK 4)

Moreover, for those CCG applicants that staff perceived as being at risk of being taken into care, staff considered that the item requested must specifically relate to their ability to remain in the community, and must not be a mere 'replacement or on-going need', which staff perceived, should be met by way of a BL.

Even if you have somebody who's disabled, you know that they are going to have to replace items, so you should be budgeting from your income and from your care component. (Respondent UK 5)

Their concerns to refuse as many discretionary applications as possible in order to manage the budget were compounded for social fund decision-makers by their targets for clearing applications. Effectively, rather than trying to change the behaviour of clients, staff were concerned to process a large number of discretionary application forms in as fast a time as possible in order to meet their targets. Targets and budgets essentially lead to a concern on the ground to control the volume of work, or demand for services. In the main office of the research study, for example, it was seen as important to deter as many potential applicants for Crisis Loans for living expenses as possible.

The Crisis Loans, um, that puts pressure on us, because we've got to clear them in one day. So that then impacts on (other discretionary Community Care Grant applications/Crisis Loans for items) who are then waiting longer, because of these damn targets. Because there was an expectation that a lot of these (Crisis Loans) were paid. And that attracted more people coming in ... *and we don't want to pay them* ... I mean we'd be awash with claims if we just rolled over and paid these. (Respondent UK 6)

Concerns to deter and refuse discretionary awards in an attempt to manage budgets and meet targets were further informed and reinforced for social fund decision-makers by the largely documentary nature of the staff-client relationship in the social fund, which in effect made it very difficult for the administrator to ascertain certainty over an applicant's exceptional need. Often for example, staff perceived that customers omitted important (and often extremely personal, sensitive and distressing) information from their application form. Because of the social fund decision-maker's targets for clearing work, rather than taking time to look for additional information and establish whether or not applicants fitted the directions, or were what staff termed as 'genuine' or deserving of payment, such applicants were often refused. The onus was then on the applicant to ask for a review, where staff could look for, and indeed often found adequate information

> You can gauge a lot from a person: talking to them, rather than what they write down on a piece of paper ... it could be a family under exceptional pressure; it could be domestic violence, and it hasn't really come out very well on the form. And then when you start to talk to them they say 'well, this happened'. And it doesn't say anything on the form about Women's Aid or that. ... And then you can find out, you can check up the information. (Respondent UK 7)

In comparison with the Netherlands therefore, the UK officers perceived that both time and financial resources were extremely insufficient in relation to the tasks they were asked to perform. A large number of 'empowered citizens' press their demands on one side, while on the other the social fund decision-maker is subjected to 'intensified forms of centralised power and control' through tight fiscal control, 'policy directions and an apparatus of audit and evaluation' (Clarke & Newman, 1997, p.29).

Conclusion

The dynamics of poverty have led some to argue that, since poverty is not (for most people at least) a long-term permanent condition, it need not be addressed by way of 'long-term social assistance programmes' (Giddens 1999, p.26). Others argue that the persistent poor are of concern since they are spread across the population and are comprised of very vulnerable groups in society. The goal of alleviating poverty that modern welfare states pursue can therefore be seen to matter a great deal more in the long run than the short (Muffels et al, 2000, p.21). Currently, both the UK and the Netherlands, along with a number of European countries, have decided to pursue the alleviation of poverty, at least in part, by tightening conditionality and increasing compulsion for certain groups of social assistance beneficiaries. This Chapter has highlighted, however, that the specific configurations of social assistance in different countries, will inform the degree to which exceptional payments within social assistance, can be used by administrators, to advance those overall policy goals.

Bijzondere Bijstand is situated firmly within the Municipal administration of an activity fare social assistance. The Dutch administrators are therefore concerned to meet exceptional need in the context of activating beneficiaries (either socially or to the labour market). The discretionary decision entails a paternalistic moral judgement regarding the client's behaviour, and, like social assistance rights and obligations, a reciprocal element; what has the client done, or will the client do for the payment requested? Administrators use their discretion to discipline or encourage able-bodied beneficiaries to 'work with them', to participate in their re-insertion trajectory to the labour market. Conversely, in the UK, social fund decision-makers consider themselves as separate from the administration, and sometimes working against the wider aims, of welfare to work. Their concerns are to administer a safety net for the most vulnerable, within a context of managerialism. This translates to providing resources for those most in need whilst managing an inadequate budget and meeting targets for clearing work. On the ground, this leads to a concern to spread a little money over a large number of CCG applicants, and deter as many Crisis Loans for living expenses applications as possible.

Notes

1 The author gratefully acknowledges the financial support of the Carnegie Trust for the Universities of Scotland.
2 Constitutes the author's PhD work in progress. The research was based on a qualitative analysis of secondary literature and legislation. In-depth semi-structured interviews were also conducted with social fund decision-makers in three local offices; Dutch (municipal) policy makers and those who administer *Bijzondere Bijstand* in two municipalities. Administrators in both countries were also asked to consider a range of hypothetical scenarios depicting applicants for a discretionary award.
3 It does not therefore concentrate on the regulated part of the social fund.
4 And Personal Advisors are responsible for the obligations or work-seeking behaviour of social assistance beneficiaries (Wright, 2001).
5 These responsibilities (in setting means tests for instance) have shifted between the two tiers of government over time, reflecting a debate between central government for standardization in national provision, and the municipal concern for increased discretion and hence diversity in national provision.
6 Presently, the social assistance scale rates are 100% of the Dutch minimum wage for a couple; 70% of the minimum wage for lone parents and 50% of the minimum wage for single people. Lone parents and single people may be eligible for a further 20% supplement, if they can prove to the municipality that they do not co-habit.
7 May also be implemented from the relatively new *Centra voor Werk en Inkomen* in the Netherlands and, which like Jobcentre Plus Offices in the UK, will provide one point of contact for social insurance/social assistance beneficiaries of working age, and in which municipal administrators may be situated.
8 Where decisions should be taken at the lowest possible level of government/as close to citizens as possible.

9   Some needs are excluded however, for example those which should be met from a beneficiary's health insurance.
10 In the second municipality a separate group of administrators were responsible for the client's re-integration plan.
11 Those that did know about them sometimes voiced that they would contact customers in these situations to inform them of where to go.
12 As well as a lack of funding/time/staff for this purpose.

Chapter 8

Undoing the Damage: Review Processes

Trevor Buck

Introduction

This Chapter examines the contribution made by the review system provided within the discretionary social fund scheme to enable applicants to challenge decision-making. The origins of the review mechanism are analysed in order to identify the political context for which this unique review system emerged, and to better explain the course of later developments in the review processes. This is followed by a brief account of how the current review processes operate and an assessment of current review practice and the available research evidence. The Chapter closes with an evaluation of the importance of the review function and a recommendation that, at least at the inspectoral stage of the review, it may be possible to develop 'systemic' remedies particularly in the social security field.

Origins of the Review Mechanisms

In the 1980s, the government intended from the outset to avoid the mainstream model of the adjudication and appeal tribunal arrangements and to provide instead merely an internal management review to deal with applicants' complaints about the operation of the social fund.

> ...the present appeal arrangements in special needs areas can have a sledgehammer effect. The full weight of legal consideration can be brought to bear on matters which may involve small sums of money for particular items with considerable delays between initial decision and formal review. We do not believe that the present system of appeals has best served the claimants' prime interest of a quick and effective consideration of decisions. The result is too slow, too cumbersome, and too inflexible. (Department of Health and Social Security, 1985b, para. 2.110)

The House of Commons Social Services Committee (1985) recommended government clarify further their proposals for a review mechanism referred to in the Green Paper of 1985 (HMSO, 1985). The Social Security Advisory Committee recommended the addition of an *external* appeal mechanism.

> An internal review by management will not be sufficient to demonstrate that decision-making is fair and has taken account of the facts. (SSAC, 1985, para. 3.83)

The White Paper, which followed in 1985, confirmed that something quite different from the well-accepted principles of adjudication in the social security system was envisaged for the social fund.

> Decisions which turned on whether it is reasonable to give or deny help in a particular case lend themselves far less readily to a separate, external assessment than do matters which turn on more specific criteria such as the amount of contributions paid or the income received. A necessary feature of any social fund review system is that it should operate quickly and effectively on the basis of knowledge and experience of local circumstances. The adjudication system would not be able to provide these features. (Department of Health and Social Security, 1985c, para. 4.50)

It was suggested that a first stage of review would consist of the local social fund officer looking again at the decision to consider whether the case had been properly handled and whether all the relevant factors had been taken into account. A dissatisfied applicant would be able to have the case reviewed again by a senior manager in the local office. It was argued that this model of review would link the task of reviewing individual cases with a general management responsibility for monitoring the operation of the social fund. However, the proposal soon drew a number of criticisms relating to the perceived attack on independent adjudication and the reduction in government's accountability that would result (Bolderson, 1988).

When the Social Security Bill was introduced in 1986 the Council on Tribunals produced a special report, which had a significant impact on Parliament's deliberations of the review issue (Council on Tribunals, 1986). It predicted (correctly) that the possibility of applying for judicial review would be impracticable in all but a minority of cases. The main thrust of the Council's argument was that the proposed review arrangements lacked independence. It pointed out that a quarter of appeals under the single payments system had been successful and that appeals against discretionary decisions were perfectly feasible as the pre-1980 system had shown (see Craig, Chapter 1, this volume).

> Very good reasons are needed before the abolition of the right to an independent appeal in such circumstances, an appeal which has existed for over 50 years. It would

probably be the most substantial abolition of a right to appeal to an independent tribunal since the Council on Tribunals were set up by Parliament in 1958, following the Franks Report. It is for those reasons that we are so critical of the proposal. In our last Annual Report we described it as highly retrograde. (Council on Tribunals, 1986, para. 12)

Given the range and authority of such criticisms and the pressures on the government over other contentious features of the fund, it was perhaps unsurprising that the government was prepared to make certain concessions over the shape of the social fund review during the course of the Bill's passage through Parliament. During the committee stage the government finally conceded that an internal administrative review contained within the normal chain of management might not of itself be fair, or be seen to be sufficiently fair. The then Minister for Social Security (Mr. Tony Newton M.P.) proposed that 'there should be an independent line of accountability to headquarters, and ultimately to the Secretary of State, which is not part of the routine line management of the day-to-day work of the DHSS local office network'.[1] It was recognised that there was a need to build in some protection against the development of office cultures which would otherwise drive particular patterns of decision-making. The government accepted the need for an additional external element to be bolted on to the two-stage internal review model proposed in the Bill. Although this 'external' review was to operate 'outside the normal chain of management' it would operate within the Department and accountability would be through the Secretary of State's directions and guidance.

At the report stage of the Bill the government's proposals for a separate body of social fund inspectors (SFIs) were brought forward.[2] In addition, in order to 'entrench the independence of the social fund inspectors', the post of a Social Fund Commissioner was inserted into the Bill at the Lords amendments stage in the Commons.[3] As the administrative head of the SFIs, the Commissioner has the power of appointment. However, both the SFIs and other support staff were to be 'made available' to the Commissioner by the Secretary of State. It would appear that the original intention of Ministers was to have an inspectorate that would only perform a limited procedural review of the local reviewing officers' decisions. As explained below, that aim is adequately met in the wording of direction 39(1) for reviewing officers and SFI direction 1 for social fund inspectors. However, the directions also included a *merits* examination under direction 32(1) (for reviewing officers) and SFI direction 2 (in relation to social fund inspectors).

This bifurcation of the review function to be performed by both the internal and external reviewer into a procedural and merits examination was confirmed in 1990 by a Divisional Court judicial review hearing. The

Court accepted in this case that although the Secretary of State did indeed have the legal authority conferred by the primary legislation to cut down the parameters of the review by secondary legislation (i.e. the 'directions'), in fact that was not what had been achieved by the wording of the directions.

> The directions make it clear that the SFI has to conduct a two-stage process. The first stage is equivalent to judicial review, but the second stage goes further. The requirement to have regard to any new evidence and any relevant change of circumstances pursuant to the second direction on the second stage indicates that the review goes beyond what would occur on an application for judicial review.[4]

Origin of the revised Budgeting Loan (BL) scheme

The revised BL scheme had been planned for two years in response to a number of concerns about its complexity and delays in processing claims prior to its introduction by the Social Security Act 1998 ('SSA 1998') (see Collard, Chapter 9, of this volume). The revised scheme was implemented from April 1999.

> We want to enable staff to take an early second look at disputed decisions, and to correct any errors there and then rather than wait for the appeal [sic] process. At the moment, decision making on applications for budgeting loans from the social fund is unnecessarily complex.   When the social fund was introduced, the idea was that it should be a simple, discretionary application of common sense, but it has not turned out like that.   The current system is confusing for customers and time-consuming for staff.[5]

It is clear that government's original intention was to entirely exclude the inspectors from reviewing the new BL regime.   When the Bill was introduced in Parliament it contained no provision for SFI review. However, the government responded to concerns that this would remove an important safety valve in the social fund system and moved at Committee stage the restoration of the SFIs' review role.[6]

The origin of 'any time' discretionary reviews

The social fund inspectors were given an important power in the 1986 legislation to review their own decisions as a matter of discretion.   The power enables inspectors to respond to the applicant's or the Department's request to review a decision a second time or initiate a review themselves. Again, this important power was inserted into the legislation at the eleventh hour.

[W]e have taken the opportunity of this change to the provisions relating to social fund inspectors to correct a minor defect in the Bill as drafted. Before amendment there was no power in the [1986] Bill to change an inspector's decision. We concluded that this was too rigid. Nevertheless, we have brought forward an amendment to give social fund inspectors the power to review their own decisions so that problems can be avoided.[7]

The 'problems', which were contemplated, were not only minor errors of bad draftsmanship in decision letters, but also the difficulties presented by decisions which could draw out judicial review challenge in the High Court and put the spotlight on more substantive errors. This power, as will be shown, has developed into an important means whereby the inspectors' decisions can be 'judicial review proofed.'

The Current Review Processes

Decision making on applications for the discretionary social fund payments can be reviewed, firstly, by the local office and if the applicant is still not satisfied, by one of the social fund inspectors of the Independent Review Service (IRS). The Social Fund Commissioner is the administrative head of IRS and has statutory powers to monitor the quality of inspectors' decisions and other matters but cannot review decisions himself. There are now three review procedures consequent upon changes in the legislation brought about by the SSA 1998: the review of community care grants (CCGs) and crisis loans (CLs); the review of budgeting loans; and, the review of overpayment decisions. The introduction in April 1999 of a 'fact-based' budgeting loan scheme in effect abandoned an important principle of the social fund scheme in its first ten years of existence, that any application to the fund would be regarded as an 'application to the fund as a whole'. That principle has only survived to the extent that an application for a CCG can be regarded as an application for a CL and vice versa.[8] There is no longer any legal authority to treat a BL application as an application for a CCG or CL.

There are a number of detailed differences in the procedures of all three review processes (see Buck, 2000, pp. 84-95 and Appendices 4(a) – (c)). The following sections highlight some of the important and distinctive features of each process.

Community Care Grant and Crisis Loan review

A reviewing officer (RO) in the local office must have full regard initially to:

(a) whether the DM applied the law correctly – in arriving at his decision. In particular:
  (i) that the decision is sustainable on the evidence;
  (ii) that the decision maker took all relevant considerations into account and did not take irrelevant considerations into account;
  (iii) that the decision maker interpreted the law – including Secretary of State directions – correctly;[9]
(b) whether the DM acted fairly and exercised his discretion to arrive at a conclusion that was reasonable in the circumstances – ie a decision that a reasonable DM could have reached;
(c) whether the required procedural steps have been followed; that the applicant had sufficient opportunity to put his case; and there has been no bias. (Direction 39(1))

The three factors, (a)-(c) above, are comparable to the traditional grounds for judicial review challenge in the High Court.[10] The RO will then proceed to consider the following factors:

(a) all the circumstances which existed at the time the original determination was made;
(b) any new evidence which has since been produced; and
(c) any relevant change of circumstances. (Direction 32(1))

Unlike the tests used at the first stage of review under direction 39, which examines the *quality* of the decision making process, this stage of the review requires in essence consideration of the *merits* of the decision. If the decision is revised wholly in the applicant's favour at this stage then the review is completed. The social fund guidance makes clear that the revised decision will be regarded as wholly in the applicant's favour 'only if it meets all the points of the original and review applications' (*Social Fund Guide*, 2002, para. 8390). If not, the applicant must be given an opportunity to attend an interview, either in person or by telephone, with an RO at the local office. The RO who conducts the interview must ensure the applicant is given '(a) an explanation of the reasons for the determination complained of' and '(b) an opportunity to make representations, including the provision of additional evidence, in relation to his application' (direction 33(3)). There are a number of procedural safeguards built into the directions and guidance. For example, the RO must make a written record of any representations made at the interview by the applicant 'and this must be agreed with the applicant' (direction 35). The guidance notes that the RO ought not to add to the record of the interview retrospectively.[11] After the interview the RO must reconsider the decision and is then under a mandatory duty to inform the applicant of the decision in writing and of the applicant's right to apply for a further review of the decision by an SFI (direction 36(2)).

An application to the local office for an SFI review will trigger the sending out of all the relevant papers to IRS in Birmingham. The SFI's review follows the pattern of the RO's action with the important exception that there is no equivalent 'interview' stage.[12] The SFI does however carry out the dual function under SFI directions 1 and 2 of conducting a *quality* and *merits* review, mirroring the powers exercised by the reviewing officer under directions 39 and 32 respectively. On a review the SFI has three powers available under the primary legislation: to confirm the original decision, to substitute his/her own decision, or to refer the matter back to the local RO for a determination (section 38(4), SSA 1998). The only remaining legal challenge available after an adverse SFI decision will be an application for judicial review to the High Court.[13] It has been estimated that from 1988 to 1999 there have 63 applications for leave granted by the High Court on social fund cases: 36 of these were later withdrawn or lapsed and 27 reached a full substantive hearing. Of these 27 cases, the SFI's decision was upheld in 20 and only quashed in seven (Buck, 2000, p.120, Table 2). One factor, which explains the relatively small number of judicial review challenges, is the availability of the 'any time' discretionary review. An SFI 'may review a determination…made by himself or some other social fund inspector' (section 38(5), SSA 1998). This power has proved to be a useful device to enable SFIs to 'judicial review proof' their decisions. If a judicial review challenge is perceived to be potentially embarrassing to IRS and/or the Department the power can be used to redo the decision in the light of the representations made. Indeed, the numbers of judicial review cases have all but disappeared in recent years.

Budgeting Loan review

A review of BL decisions follows the pattern of review for CCGs and CLs but there has been a narrowing of the review powers in relation to BLs which reflect the policy intention to create a more automated, 'fact-based' and simplified BL scheme (Department of Social Security, 1999). In the case of CCGs and CLs, the directions spell out three circumstances where a determination must be reviewed: where the decision was based on a mistake of law, or given in ignorance of or based on a mistake of material fact; or where there has been 'any relevant change of circumstances since the determination was made' (direction 31(a)-(c)). However, in the case of BLs the 'change of circumstances' factor is omitted. This has the effect of cutting down the discretion of both the RO and SFI in looking at the applicant's changing circumstances since the application was originally made. That is arguably inconsistent with the claim that the social fund provides a mechanism to track and target needs. Again, the open-ended 'unreasonableness' head in direction 39(1)(b) (see the text above), does not appear in relation to the parallel direction for BLs. Direction 39(2)(b) narrows the scope of review by inserting a formulation which in effect constrains the territory of 'unreasonableness' which the SFI may examine. In fact, the core of the discretion available to decision makers, ROs and SFIs, i.e. a consideration of 'the nature, extent and urgency of the need' (section 140(1) Social Security Contributions and Benefits Act 1992 ('SSCBA 1992')), does not appear in the revised budgeting loan scheme. The SFIs act under parallel directions (SFI directions 3 and 4). In short, not only has the reviewing power been narrowed in relation to BLs but the substance of the discretionary determination has also been squeezed into an area which is less vulnerable to effective legal challenge.

Overpayment review

ROs and SFIs took on this additional jurisdiction from October 1998. The legislation now provides that an officer 'may review such a determination on the ground that the person who applied for the [social fund] payment to which the determination relates misrepresented, or failed to disclose, any material fact' (section 38(1)(b) SSA 1998). In essence, under directions 43-48 what must happen is that the decision maker must first review the social fund payment decision where an overpayment question arises. The applicant will then have the right to request a further review from the RO. That officer will then apply the bifurcated review function (see directions 45 and 46) suitably adapted to this context. The SFI acts under parallel directions (SFI directions 5 and 6).

Current Review Practice

Review caseload

It can be seen from Table 8.1 below that there are about 99,000 (internal local office) applications for review of CCGs, 42,000 reviews of CLs and 43,000 reviews of BLs. However, the proportion of reviews of initial refusals is only 28.7 per cent, 13.3 per cent and 9.5 per cent for CCGs, CLs and BLs respectively. It is revealing also to know the huge percentage figure for ROs upholding BL decisions under the revised scheme (90.6 per cent). This is good evidence that the review function in relation to BLs has indeed been severely curtailed since the changes introduced in April 1999. The caseload profile for IRS reviews also shows how BL review activity accounts for only a small proportion of both its own total caseload and of initial applications. The total workload of IRS for 2001/02 was 25,681 cases, slightly greater than the sum of reviews in row 5 of the Table 8.1

below. One also must add in 251 cases found to be 'outside jurisdiction',[14] 47 cases withdrawn and 530 cases determined under the 'any time' discretionary reviewing power.

Table 8.1   Numbers and Percentages of Initial Applications, Refusals, Internal Reviews, SFI Reviews by Type of Social Fund Payment, 2001-2002

	Community Care Grants		Crisis Loans		Budgeting Loans	
1 Initial applications	579,000		1,330,000		1,748,000	
2 Initial refusals	346,000		317,000		460,000	
% initial refusals		*59.8%*		*23.8%*		*26.3%*
3 Applications for RO review	99,313		42,062		43,660	
% refusals going to RO		*28.7%*		*13.3%*		*9.5%*
4 Decisions upheld by RO	49,923		25,364		39,555	
% RO applications upheld		*50.3%*		*60.3%*		*90.6%*
5 IRS reviews	14,444		6,847		3,562	
% IRS review i) of initial apps		*2.5%*	*0.5%*		*0.2%*	
ii) of initial refusals		*4.2%*	*2.2%*		*0.8%*	
iii) of apps to RO		*14.5%*	*16.3%*		*8.2%*	
iv) of ROs' refusals		*28.9%*	*27.0%*		*9.0%*	

Source: Derived from Social Fund Commissioner (2002), Tables 2, 3 and 6.

Quality of reviews

The quality of reviews at the local office is clearly dependent on levels of training, seniority and a number of other factors. As explained above the original intention was to provide a basic grade civil servant to perform an initial review and then by a more senior officer in the local office. Until 1994 this was achieved by the appointment of a 'social fund officer' (SFO) and 'a social fund officer not below the rank of higher executive officer' (HEO(SF)) respectively. However, two reforms in April 1994 and September 1995 have rolled up these two officers' reviews into a single review performed by an RO who will not need and invariably is not an HEO (see Buck, 1996, pp.78-79, 401-403). SFIs have for many years been of HEO grade. However, that practice has been altered by the appointment of EO grade officers in IRS to handle BL reviews and other matters. There has also been a remarkable increase in the SFIs' review productivity rate and frequent exercises to increase 'clearance' rates.   Indeed, one of the problems has been the slower and more variable clearance review rate achieved in the district offices. The Select Committee on Social Security recommended that internal reviews should be handled within two weeks of receipt (House of Commons, 2001). However, the Social Fund Commissioners Annual Report for 2001/2002 observed that district offices only processed on average, 72 per cent of its reviews within 15 days and 48 per cent within 10 days. Furthermore, there was 'a wide range of clearance times across the 129 district offices'.

The profile of disposals by the SFIs also tells us something about the overall quality of inspectoral reviews: see Table 8.2 below. Overall, the SFIs confirmed more than half of all applications for review. However, the rate of substitutions for CCGs (60.3 per cent) shows evidence of fairly vigorous scrutiny of ROs' decisions for that payment.

Table 8.2   Numbers and Percentages of SFI Reviews by Outcome and Type of Social Fund Payment, 2001-2002

	Community Care Grants		Crisis Loans		Budgeting Loans		All payments	
Confirmations	5,563		4,467		3,191		13,221	
		38.5%		65.2%		89.6%		53.2%
Substitutions	8,706		2,345		371		11,422	
		60.3%		34.2%		10.4%		46.0%
Refer Backs	175		35		0		210	
		1.2%		0.5%		0.0%		0.8%
TOTALS	14,444		6,847		3,562		24,853	

Source: Derived from Secretary of State for Work and Pensions (2002), Annex 12.

Conversely, the proportions of substitutions and confirmations of CLs are the other way round with 65.2 per cent of these being confirmed by inspectors. The rate of substitutions for BLs (10.4 per cent) is strikingly low but perhaps this is to be expected given the 'simplified' legal structure of the revised BL scheme.

The development of IRS under three successive Commissioners has often demonstrated the difficult balance to be achieved between the desire to increase the accessibility of the review process against the need to achieve legal accuracy and rigour. This has shown itself over the years by varying approaches to decision letter writing and more recently there has been a significant change in paperwork distributed to applicants to comment upon. The IRS has now implemented a system whereby applicants only receive the key documents to comment upon rather than the more comprehensive bundles of paper which used to be disclosed.[15]

'Any time' discretionary reviews

Section 38(5), SSA 1998, states that '[a] social fund inspector may review a determination ... made by himself or some other social fund inspector'. Although section 38(5) reviews are numerically small and only accounted for 2.1 per cent of IRS's total workload in 2001/02,[16] they are of key significance in the review process.

This special reviewing power is entirely at the discretion of the SFI. There is no further guidance as to how it should be exercised in the statutes, directions or the *Social Fund Guide*. In essence, it is used to correct an error of law or fact in the inspector's original review decision. The Social Fund Commissioner issued some advice on how to approach the use of section 38(5) in February 2002 which seeks to delineate when an error is sufficiently 'important' to justify using the power.[17] However, the regulations[18] governing review applications do not formally apply to section 38(5) reviews, thus there is no time limit for an application under this power. There are advantages in the use of the 'any time' review for welfare advocates to obtain a subsequent review from the SFI. The power also provides the inspectorate with a powerful device to forestall judicial review challenges. There is evidence that the discretionary nature of 'any time' reviews has in fact been exercised and recorded inconsistently over the years and IRS policy towards its use is vulnerable to the particular views of the incumbent social fund Commissioner (Buck, 2000, pp.98-99, 157-161, 298).

Research on the Review Process

The Policy Studies Institute conducted an important piece of research in 1990, which focused on the social fund review process (Dalley and Berthoud, 1992). This study found little understanding by applicants of how the review process worked. Few were aware, for example, of the existence of SFIs unless they had already used the procedure. Applicants tended to regard the internal review at the local office as a second stage of their original application. The study also found that the majority of BL decisions tended to turn on technical errors while revised CCG decisions often depended on further information gathered. Those who attended review interviews generally felt they had had an adequate explanation for refusal and an opportunity to state their case. The study also confirmed that the initial judicial review cases in the High Court had 'had a profound effect on the social fund, and especially on inspectors' reviews'.

Interestingly, the researchers concluded that the social fund review contained all the elements of the tripartite model of 'bureaucratic justice' advanced by Mashaw (1983). The legal structure of the social fund, i.e. the primary legislation and its directions and guidance, were sufficient to meet the conditions of 'bureaucratic rationality'. There were elements of 'moral judgment' to be found in the way some of the discretion found in the directions was exercised. There were also elements of 'professional treatment' in respect of certain decisions. The report discusses in some detail the difficult balance to be struck between certainty, appropriate use of discretion and the applicant's accessibility. In general, the study approved of the inspectors' role.

> They are able to offer a level of scrutiny in relation to each individual case which the members of a tribunal could not hope to achieve. And they can explain their decision in detail, whatever the outcome. It is this aspect of the current system which is most positively approved of by applicants. (Dalley and Berthoud, 1992, p.157)

The study identified some concern in local offices about the criticisms sometimes made in SFIs' decision letters and that applicants were impressed with these. On a broader level, the researchers suggested the possibility of extending the inspector's role to one along the lines of the (then) HM Inspectors of Schools. They suggested an annual review of cases from each district office would be useful to identify any patterns of problems arising. The researchers concluded however that no review mechanism could rescue a scheme from its inherent weaknesses: 'perhaps the greatest value of the review procedure is the clear light it sheds on the design of the social fund as a whole.' (Dalley and Berthoud, 1992, p.163).

The unique dual function of the social fund review, explained above, has inevitably drawn interest from administrative lawyers, in particular because the inspectors not only have to apply a judicial review type test in their review work, but also because they are potential targets for judicial review challenge. There has not much research available on the influence of judicial review on the respondents to judicial review, like the IRS. However, one exception has been a research study, conducted in 1999, which examined the influence of judicial review on decisions taken by the SFIs (Sunkin and Pick, 2002). This research examined, inter alia, the extent to which such organisations can digest juridical norms. Earlier work had questioned whether juridical norms were capable of infiltrating administrative cultures and speculated that 'certain values those associated with process for example, are more readily internalised than others' (Richardson and Sunkin, 1996). The research found that:

...[W]hile of central importance during the early years of the IRS's existence, the influence of judicial review declined as the organisation's goals shifted from a concern to establish its legitimacy to a concern to ensure efficient service delivery. The decline in the external influence of judicial review does not by itself signify that juridical norms are no longer important to the general operating ethos of the IRS. However, it does imply that such norms are expected to serve organisation goals rather than to drive them. (Sunkin and Pick, 2002, p.759)

The extent to which the organisation culture of IRS has been affected by judicial review challenge has also been the subject of commentary in Buck (1998) which details the way in which IRS developed and attempted to cope with varying roles demanded of it. There are also particular concerns raised about the way in which the more recent organisational 'customer care' focus can in fact be utilised as a sleight of hand method to conform with Departmental policy demands rather than the demands of legal propriety (Buck, 2001).

The Importance of the Review Mechanisms

From the applicant's perspective, the review mechanisms may offer opportunities to challenge decision-making and obtain payments, and to achieve that important, but often indefinable benefit, of securing justice. It must always be important in designing appeal/review mechanisms to ensure that those mechanisms are capable of arriving at the 'right' legal answers. But it is also important that the review delivers the answers in an appropriate manner. The various features of the *processing* of reviews lies at the important interface with the users of the system many of whom are vulnerable and in poverty. Such mechanisms ought in principle to be highly accessible and capable of empowering individuals: they should not operate to exclude or stigmatise applicants.

It will also be in the interests of the Department for Work and Pensions to have an effective review system, which can put right incorrect decision-making in individual cases and perhaps provide more durable lessons for future decision-making. More generally, any system of legal review or appeal ought to confer some kind of legitimacy on the system that is the subject of review.

From the perspective of the policymaker, the social fund review system is of particular importance and interest in that its underlying dual function – to assess both the *quality* and the *merits* of decision making – is unique in the larger context of the UK's various tribunal systems. The quality evaluation inherent in social fund reviews also resonates closely with the legal tests developed by the common law which constitute the grounds for an application for judicial review in the High Court.   The question that then arises is whether there are wider administrative law implications? If a group of civil servants (as opposed to a High Court judge) can be shown to have succeeded in applying those tests is there a generalisable case to extend this type of remedy into other important areas of dispute resolution?

Finally, it should not be forgotten that the question whether a review/appeal mechanism is made available at all and the manner in which it is structured is a political question. The history of the provenance of the review outlined in this Chapter demonstrates the way in which the offer of a review mechanism as originally conceived, was based on a particular political position. The government simply believed that the spiralling cost of appeals against single payments decisions was providing an over-effective weapon of welfare advocacy and poverty lobbying (see Craig, Chapter 3, this volume).   Yet there were also strong forces at work to remind government of the importance of providing an independent element to any review mechanism. The last minute addition of the inspectors in the legislative review framework underlined the political bartering which was conducted from the beginning of the social fund's existence.   However, independence is a quality that does not lend itself easily to neat measurement and categorisation.

In the early years of the social fund, under the leadership of the first Social Fund Commissioner, there was undoubtedly a strong policy to support the establishment of the inspectors as an independent element in the review scheme.   However, this was driven more by a political understanding of the necessity to achieve the public *perception* of independent scrutiny rather than a genuine ideological commitment to the intervention of legality in this particular arena. Governments of all political persuasions are also well aware of the potential dangers of applicants' grievances leaking out to a well-publicised case in the High Court. The late insertion in the Social Security Bill 1986 of the discretionary review provides an effective longstop to field such unpredictable criticisms of the social fund scheme.   That function of the inspectors has been fully recognised in the government's change of mind in relation to the review arrangements applicable to the revised BL scheme introduced in 1999.

It should also be remembered that any appeal/review system is essentially a 'filtering' process and must be evaluated on the basis of how effectively it resolves applicants' grievances along all the various stages of the review.   There is not any available research which will reliably tell us, for example, what has happened to the 246,687 applicants in 2002/02 (see Table 8.1 above, row 2 minus row 3) who were refused a CCG by the decision maker and who did not take the first step into the review process and apply to a local RO.   One must also consider the shortfall between the numbers of those whose cases have been rejected by the RO and those who have chosen to pursue a further review to the inspectors (row 4 minus row

5), a total of 35,479 review applicants. The way in which the review is made known to applicants, and the help available along key points in the review process, is therefore of crucial importance and integral to any proper assessment of the process. The reality for social fund applicants is that they will belong to the most numerous category of persons who will either not have the resources and stamina to pursue a review and/or will be persuaded by the management of review processes in the district offices that there is no point in pursuing their claims any further.

The Review Process and the Provision of a 'Systemic' Remedy

This section briefly explores three propositions. Is there any evidence that the social fund review process currently provides avenues whereby flaws in the social fund scheme itself can be highlighted? In principle, should a review/appeal process in social security matters provide more than individual justice? Are there ways in which the review processes could be adapted or extended in order to deliver a 'systemic' remedy?

Highlighting flaws

An inspector's decision does not set a binding precedent in law comparable to the status of Social Security Commissioners' decisions. Consequently, the lessons learned from individual inspectors' decisions may often be lost in terms of more general application. This has been the legacy from the policymakers in the 1980s who had set their faces against accepting a grievance procedure which let in this strong version of judicial accountability. The Social Security Commissioners' decisions on single payments had done much to assist the challenges made to Departmental policies in this area.

However, the underlying dual legal function of the social fund review has provided the opportunity, in particular at the level of the SFIs' review, to expose a range of criticisms which can be made relating to *process* values. SFI direction 1 provides the vehicle by which original decision-making and the RO's decisions can be matched against the standards set by the High Court on an application for judicial review. Furthermore, the power to refer decisions back for re-determination provides a mechanism whereby decision makers and ROs can be made more aware of such process values and be given clear guidelines in individual cases as to how to conform with such standards within the larger framework of legality. However, as Table 8.2 above makes clear, the refer back power is being used very sparingly: in 2001/02 only 1.2 per cent of CCG cases and 0.5 per cent of CL cases were referred back and no cases at all are referred back under the revised BL scheme. There has been a very clear decrease in the proportion of cases dealt with by referring them back since the 59 per cent of cases managed in this way in 1989-90 (Buck, 2000, p.90, Table 2). In principle, the refer back power has the ability to ensure, like the High Court on a judicial review, that not only are the proper procedural values identified, but that they are also actively digested by the decision makers further down the line of authority. This would generate a truly 'supervisory jurisdiction' with the SFIs. However, the downgrading of this function is emphasised not only by the decrease in the use of the refer back power, but also by the way in which an SFI direction 'flaw' which is adjudged not to have made a difference to the actual outcome of the case, will be counted as a 'technical confirmation' of a decision.[19]

More than individual justice?

Liberal conceptions of justice are saturated with an emphasis on the individual rather than any collective entity. However, in the arena of social security, a policy area which is intimately concerned with collective responsibility, there is perhaps a case to be made to structure an appeal or review to provide more than a mechanism constrained to resolving an individual matter. What is needed is a system of review which is also capable of providing clear indications of where the administrative system of the social fund itself has failed. In principle, the systemic aspects highlighted by the exercise of administrative justice should be addressed in a more organised manner than is possible with the current review model. The counter-argument is that such an approach would undermine the necessary independence of a judicial function. The IRS, which has an essentially judicial function, does risk some dangers in synthesising its experience of individual reviews in order to make a contribution to the wider objectives of system efficiency. In short, such organisations must carefully balance the maintenance of their legitimacy as independent bodies who can credibly adjudicate citizen/state disputes, with the more general advantages of providing authoritative evidence of system failures.

Adapting social fund reviews to provide systemic justice

There are already indications that the lessons learned from the core review activity undertaken by IRS are being utilised to flag up general disorders in the administration of the fund and to make recommendations for their resolution. In the Social Fund Commissioner's Annual Report (2001/02), for example, there is clearly some concern that decision making at the ground level is far too budget driven and that the area budgets which vary from one region to another are causing problems of 'territorial injustice'.

> Our research indicated that the errors about qualification and priority arose from significant and growing pressures on districts' grants budgets, which were improperly influencing the Agency's decisions. The law requires that decisions on both of these must be made without reference to the state of the local office budget. ...
> Having identified the budget as a root cause of the increased error rate at the Agency and the consequential increase in our substitution rate, we carried out further analysis of grants budget allocations and social fund activity at the Agency. For each of the 128 districts, we examined funding levels, and the level of activity and outcomes at each stage of the decision making and review processes. Our findings showed wide variations across the districts and included the following:
>
> - the level of funding available per application made to the fund ranged from £107 to £294, with an average of £169;
> - the proportion of applications where an award was made at the initial stage ranged from 26 per cent to 56 per cent, with an average of 38 per cent;
> - of those seeking a review, the proportions which received an award ranged from 28 per cent to 63 per cent, with an average of 46 per cent; and
> - the average amount awarded at the initial stage and on review ranged from £219 to £578, with an average of £352.

The same annual report also makes a strong recommendation for the need to conduct more research on the operation of the social fund.

> In recent years, research into the social fund has been small scale and focused on narrow aspects of the fund. Little is known about the effects and outcomes for those who use the fund, nor about why the level of take-up by eligible people is low. I understand that around 13 applications are made nationally for every 100 eligible people.
> I have suggested some in-depth research to address the following questions:
>
> - why do significant numbers of eligible people not use the discretionary social fund?; and
> - of those who do use the fund, what difference does it make to them and how regularly do they return to the fund for help?

The IRS has also incrementally developed a 'maladaministration' jurisdiction of its own. Its recent annual reports note the numbers of 'complaints' (i.e. not form legal 'reviews') received and how these were dealt with by the organisation. Many of these purely administrative matters will fall outside of the inspector's jurisdiction and SFIs are not (at present) subject to investigation by the Parliamentary Ombudsman. Nevertheless, this is a part of IRS's work that has been given greater focus.

The IRS has developed a role over and above its case review work under the leadership of successive Social Fund Commissioners. It organises its liaison activity with the Department for Work and Pensions and welfare rights groups with the deliberate intention to better inform policymakers and other stakeholders in the social fund system. It was perhaps in recognition of the IRS's proactive role that the House of Commons Select Committee on Social Security (2001) recommended that the applicant ought to apply directly to the IRS for a review rather than having to go via the local office. It is useful to reflect that the nineteenth-century 'poor law inspectors', (Brundage, 2002) although forever associated with a repressive regime of social control, nevertheless produced an invaluable and detailed documentary account of the circumstances of those in poverty: perhaps an early example of 'evidence-based policy making'. Social fund inspectors are similarly tied in to an association with a largely discredited system of one-off discretionary benefit payments. However an examination of the development of IRS's organisational activities and goals arguably demonstrates the emergence of a significant prototype of administrative justice that may well outlive the existence of the discretionary social fund scheme itself. The social fund review mechanism may well 'undo the damage' in some individual cases, but the system is set up to ensure that this will only happen for relatively small numbers of applicants. What is required is that any reformed social fund scheme is able to build purposefully upon the IRS model of review. The valuable lessons learned from review activity could then have some chance of being appropriately captured and reprocessed to the advantage of its users and the integrity of the system as a whole.

Notes

1 *Hansard*, H.C. Official Reports, Standing Committee B, col. 1306 (April 10, 1986).
2 *Hansard*, H.C. Debates, Vol. 98, cols. 29, 123, 206 (May 19-20, 1986).
3 *Hansard*, H.C. Debates, Vol. 102, cols. 426-439 (July 23, 1986).
4 Woolf L.J., *R v Secretary of State for Social Services and the Social Fund Inspectors, ex parte Stitt (No.1)*, *Sherwin and Roberts*, Divisional Court, 21 February, 1990.
5 *Hansard*, H.C. Debates, Vol. 298, col. 783 (July 22, 1997). Ms Harriet Harman M.P., Secretary of State for Social Security.
6 'These changes have emerged as a result of the consultation exercise on the new budgeting loans scheme. We have listened carefully to the responses received and think it proper that all budgeting loan determinations should carry a further right of review with a social fund inspector.' *Hansard*, H.C. Official Reports, Standing Committee B (November 18, 1997), Mr. Denham, Parliamentary Under-Secretary for Social Security.

7 *Hansard*, H.L. Debates, Vol. 479, col. 431 (July 24, 1986), Baroness Trumpington. There is also a parallel, discretionary power (section 38(1)(c), SSA 1998) to review by the RO but the SFI's power is more significant as it lies at the end of the statutory review process and affects the applicant's access to the High Court.

8 Social Security Contributions and Benefits Act 1992, s.140(4)(aa).

9 Following *Stitt, Sherwin and Roberts* the text of relevant social fund guidance and the directions were changed so that the word 'correctly' replaced the original wording 'properly' in order to put an end to the notion that the social fund review was merely a limited procedural review.

10 These are, respectively; 'illegality', '*Wednesbury* unreasonableness' and 'procedural impropriety'. See Lord Diplock's classic statement of the grounds for judicial review in *Council of Civil Service Unions v Minister for the Civil Service* [1985] A.C. 374 at 408 (the 'GCHQ case').

11 *Social Fund Guide*, paras. 8602, 8621.

12 However, the Northern Ireland inspectors have tended to carry out a limited number of home visits and at varying times the IRS has considered whether to increase this type of activity: see Buck, 2002, para. 5.26.

13 Civil Proceedings Rules, Part 54 and Supreme Court Act 1981, sections 29-31. The specialised element of the High Court which dealt with judicial reviews used to be called the 'Crown Office List'. This was renamed in July 2000 the 'Administrative Court' following recommendations made by the Bowman review.

14 Applications which are not made in the appropriate 'time, form and manner' or otherwise outside of jurisdiction. For example, a maternity item would not be regarded as falling within the inspector's jurisdiction as these are provided for under the regulated social fund scheme.

15 See Social Fund Commissioner's Annual Report for 2001/02, p.25.

16 Higher figures for the SFI's discretionary review have been recorded in previous years, a peak of 1,682 cases were noted for 1995-96, 5.7 per cent of all SFI cases cleared in that year (Buck, 2000, p.158, Table 4).

17 See Commissioner's Advice on the approach to take when considering whether to exercise the discretionary power in Section 38(5), effective from 02/04/02, at http://www.irssf.gov.uk/infocent/commad/38(5)/38(5).htm.

18 Social Fund (Application for Review) Regulations 1988, SI 1998 No. 34.

19 For example, see Social Fund Commissioner's Annual Report for 1998/99 at p.23.

PART III
THE PROSPECTS FOR REFORM

Chapter 9

Making it Better? The Impact of Reform

Sharon Collard

Introduction

The Budgeting Loan (BL) scheme was set up in 1988, following a major review of social security provision, to replace the single payments system that had previously been available to claimants of Supplementary Benefit. It was the latest in a series of government measures that aimed to help people on basic means-tested benefits meet the lump sum needs which they might not be able to afford out of their weekly benefit (Kempson *et al*, 1994). As such, it was not designed to provide a source of low-cost credit for people without access to mainstream sources, but was rather an advance on benefit income that had to be repaid.

The BL scheme continued unchanged until the Social Security Act 1998, when a number of reforms were introduced to simplify the application, decision-making and review processes (see Buck, Chapter 8, this volume), and to make the scheme less costly to administer. Despite sustained criticism from lobbyists, however, the discretionary social fund has so far remained cash-limited, and gross expenditure on BLs and Crisis Loans far outweighs that spent on Community Care Grants.

The main aim of this chapter is to assess the impact of the 1998 reforms from the point of view of BL recipients, mostly using information drawn from depth interviews with benefit recipients who successfully applied for a BL under the revised scheme (Whyley *et al*, 2000).[1] In addition, drawing on this and another study, of social fund use among older people (Kempson *et al*, 2002),[2] a number of other possible reforms are suggested that would arguably improve the social fund's effectiveness further, including changes to the repayment levels of BLs and measures to increase awareness of the discretionary social fund. The idea of extending the BL scheme to other low-income groups is also considered. The chapter begins, however, by describing the types of people who use the BL scheme and examining the reasons why they use it.

Who Uses the Social Fund Budgeting Loan Scheme?

BLs are currently only available to people who have been receiving either Income Support (IS)[3] or income-based Jobseeker's Allowance for at least 26 weeks. There is some evidence to suggest that applicants to the scheme are among the most vulnerable recipients of these benefits. Recent research, largely carried out among non-pensioner BL applicants, found a high incidence of physical and mental ill-health; family instability and breakdown; and insecure housing among applicants. For the most part, applicants had also been receiving benefit for long periods of time and, consequently, had little or no money in savings to draw on when faced with unexpected expenditure. In addition, because of the high incidence of family breakdown, many had no relations to turn to when they needed to borrow money (Whyley *et al*, 2000).

But take-up of the scheme varies widely among the different groups of eligible benefit recipients. As Table 9.1 indicates, lone parents are among the heaviest users of the scheme. In May 2001, 19 per cent of all people eligible to apply to the social fund were lone parents (National Statistics, 2001), yet they accounted for nearly half the expenditure on BLs. In contrast, people over state pension age make very little use of the scheme. Not only do they account for the smallest proportion of expenditure, they are also greatly under-represented relative to their proportion in the eligible population.

Table 9.1   Budgeting Loan Expenditure by Claimant Group

		Percentages (%)
	Percentage of expenditure in 2000	Percentage of all receiving IS or income-based JSA (May 2001)
Pensioners	4	37
Unemployed	12	15
Disabled	24	22
Lone parents	49	19
Others	10	7

Sources: *Secretary of State for Work and Pensions, 2001; Quarterly Statistical Enquiry: Income Support*, May 2001.

This is not to say that people who apply for social fund awards are in greater need than those who do not. Recent research among eligible pensioners, for example, found that applicants and non-applicants had similar levels of need for the type of items for which they could apply to the social fund. In fact, the people who had the most pressing needs were almost all people who had *not* applied to the social fund (Kempson *et al*, 2002). What distinguished applicants from non-applicants was not need, but rather awareness of the social fund.

Why Do People Use the Budgeting Loan Scheme?

On the whole, people living on IS or Jobseeker's Allowance have few choices when faced with 'lumpy expenditure' such as buying furniture or white goods. Indeed this was why most applicants had applied to the BL scheme.

> I'm not working or anything, and I'm on my own with no income other than Income Support, so I know I can't get a loan from anywhere else. (26 year old lone mother)

People who are not working are almost certain to have applications for any form of mainstream credit rejected and so do not even bother applying. Even if they had overdraft facilities, or credit or store cards when they were in employment, they almost certainly stop using them while on benefit.

Informal help among family and friends, both in cash and kind, is widespread among people living on low incomes (Kempson *et al*, 1994). But many people who are eligible for a BL have friends or family who are no or little better off than themselves. So, while they may help out with small sums of money to help make ends meet, they are unable to lend larger sums of money.

Access to loans through community-based credit unions is also restricted. Despite important developments in the past few years, the availability of credit unions for people who do not work remains patchy. Even if there *is* a credit union available locally, not everyone on IS or income-based Jobseeker's Allowance wants, or is in a position, to join. Moreover, parents with young children who have been on a low income for some time are rarely able to save enough to qualify for the amounts of money they typically need to borrow. And once they start using high-cost commercial credit this further reduces their capacity to save. As a consequence, only a small number of people who are eligible for BLs are also members of a credit union.

Other types of community-based lending organisations, such as community reinvestment trusts,[4] are as yet relatively small-scale. Some are limited to certain groups (such as local authority or housing association tenants) while others only operate in certain locations.

Consequently, apart from the BL scheme, only mail order catalogues and the 'alternative' credit providers[5] are widely available to people claiming IS and income-based Jobseeker's Allowance. Indeed, they represent the main sources of credit for large numbers of benefit recipients.

Although easily accessible to people on low incomes, these forms of borrowing are, without exception, high cost and often have loan conditions that are unfavourable to the consumer, such as punitive penalties for late payment. For example, a washing machine that could be bought in the high street for £400 using a BL would cost £500 if bought from a mail order catalogue with repayments spread over 50 weeks. If it were bought through a rental purchase outlet, such as *Crazy George's*, it would cost around £600, with a risk of it being repossessed if repayments were missed at any time during the agreement.[6] A 50-week loan from one of the weekly-collected credit companies, such as *Provident* or *Greenwoods*, would be the most expensive option, costing £700. Compared with these types of borrowing, the advantages of BLs for people living on low incomes are clear: they are interest-free and, because repayments are deducted from source, there are no penalties for late payment.

What do People use Budgeting Loans for?

Broadly speaking, there seem to be four main reasons why people on IS and income-based Jobseeker's Allowance need to borrow money:

- to buy essentials such as household appliances, furniture or clothing;
- to pay bills;
- to meet the costs of discretionary items, such as holidays, Christmas or family events; and
- to make ends meet.

In keeping with the aims of the scheme, the research indicates BLs were mainly used for the first two of these reasons. Alternatively, people bought items from mail order catalogues or borrowed money from weekly-collected credit companies to meet these needs, both of which were high cost.

Applicants generally felt that it was inappropriate to apply for a BL for discretionary items, and on the whole were not in favour of borrowing for this purpose at all. Most spent very little on holidays or days out, Christmas presents or family events, and these were usually the first candidates for economies if there was a drop in income (Kempson, 1996; Whyley *et al*, 2000).

Nor were BLs used to make ends meet. This need was met by borrowing from friends and family wherever possible or else by pawning valuables. As a very last resort, people would consider borrowing from an unlicensed 'loan shark'.

Reform of the Budgeting Loan Scheme

Until the Social Security Act 1998, there had been little substantive reform to the discretionary social fund since it was set up in 1988. The provisions of the Act were designed to simplify BL applications, decision-making and review processes, and make it less expensive to administer.

Prior to the reforms, applications for all three elements of the discretionary social fund (BLs, Crisis Loans and Community Care Grants) were decided by staff who exercised discretion within a framework of set parameters. In order to make sure that local budgets for the social fund were not exceeded, applications were prioritised. In the case of BLs, priority was determined by the types of items that had been applied for, and an assessment of why and how badly these items were needed (Department of Social Security, 1999).

The need for reform was driven by a number of criticisms. First, the complex nature of the decision-making process was confusing for applicants and staff alike. Moreover, the exercise of discretion was considered unnecessary in deciding people's need for the types of commonplace items covered by BLs. Second, because the same application form was used for all three elements of the discretionary social fund, it was lengthy and asked for information that was not necessarily relevant to the reason for the application. Third, questioning applicants about the extent of their need was felt to be unnecessarily intrusive. Fourth, its focus on particular items had been shown to promote dishonesty, because it encouraged applicants to apply for items that were known to be afforded a high priority, rather than applying for the items they actually needed (Huby and Dix, 1992). Finally, the scheme was costly to administer.

In an attempt to tackle these problems, a number of key changes were made to the scheme. Firstly, the application procedure was simplified. A separate and shorter application form for each type of payment replaced the combined application form for all types of social fund payment. In addition, the BL application form listed the categories of allowable expenses,[7] so that the applicant no longer had to undergo intrusive questioning to demonstrate the need for specific items.

Secondly, in order to make the decision-making process more transparent, social fund officers no longer exercised discretion in awarding loans. Instead, the priority afforded a claim was based on weightings linked to the applicant's personal circumstances, including family size and length of time on benefit. The size of the award was then calculated according to these weightings.[8] Moreover, to enable the BL scheme to provide assistance to as many people as possible, individual maximum possible amounts of BL debt were set, determined by the circumstances of the applicant. Consequently, outstanding BL debt acted as a rationing mechanism, so that the amounts awarded in subsequent applications might be reduced.

Overall, the changes were designed to make it easier for potential applicants to understand the circumstances in which they could apply and to make some self-assessment of the likelihood of being successful. Consequently, BLs were no longer linked to a specific need for credit and decisions were now supposed to be made according to fact-based criteria rather than on a discretionary basis. The changes were also intended to remove any incentive for applicants to make dishonest applications in order to 'work the system'. The revised scheme was implemented on 5th April 1999.

Applicants' Views and Experiences of the Revised Budgeting Loan Scheme

Even among successful applicants to the revised BL scheme, awareness of the reforms was low (Whyley *et al*, 2000). For the most part, people did not realise the scheme had been changed until they were in the process of applying for a BL. Even then, they were only aware of changes such as the shorter form and broader categories, rather than changes to the rules governing the scheme. The most likely explanation for this is that most people found out about the scheme by word of mouth rather than from official sources, and so would not have realised that it had changed. Even so, it is worth noting that the changes were not widely publicised by the Benefits Agency.

Views and experiences of the application process

For the most part, applicants to the revised BL scheme found the application process relatively straightforward (Whyley *et al*, 2000). Positive views about the changes to the application process since April 1999 were centred on the simplified application form and the faster processing of applications. And, although people tended to request the same items as before, there was some indication that they were gradually starting to apply for items under the new broader categories that had previously been afforded a low priority.

Several people who had made applications before April 1999 had found the previous, lengthier application form off-putting. A lone parent with four children had found the form so daunting that she did not proceed with her application, and instead bought the goods she needed from a rental purchase shop.[9] In comparison, the new BL form was generally considered clearer and simpler to complete.

> ... it seemed far less, far less questions they're asking you. Much simpler and easier. You had to go through before writing down all the figures, what were the amounts of the things that you needed. I think that's been cut out, you just put in what you want and a grand total of what it will cost. You don't have to price every item. (50 year old single man)

Indeed, some people thought that the new form would encourage more people to apply to the scheme. Official sources note that, since the introduction of the revised BL scheme, applications have increased and more of them have been successful (Department for Work and Pensions, 2001). It is difficult to ascertain how far these trends can be attributed to the simplification of the application form and application process, but it is likely that the changes played at least some part.

In addition, several people mentioned that, under the revised scheme, applications seemed to be processed considerably faster. Most received a response to their application within seven to fourteen days.

Earlier research indicates that, under the previous system, the items applied for largely reflected those given high priority in the guidance notes used by social fund officers, that is, bedding, essential furnishings and household equipment (Huby and Dix, 1992; Kempson *et al*, 1994). In this respect, little seemed to have changed. Among successful BL applicants, the most common items applied for (as in the past) were furniture, beds and bedding, and white goods.

It was noticeable, however, that several people applying after April 1999 had requested loans for decorating, clothing, and household goods such as crockery and cutlery under the new, broader categories. So it does seem that people are starting to apply for items that previously were considered low priority, rather than applying for items of known high priority in order to increase the chances of receiving an award. Nonetheless, the fact that applicants only realised they could apply for a wider range of items once they had started the application process suggests that better communication of the changes is still required among eligible benefit recipients to enable them to make more effective use of the scheme.

For some older people, however, even a simplified application process proved to be problematic (Kempson *et al*, 2002).[10]   In particular, poor physical health, mental health problems and language difficulties made it almost impossible for half of the older applicants who were interviewed to complete a form of any kind. Family or friends helped some, while social workers or other formal carers assisted others.

Most of these people suffered from physical ailments that meant they needed help to apply to the social fund. Some had multiple health problems that left them too ill to complete a form, while others had difficulty communicating either in writing or orally because they had suffered a stroke. A minority had been unable to apply personally as a result of poor mental health, including severe long-term mental illness; senility; and memory loss.   Lastly, one or two people needed help because their command of English was poor.

These communication problems point to a need for information about the social fund to be promoted using non-print media. But it also highlights a need for the Benefits Agency to ensure that people who have literacy problems or suffer from mental confusion can get personal help with form-filling. Such changes would improve awareness and take-up of the social fund among pensioners and non-pensioners alike.

Views and experiences of the decision-making process

In order to make decision-making more transparent, under the revised BL scheme, the outcomes of applications are decided using fact-based criteria; the amount of BL debt outstanding is also taken into account.   Early evaluation of the revised scheme, however, indicates that many applicants remain confused about the rules governing the scheme, and are especially unsure about how loan awards are decided (Whyley *et al*, 2000).

Most of the successful applicants who were interviewed for the study were awarded less than they had applied for - typically around half the amount. In addition, a small number of applicants had had very recent applications to the BL scheme rejected outright.[11] Hardly anyone questioned these decisions. Instead, they either bought fewer or cheaper items than they had intended; borrowed elsewhere, often from high cost commercial companies; or went without.

At the root of this unquestioning acceptance was an almost complete lack of understanding about how decisions were reached. A small number of people, for example, had simply applied for more money than they actually needed, in expectation of receiving less. This practice was often based on their own experiences or what they had been told by other people.

> [W]hen you apply you never expect to get the amount you apply for, you expect to get less. Some people say, 'Well, if you want £500 apply for £1,000, if you want £1,000 apply for £2,000', because you're never going to get that, like they'll cut it 50 per cent. (50 year old single man)

> I did have enough for the washing machine and the bed. But I put a bit extra on, just in case, because sometimes they do knock you down. So I thought, well, if I put £150 for the bed, they might knock me down a little bit, but I'll still have enough to buy the bed. (24 year old lone mother)

In addition, several applicants already had a loan or arrears from a previous BL, and only realised the impact this had on their application when they were offered less than they had applied for or had their application rejected. Put another way, they had no idea what their maximum possible debt or 'credit limit' was when they were applying for a further loan, nor was this clarified when they received written notification of the outcome of their application. The problem seemed to arise, in part at least, because the BL scheme operates quite differently from the other sources of borrowing that applicants would be familiar with. 'Top up' loans from a weekly-collected credit company, for example, are discussed in advance of the customer's application. Moreover, most customers know their credit limit and how much is still available to them because it is a much simpler calculation than the one used for BLs.

As well as a lack of understanding about how existing BL debt impacted on subsequent applications, there was also some evidence that applicants were not familiar with the new fact-based decision-making process. One woman, for example, believed that the chances of her being awarded a BL in the future could be jeopardised by the fact that she was currently appealing against a Benefits Agency decision to withdraw her Incapacity Benefit.

Better information about the workings of the BL scheme would undoubtedly help eligible benefit recipients make fully informed decisions about applying to the scheme. In particular, letting all applicants know in advance how much they are eligible to receive in BLs and when they can apply for further loans would enable them to plan ahead. Administrative costs might also be reduced if fewer people deliberately increased the amounts they applied for in the expectation of receiving less.

Overview of the revised Budgeting Loan scheme

On balance, the impact of the revised BL scheme from the viewpoint of successful applicants has been mixed. While they generally appreciated the simplified application forms and the speed with which decisions were reached, they were still confused about the rules governing the scheme, particularly in relation to the impact of outstanding debt on further applications. As a result, people continued to apply for BLs when they had reached their maximum 'credit limit', and were none the wiser when they were awarded less than they applied for or had their applications rejected. Further work is clearly needed to make the process more transparent to applicants. Not only would this help increase the effectiveness and efficiency of the scheme, by reducing the number of ineligible applications, it might also help to reduce the sense of frustration and injustice felt by applicants who receive a reduced award or have their application rejected.

Further Reform?

So far, this chapter has focused on evaluating the changes to the BL scheme instituted by the Social Security Act 1998 from the viewpoint of users of the scheme. Our research has, however, highlighted two further areas where reform could potentially have a considerable impact on benefit recipients' use of the social fund. The first, related specifically to the BL scheme, is the level at which loans have to be repaid. The second, more general issue concerns the lack of awareness of the social fund among eligible benefit recipients, and particularly pensioners. Furthermore, on the basis of this research, there seems to be a strong case against extending the BL scheme to other low-income groups, and this is the final point to be considered.

Repayment levels

The level at which BLs have to be repaid, and the problems this can create for applicants, have been the main criticisms of the BL scheme, among applicants and commentators alike (Kempson *et al*, 1994; NACAB, 2000; Whyley *et al*, 2000; Kempson *et al*, 2002).

Published guidance on the social fund indicates that there are three rates of BL repayment that normally apply: fifteen per cent, ten per cent and five per cent of applicable benefit payments. Repayments are normally fifteen per cent of the applicable benefit amount (excluding housing costs) where the applicant has no other credit commitments or arrears to be repaid. If the applicant has other direct deductions made from their benefit, for example for rent or fuel arrears, the repayment rate may be lowered to ten per cent. If these direct deductions are high, the rate of repayment could be reduced to five per cent.

Although high repayment levels were a cause for complaint among applicants (Whyley *et al*, 2000; Kempson *et al*, 2002), most were still able to make ends meet on the reduced amount of benefit they received. Some, though, clearly struggled, and this was often because of a change in their circumstances or a high expense like a household bill. In one case, for example, a lone mother, who was repaying £12 a week on a loan of £800, could usually manage on the reduced amount of benefit she received, except when she was faced with a large household bill. When that occurred, she borrowed money from her family to tide her over.

> It's been okay apart from when I've had a big bill to pay like my TV Licence. But then I've just borrowed the money to do that and I'm paying it back. I borrowed that off my mum, so that's not a problem. (35 year old lone mother)

In addition, high levels of repayment would deter a number of older applicants from re-applying to the scheme in the future. Couples were particularly worried about leaving their partner with an unmanageable commitment (Kempson *et al*, 2002).

Several people did not understand why the repayments on smaller BLs were higher, and felt that this was unreasonable, particularly when commercial credit companies offered smaller repayment amounts over a longer period of time on loans of a similar size. One man was surprised at having to repay £16 per week on a loan of £500, because on a previous occasion he had been repaying £16 a week on a loan of £1,000.

> I was taken aback by the £16. I think the last time I got a bit more, I got nearly £1,000 and I was paying about £16 per week and this time it was £500 and £16... which I think is really heavy, you know. I think, to my way of thinking, £16 a week for £500 that's too high, that's my main complaint. You have to pay back too much, too soon, they should spread it out a bit more. (50 year old single man)

Others also questioned why repayments could not be spread over a longer period, to make it easier for them to manage, particularly as repayments were deducted directly from their benefits.

> [W]hat I'm saying is this, Why should they take £20.06 off you? I mean they know they've got the money because they give you it in the first place.
> (80 year old widowed man)

Despite these criticisms, most people simply accepted that the repayment level was fixed, and did not apply to have the amount reduced. This mirrors other research which has suggested that review and subsequent re-negotiation of repayment levels are a rare occurrence (NACAB, 2000).

In order to better meet the needs of benefit recipients, then, BLs would ideally be repaid in smaller weekly amounts over a longer period of time.[12] However, given that repayment levels are set to ensure that loans are repaid as quickly as possible so that the money is available to other applicants, this may be difficult to achieve without a significant increase in the social fund budget. It would also mean that applicants would have to wait longer before they could apply for further loans, which might be a drawback for some people. An alternative might be to make the repayment system more flexible so that, in times of particular financial strain, applicants could miss a repayment. This method of working has proved very effective for weekly-collected credit companies that often set repayments at similar levels to BLs.

Levels of awareness

People's use of the discretionary social fund is, without doubt, hampered by low levels of awareness, both of the fund itself and how it works. Among applicants, word of mouth was by far the most common way of finding out about the social fund. Consequently, if eligible benefit recipients do not come into contact with people who know about the social fund, such as friends, relatives or care workers, their chances of finding out about it are significantly reduced. As we have seen, even among applicants, knowledge and understanding of how the fund operates was patchy at best.

Although not the only barrier to take-up, lack of awareness is certainly one of the main reasons why older people make so little use of the discretionary social fund. Nearly all the non-applicants who were interviewed as part of a recent study (Kempson *et al*, 2002), said that they had never heard of the social fund. Moreover, fewer than half of applicants knew enough to make an informed application; the rest had either only a vague awareness or said that they knew nothing at all about the scheme. Of most concern, though, was the fact that knowledge and use of the fund was in no way related to people's needs. Consequently, most eligible pensioners who had never applied to the social fund had needs every bit as pressing as those who had applied.

Among pensioners who were aware of the social fund, information had invariably been gleaned in a rather hit-and-miss way from a range of sources. Some had found out informally through family, friends or neighbours; others had been told about the social fund by more 'official' sources, such as social workers, advice workers and home helps. Rarely had people sought information about the social fund, nor had they been told about it as part of a systematic assessment of their needs.

More effective methods for disseminating information are clearly required to enable eligible benefit recipients, and particularly older people, to make fully informed decisions about using the social fund. Indeed, when asked for their ideas about how the social fund could be better publicised, older people mentioned several methods that could be used to raise awareness among potential applicants of all ages.

Firstly, everyone could be sent details of the social fund as soon as they began to receive qualifying benefits and periodically thereafter. Secondly, Benefits Agency staff could be more proactive in providing information about the social fund. Certainly, there was little evidence of any discussion taking place between staff and benefit recipients around issues such as eligibility to apply to the fund. Older people also thought television adverts would be a good way of raising awareness about the types of help available from the social fund, perhaps linked to a pre-recorded message on a freephone number. Finally, they called for closer links between the Department for Work and Pensions, the Benefits Agency and other statutory and voluntary caring agencies, to widen the number of sources from which information about the social fund could be received.

Extending the budgeting loan scheme

It has been argued that BLs should be extended to other groups, such as people in low-paid work (HM Treasury, 1999). Apart from the many practical problems that are associated with this, it raises important questions about the most effective use of limited resources. On one level, it would be desirable for interest-free loans to be made more widely available. Yet unless this was accompanied by a significant increase in the social fund budget, the net result would be a reduction in help for some of the most vulnerable people in society.

Further, while people in low-paid employment may have *limited* access to mainstream sources of credit, they are nonetheless likely to be able to borrow money for the types of essential items that BLs are used for, for example by using hire purchase or store cards. Our research indicates, however, that recipients of IS or income-based Jobseeker's Allowance have very little, if any, access to mainstream credit and instead must use high-cost, alternative providers if they need to borrow money (Whyley *et al*, 2000). The extent of unmet needs for credit that remains among this group therefore provides a compelling argument for concentrating resources among them.

Summary

The undeniable strength of the BL scheme is that it provides a source of interest-free borrowing for benefit recipients who have few affordable options when faced with lump-sum needs such as buying large household items or repaying debts.

Reforms brought about by the Social Security Act 1998 have made the scheme simpler and easier for applicants to use. But there is still room for improvement. Most importantly, applicants need to be better informed about the rules governing the scheme, so that they can make more effective use of BLs. In particular, the fact that the scheme is no longer limited to needs for specific items should be communicated to eligible benefit recipients. Applicants also need to be able to assess their own 'credit limit', so they know how much and when to apply for a BL. Ideally, applicants would prefer reduced levels of repayment spread over longer periods of time. Failing this, more flexible payment arrangements would make it easier for applicants to make ends meet in times of particular financial strain. Finally, raising awareness of the discretionary social fund in general would overcome one of the fundamental barriers to applying for financial assistance, particularly among older benefit recipients.

Compared with these changes, the case for extending the BL scheme to other low-income groups is much less compelling. The extent of unmet needs for borrowing that remains among recipients of IS and Jobseeker's Allowance provides a strong argument for focusing resources upon them.

Notes

1 The study included in-depth interviews with 20 people who had current BLs that had been taken out between April 1999 (when the rule changes came into force) and October 1999.

2 The study comprised in-depth interviews with 37 people who were aged 60 or over and in receipt of Income Support/Minimum Income Guarantee. Of these 37, 19 had applied successfully to the social fund since October 2000 (ten for BLs and nine for Community Care Grants); and 18 had never applied to the discretionary social fund. Both these studies were commissioned and funded by the (now) Department for Work and Pensions.

3 Minimum Income Guarantee for people over state pension age.

4 A number of community reinvestment trusts have been developed around the UK, including Portsmouth Area Regeneration Trust (PART) and Salford Moneyline. They are not-for-profit mutual organisations designed to offer loans to those excluded from mainstream financial institutions, and in particular to people living on low incomes. Consequently, eligibility for loans is assessed according to the applicant's financial circumstances and ability to pay.

5 The 'alternative' credit market comprises companies that target people on low incomes, including door-to-door money lenders, sometimes known as home- or weekly collected credit companies; rental purchase shops such as *Crazy George's*; sell and buy back outlets such as *Cash Convertors*; and pawnbrokers.

6 This is in contrast to hire purchase, where goods cannot be repossessed once a third of the cost has been paid.

7 BLs may be awarded to meet any of the following expenses: furniture and household equipment; clothing and footwear; rent in advance and/or removal expenses to secure fresh accommodation; improvement, maintenance and security of the home; travelling expenses; HP and other debts.

8 Although the criteria are applied nationally, the amount received depends on the budget within each particular district.

9 Rental purchase shops (such as *Crazy George's*) offer retail credit for 'white goods', with an optional service charge which entitles the customer to return the goods if they cannot afford the repayments and then reclaim them when they can afford to start repaying. Concerns have been raised in relation to the costs and terms of these optional charges.

10 This research refers to older people's experience of the discretionary social fund in general, rather than the BL scheme in particular.

11 Although the focus of the research was on the experiences of successful applicants, three people had had very recent loan applications turned down.

12 The maximum period for the repayment of BLs is currently 78 weeks.

Chapter 10

Achieving Policy Goals

Beth Lakhani

The Government's Agenda and the Commitment to Abolish Child Poverty

There has been copious research evidence available for many years to demonstrate that children's life chances are directly affected by their living circumstances during childhood. In general terms, 'children from poor homes have lower life expectancy and are more likely to die in infancy or childhood; they have a greater likelihood of poor health, a lower chance of high educational attainment, a greater risk of unemployment.' (Holterman, 1995). It was therefore, of some concern to the poverty lobby that the New Labour government began its period in office in 1997 by implementing conservative legislation relating to social security inherited from the previous Conservative administration. It also committed itself to the previous government's public spending plans and reduced benefits for lone parents, 'arguably the first time since 1948 a government had cut a social assistance benefit' (Fimister, 2001, p.13).

However, other indications of policy direction were more positive. The government soon declared its intention to 'make work pay' for those who can work and to provide security for those who cannot. In March 1999 the Prime Minister, Tony Blair, gave the following commitment:

> Our historic aim will be for ours to be the first generation to end child poverty, and it will take a generation. It is a 20-year mission but I believe it can be done. (Blair, 1999)

The first pledge resulted in the introduction of the minimum wage and an improved top up to low earnings for low paid families through the Working Families Tax Credit (WFTC). A new scheme to encourage people into work, the 'New Deal', was targeted not just at the unemployed but also at lone parents and disabled people. A hesitant start was made to improve access to childcare facilities.[1] Other small changes to benefits have eased the transition into work. However, other changes have worked in the opposite direction: the loss of some passported benefits and automatic maximum housing benefit can be a disincentive to work. The government insists that for most the route out of poverty lies through work.

The second pledge, to tackle child poverty, has resulted in benefit increases for children less than 11 years at well over the rate of inflation, both for in-work and out-of-work benefits, and sizeable increases to child benefit. There is now one rate of allowance for all dependent children under the age of 16 years. However, because most increases of benefit over the rate of inflation have been targeted at younger children, those over 11 years are generally not proportionately better off. It has been calculated that by October 2000 couples with two children were nearly £30 better off in real terms than they were in 1997 and those on WFTC made a similar gain. (Department of Social Security, 2000, p.6). Lone parents, however, lost some of the gains as a result of the cuts to lone parent benefits. It has also been estimated that there has been a reduction in numbers living below the poverty threshold (defined as below 60 per cent of median income). The number of children in low income households fell by half a million. From 1996/7 to 2000/1 and the number of people as a whole in low income households fell by a million in the same period (New Policy Institute, 2002). The improved incomes are partly explained by the fact that more people went to work, which reflected the general downward trend in unemployment at the time the New Labour government took office and which has continued.

There have been a number of 'joined up' government initiatives to provide a more substantial programmatic infrastructure to tackle deprivation and exclusion. A new Social Exclusion Unit was established to investigate and remove some of the causes of exclusion and poverty. Particular programmes have included, for example, the Health Action Zones and healthy living projects. There has also been the 'Sure Start' programme that aimed to provide additional support for families in deprived areas through £540 million for targeted pre-school activities. There was more cash help targeted at maternity expenses and to encourage young people to stay on in education, via the Sure Start Maternity Grant, now worth £300, and new educational maintenance allowances in pilot areas, worth up to £40 per week.

The size of the problem

A battery of statistics demonstrates the large numbers of children that continue to live in poverty. Current figures and the government's target have to be seen in the context of a significant increase in poverty between

1968 and 1995. Nine per cent of children in two parent households were poor (below half mean income) in 1968 but this had risen to 24 per cent by 1995 (Gregg, Harkness and Machin, 1999). Children are more likely to live on means-tested benefits such as Income Support. "Seventeen per cent of households with children receive half or more of their income from means tested benefits compared with only seven per cent of households without children." (Department of Social Security, 2000, p.46). In 1998, there were over 800,000 children who had spent at least five years on means tested benefits (HM Treasury, 1999a).

There are concerns too about the *depth* of poverty. It has been estimated that this is severe in non working households: 2½ million people (including ¾ million children) were more than £50 a week short of the poverty threshold and four in every ten were more than a £100 short (Kenway and Palmer, 2002). The depth of poverty is also a problem in working households, particularly where adults are working part time or are self-employed. It is arguable that in those families where the depth of poverty is most severe a new system of grants would be most beneficial.

In short, the figures show that the government has a considerable task ahead of it to eradicate child poverty and would be well advised to be flexible in the approaches it takes. Paying out grants in specified circumstances is a necessary complement to increasing the basic weekly allowances. Even if the government achieves its ten-year target of halving child poverty, the level of poverty in 2009 will still be higher than in 1979 (Howard, Garnham, Fimister and Veit-Wilson, 2001, p.64).

Family and Child Poverty: the Evidence

The dry statistics do not demonstrate the picture as graphically as particular stories or evidence of particular kinds of deprivation. People on lower incomes will try to cut back their spending on even essential items, whilst those on the lowest incomes will not only get into a range of debt problems but may also go without food or fuel.

Food poverty

Low income is one of the main causes of food poverty. The Family Expenditure Survey shows that households in the lowest ten per cent income group spend the highest proportion of their income on food; 21 per cent of their income goes on food as against 14 per cent by those in the highest 10 per cent (Department of Social Security, 2001). However they spend much less in absolute terms. The type of food bought also varies. Households with incomes above £940 spend £4.40 a week on fruit alone, households with incomes under £96 spent £0.20 a week (Dowler, Turner and Dobson, 2001, p.18). A Leicester study showed that a poor family could afford to spend overall on food a total of £30-£35 and this amounted to £1.16 a person per day – less than the cost of a school meal (Dobson, Kellard and Talbot, 2000). A recent national survey (Gordon *et al*, 2000) revealed that 'almost 2 per cent of children did not get three meals a day because there was not enough money and almost 5 per cent of parents could not afford to provide fruit at least once a day'.

There is abundant evidence that pregnant women on low incomes are unable to afford an adequate diet. In some cases they were missing meals either because they could not afford to feed themselves or there were children in the family already. Iron intakes were unhealthily low (Dallison and Labstein, 1995). Food patterns are generally different for poor families. Poorer children are much less likely to eat higher fibre foods, including fruit and vegetables, and this has consequences for dental infection and generally slows the recovery from infections (Nelson, 2000). Low-income families have strategies for saving money on food, In particular, mothers will often go without in order to save for the children or buy a limited amount of food at a time in order that there is sufficient to last a week. When money and supplies are short they make do:

> One week I had only milk and flour so I made milk buns; they really filled us up. I normally buy four packets of bread, [but if I'm running out of money for food] we just buy two. So those who have 6 slices I tell them to take 4, those taking 4 I tell them to take 3 and I don't eat. (Dowler, Turner and Dobson, 2001)

Food is also one of the more potentially flexible items in the budget and over which adults may have some control. It is common practice for families to cut back on the food budget in order to meet bills or other emergency needs.

Survey of poverty findings

The recent national survey of poverty and social exclusion in Britain (Gordon et al, 2000) examined poverty by investigating 'whether people lack items that the majority of the population perceive to be necessities, and whether they have incomes too low to afford them…'. Goods and services identified by more than 50 per cent of a representative sample of people as items that no one should be without were regarded as necessities for the purposes of the research. A person would be counted as poor or deprived if that person were unable to afford at least two such necessities. The survey found that:

- 27.7 per cent of individuals lacked at least two necessities.
- Over 10 per cent of adults lacked 'regular savings (of £10 per month)', 'money to keep the home in a decent state of decoration', an amount 'to replace or repair broken electrical goods and replace worn out furniture'.
- Children were considered poor if they lacked one necessity. 34 per cent were poor according to this definition. 18 per cent lacked two necessary items.
- Children were more likely to be deprived of two or more items if they were living in a larger family, local authority property, rented accommodation or were in families on income support/income based JSA.
- Of children lacking two items, 9 per cent did not have fresh fruit and vegetables daily, 12 per cent and 11 per cent did not have new fitted shoes or a warm waterproof coat. (Gordon et al, 2000)

Poverty also generates a number of significant consequences for education and health. It is arguable, for example, that low income, as measured by school meal eligibility, may account for 66 per cent of the difference in GCSE attainment (West A. et al, 1999). A clear link between poverty and ill-health has been acknowledged for many years: '[i]n nearly every case the highest incidence of illness is experiences by the worst off social classes.' (Whitehead, 1988). Another study noted that about two thirds of the families interviewed reported sickness or disability; for example asthma, bronchitis and eczema. Ill health was linked to the stress of poverty and the inability to meet the extra expenses caused by illness. In addition there were problems heating homes (Cohen et al, 1992).

Measuring Poverty

This section examines the measurement of poverty and the role of minimum income and family budget standards as means to assess a reasonable income on which to live. Such standards will determine the level at which government targets will be set to raise weekly benefit income. They also demonstrate the necessity for a system of grants for low-income families, at least in the short term, as the programme to lift children out of poverty progresses.

There are a variety of methods of measuring poverty (see the four options currently under consultation in Department of Work and Pensions, 2002). Academics often use a 'below half average earnings' measure particularly for comparative purposes. Benefit rates, set annually by Parliament, are theoretically the agreed level of income which people need.

However, weekly benefit rates have never been based on an up to date measurement of the cost of living. They are derived (updated and significantly modified in structure) from the 1948 allowances introduced by the post war Labour government. Since the 1930s there has also been a system of grants to complement the weekly allowances. It was assumed that the weekly allowances were insufficient over a period of time to allow claimants to budget to replace clothing and other more costly items. From 1988 most people have had to rely on loans with the repayment requirements effectively reducing the value of future benefit. Consequently, many people have less than the standard benefit rates coming in each week: money is deducted from benefit to pay arrears, social fund repayments, sanctions/penalties of one kind or another are applied. In addition, as help with mortgages and rent is restricted many claimants may have to pay some of these housing costs from their benefit, thus further reducing any linkage between benefit amounts and the measurement of poverty.

One standard measure is to define the poverty line at 50 per cent of the mean disposable income, (often used internationally), or 60 per cent of the median income (used by the government). The figure may be before or after housing costs. This measure of 'household below average incomes' (HBAI) is derived from looking at the *spread of income*; it does not measure what would be an *adequate level of income* for living. The figures are derived from the Family Resources Survey, an annual government survey, which arguably underestimates the numbers on lowest incomes because people in bed and breakfast and homeless people are not included. The resulting percentages of the HBAI are therefore likely to be an underestimate (Howard, M., Garnham, A., Fimister G. and Veit-Wilson J. 2001, p.32). As standards of living rise so the HBAI figure rises. If the HBAI figure is used as a measure of poverty the target for lifting people out of poverty rises. This is fair, as the poverty threshold should rise in line with standards across society.

Another approach is to measure poverty by reference to a minimum income standard or budget standard that will enable a family to live adequately and not be forced to do without certain necessities. This approach can be used as a benchmark by which benefit levels can be judged, and/or as a target at which benefits should be paid in the future, or to justify increases in financial support now. A person or family who has an income which forces them to live below this standard may be said to live in poverty. However, this approach begs further questions, for example, about what is meant by 'adequate' in this context. For what and for how long must the budget standard be 'adequate' and who should have the power to determine what is adequate (see Veit-Wilson, J., 1998). Some of the methods used to measure adequacy or set minimum incomes have attempted to deal with these questions. A budget standard approach can vary to reflect changing standards. Experience has already shown that there are different and complementary methods for establishing budget standards and more than one standard may be set at the same time. The Family Budget Unit at the University of York originally worked out a 'modest but adequate' standard and a 'low cost' standard, in relation to a child: the latter being almost half of the former standard (Oldfield, N. and Yu, A.C.S., 1993). In 1998 it produced a 'low cost but acceptable' budget standard for families with children. The Unit's report (Parker, H., 1998) identified standard costs including food, clothing, household goods and services and also core variable costs, including housing, fuel, transport, job related costs, debts, maintenance and lifestyle variables including leisure costs. It priced essential furniture and household appliances. A weekly figure for an item was its total value divided by its expected life and then divided by 52. A gas cooker (then priced at £312) translated into a weekly figure of 50p.

The Child Poverty Action Group (CPAG) has described this budget as 'cautious'. The gap between the budget and income support allowances has narrowed with above-inflation increases for younger children. Even so, it is clear that a person living on this kind of income would not be able to save or repay a loan at a commercial rate or the rate set by the social fund budgeting loan scheme. The national study on poverty and exclusion produced a comprehensive list of indicators for establishing a poverty standard and, as explained above, counted a person in poverty if that person could not afford two or more items identified as necessities (Gordon, D., 2000). Other methods of assessing poverty were also used including those at risk of poverty. It must also be remembered that what are accepted as 'necessities' may also be a reflection of fashion and habit and the consensual approach could therefore tend to be somewhat conservative.

The Social Fund: The Forgotten Element Of Social Security

The House of Common Select Committee on Social Security (2001) noted that the discretionary social fund had become the forgotten element of social security and that '[l]ess is spent on the social fund today than five years ago with no evidence of diminution of need.' Despite frequent criticisms of the social fund, it is one area of social provision that the current government has left virtually unchanged since 1997. There have been some alterations to the budgeting loan scheme, but arguably these changes mean the resources are more widely dispersed at the expense of those in greatest need. It should therefore be questioned why a government that has initiated so many other welcome and innovative anti-poverty schemes has not turned its attention to the social fund? The Select Committee has tried to attract the government's attention to this issue:

> We urge the government to use the opportunity offered by the re-organisation of DSS (DWP) to take a radical look at the social fund, so that it may work to enhance the strategy to reduce child poverty rather than work against it. (House of Commons Select Committee on Social Security, 2001)

The Select Committee also questioned whether the Fund was achieving its original objectives and recommended that 'the scheme in its current format needs urgent overhaul and an injection of funds.' The government's response to these conclusions was dismissive. It simply disagreed that the social fund worked against its objectives to end child poverty but without demonstrating why and said it would keep under review 'in the light of its overall priorities' the 'best way …of supporting vulnerable people with the cost of intermittent expenses' (Department for Work and Pensions, 2001, p.13). The Select Committee had recommended that the government establish 'a specific budget to fund research into the levels of income needed to avoid poverty'. However, the government asserted in its response that there was 'no simple answer to this question' and that 'different research methods tend to make different assumptions and generate a range of estimates' (Department for Work and Pensions, 2001, p.12). Whether these range of estimates could be a helpful guide to policy making was simply ignored and the government fell back on their old rhetoric that they were helping people into work and providing extra help for those who were not going into work. It did not to say what the additional help was.

On the question of interest free loans and expanding credit to a wider group it commented:

> The Government does recognise that there are some people who are currently excluded from normal credit markets who do not qualify for help from the social fund as they are not entitled to Income Support or income-based Jobseeker's Allowance. At the same time it is important to concentrate limited resources where they are most needed. (Department for Work and Pensions, 2001, para. 50)

It should be remembered however, that it is the government that have decided that only 'limited resources' are available to those living in poverty and who need to use the social fund.

In the adjournment debate on the government's response to the committee's recommendations on the Social Fund (House of Commons, 2002) Archy Kirkwood, M.P., the Chair of the Select Committee, argued that the operation of the fund was inefficient, expensive, unfair and conflicted with other government objectives, such as initiatives to tackle homelessness, supporting vulnerable people and helping victims of domestic violence. He stated that in 1999/2000 it cost £250 million to administer, a figure that was twice the budget for grants and six times the real cost of the amount paid out in loans in that year. This was reason enough for change. He emphasized the need for the government to target more help on those who have no chance of working and 'who experience long periods on benefit'.   Karen Buck M.P. pointed out that 50 per cent of low income families had no household insurance, yet were three times more likely to experience domestic burglary than families with insurance, and more low income families, particularly those in private rented accommodation, are more likely to be the victims of domestic fires. The needs that thus arise may not be met by the social fund and only by a loan thereby reducing future income.

Principles For Reform

Any reform of the social fund may result in the development of new rules and perhaps different departments of government taking responsibility for different types of payments. It is important however, to consider what principles ought to be present in arriving at any model of reform to the social fund. At present, social security is a national scheme, yet the discretionary social fund scheme does contain an element of variation by postcode, as there are differences in the way local budgets are arranged.

Furthermore, the legal structure of the social fund is underpinned by concepts of *eligibility* and *qualification* for payment, rather than a clear set of conditions of *entitlement* (see Buck, 2000, pp.75-78). CPAG and other commentators have supported a rights-based system as less stigmatising. Discrimination is possible but less likely and is easier to monitor and guard against than in a system that is heavily dependent on the exercise of discretion.[2] The government has always argued that parents have responsibilities. It is therefore reasonable that they should have the means necessary to exercise those responsibilities effectively. In a system based on clear rules needs can be openly recognised and provided for. Parents would be able to better plan household and family expenditure if there was a clearer set of rules determining entitlement to social fund payments.

Some of the research evidence on the operation of the fund has shown that claimants had no way of knowing that they would get a payment and this built in a deterrent to take-up. Furthermore, loans and grants were not going to the most needy (Huby and Dix, 1992). Recently, the Social Fund Commissioner has expressed concern that only 13 in every 100 people eligible to use the social fund apply (Social Fund Commissioners Annual Report, 2001/02, p.14). Clearer rules of entitlement would enhance take-up rates: they are also a necessary condition for fighting child poverty.

The government has stated in its response to the Select Committee that it is committed to ensuring that the Social Fund fulfils the aim of helping the poorest and most vulnerable (Department for Work and Pensions, 2001, para.6). However, it is unclear how this commitment can be achieved with a cash limit. The only part of the social security system which is currently cash limited (apart from discretionary housing benefit) is the social fund. The budget and the cash limit are a means to exclude and limit expenditure. Inevitably some claimants who have severe needs are excluded. The process of decision making in a discretionary cash limited scheme lacks transparency. The cash limit creates inconsistencies in decision-making during the course of a year within one office and between offices at the same time because of different levels of demand on the budget.

The detailed operation of the social fund depends on guidance and on directions issued by the Secretary of State that do not go before Parliament in contrast to clear conditions of entitlement incorporated into acts and regulations which must be agreed by Parliament. The use of discretion and the budget are tools to ration access and are used by local officers. This structure allows the government to abdicate its responsibility for the results of decisions. It can state that it is committed to helping the poorest and most vulnerable people in society having created a rationing process that is arbitrary and hidden from view and does not guarantee that certain needs are met. The government ought to be accountable for any new system of support through lump sum payments.

Any reform of the social fund must take account of the fact that large numbers of children do live in poverty or live in families where income is very low and parents go without to try to protect their children. A programme to combat child poverty requires both an increase in weekly incomes and access to a range of grants to meet those additional costs not covered by the weekly allowances. But poor families cannot afford loans. Repayment rates from social fund loans reduce benefit rates making people even poorer. The numbers of claimants who are subjected to deduction from their benefit amounts to 31 per cent for Income Support (IS) claimants and nearly 27 per cent for income-based Jobseekers Allowance (IBJSA) claimants. The most common form of benefit deduction in both the case of IS and IBJSA is a social fund recovery. The proportions of both IS and IBJSA deductions subject to social fund recovery have been steadily rising as shown in the Tables below.

Table 10.1   Deductions from Income Support Payments by Type: May 1998 to May 2002

Thousands/(Percentages)

Type of deduction	May 1998	May 1999	May 2000	May 2001	May 2002
All types	1,535	1,530	1,620	1,688	1,683
Social fund loan recovery	577	622	734	786	806
	(37.59%)	(40.65%)	(45.31%)	(46.56%)	(47.89%)

Source: Derived from *Income Support Quarterly Statistical Enquiry* (DWP), May 2002, Table 12.1.

Of the (806 thousand) social fund deductions in 2002 made to income support, 49 per cent were to those classed as lone parents, 36 per cent disabled, 8 per cent aged 60 or over and 8 per cent 'other'.[3]

Table 10.2   Deductions from Income-Based JSA Payments by Type: May 1998 to May 2002

Thousands/(Percentages)

Type of deduction	May 1998	May 1999	May 2000	May 2001	May 2002
All types	375	347	309	260	224
Social fund loan recovery	153	151	150	134	114
	(40.80%)	(43.52%)	(48.54%)	(51.54%)	(50.89%)

Source: Derived from *Jobseekers Allowance Quarterly Statistical Enquiry* (DWP), May 2002, Table 10.1.

The average weekly amount of deduction for social fund repayments from IS in May 2002 was £10.40 and from IBJSA £7.17.[4] The projected £9 a week increase for a family with two children on income support in the first year of the new tax credits scheme will still not remove the need for grants.

Social fund payments should increase income; they should be grants not loans.

In short, the guiding principles for reform should be to create a national scheme where payment is based upon entitlement without any cash limited budget. The government should be properly accountable to Parliament for the detailed rules of its operation and payments should be by way of grants not loans.

Any reform of the social fund ought also to reflect the need for income to be sufficient to meet the balance between everyday costs and lump sum expenditure.   Lump sum expenditure can be considered in three (overlapping) categories. Firstly, there are large expenses associated with the home, which may be predictable or unforeseen, such as replacing major household equipment.[5] Secondly, there are smaller expenses, which if benefits were considerably higher, could arguably be met from weekly benefit. These may be predictable or sudden and include in particular clothing and travel costs. Some of these costs may be bunched; for example when a child grows quickly or moves to a new school. In addition there are utility bills. Finally, there are 'event related' items of expenditure.

There is no compelling reason to retain the current structure for social fund payments. It is important in principle that the needs to be met by grants should first be identified followed by a discussion of the mechanism for delivery. A new system of financial support through grants could be spread through a number of departments or retained largely within a new scheme operated by the Department for Work and Pensions. The delivery of the grant may reflect the type of need or the fact that it is a financial payment. It may be most practical to make most of the proposed new payments the responsibility of the Inland Revenue and/or the Department for Work and Pensions as the departments concerned with financial support. But in some cases, where grants are closely associated with the delivery of other services, then that department may take responsibility.

The proposed reforms accept that it is not possible to go back to the pre-1988 single payments scheme and that the new grants must generally be administratively cheap and easy to operate. As far as possible any necessary evidence should be easily available to the department concerned. Some payments might only be accessible if a claim is made, some could be automatic provided conditions are satisfied.

The introduction of 'Jobcentre Plus' and the development of the role of the 'personal adviser' give new scope for efficient delivery of grants either directly or indirectly by Jobcentre Plus. The personal adviser has a wide-ranging role which links into welfare to work but also to benefit take-up. A potentially new enabling philosophy could allow a new grants system to work effectively without the administrative problems associated with single payments and the social fund.

Take-up is simplified if specified benefits can act as passports to the proposed grants. In general, IS, IBJSA and maximum child tax credit would be appropriate passporting benefits. Benefits for adults and children will be separated with the introduction of new tax credits. Child tax credits will be paid for the children on top of child benefit. For adults the applicable amounts for IS and IBJSA could be more than halved, comprising the adult personal allowances, the adult related premiums but not the family premium.[6] Many people who would now qualify for IS or IBJSA will not do so. Instead entitlement to maximum child tax credit should be an alternative route, paid up to an income of £13,230 p.a. for those out of work.

Proposals: A Model for Change[7]

The following proposals are based on the CPAG's ideas in its submission to the Select Committee (Child Poverty Action Group, 2001) and more detailed options developed in a discussion document (Howard, 2002). A series of grants, subject to clear conditions of entitlement with a right of appeal, are proposed. The new grants focus on the needs of children, health and safety in the home and the need to give families the means to purchase basic furniture and household equipment when setting up a home. They also include a grant relating to costs associated with returning to the labour market or entering work.

Grants are a means to target financial help so that low-income families are not forced to repay large loans from benefit, and not forced to cut back on food in order to pay for other necessities. They are, with one exception, interim measures to help those still living in poverty before the government achieves its objective of abolishing child poverty.

Child Development Grant

The purpose of this grant is to give families additional resources on top of their weekly allowance to pay towards lump sum expenses connected with children. There are additional costs associated with the different ages of childhood. Babies become toddlers with different needs. Parents need to replace a cot with a bed and different bed linen. There are costs associated with childcare and nursery attendance and new costs again when a child starts school or moves up to another school. There are additional costs, as children become teenagers, additional nutritional requirements as well as adult sized clothes which are not VAT free. Children wear out clothing, have sudden growth spurts, girls need sanitary products which are expensive. Attending new schools may require new clothing and different equipment. These are examples.

Some parents cannot afford to provide a warm waterproof coat and/ or new fitted shoes for their children. Additional heating costs in winter also put extra burdens on the family budget. Research has shown that adults may have to cut expenditure on food to pay fuel bills (Gordon et al, 2002). The child development grant could be paid periodically to reflect these additional costs. The regularity of payment and its timing are matters that need further discussion. It could be limited to years when major changes in the child's life are likely, for example at three, five, eleven, thirteen and sixteen years. Alternatively it may be easier to pay a smaller size grant annually in recognition that it is sometimes difficult to predict when these additional costs will arise. Whether or not paid annually it may be appropriate to time the payment to coincide with the beginning of the school year. Alternatively the payment could be made in the New Year to coincide with the time when heating costs are higher.

The payment could be via Jobcentre Plus or the Inland Revenue (if the latter it could be called a 'child development credit'). Age would trigger the payment subject to rules of entitlement. If the conditions to be satisfied are decided by Jobcentre Plus that agency could authorise the payment but it could be paid with the child tax credit.

Who qualifies IS and IBJSA should be automatic passporting benefits. In addition, maximum child tax credit (for those not in work) should be a passport. As this payment is essentially a top up to the child tax credit when paid at the maximum rate, it may be reasonable to apply a capital test. To ease processing a maximum of £3,000 could be considered. This is the current amount disregarded for awards of IS and IBJSA. Arguably, a family with capital over £3,000 could meet these additional costs from their savings. Tapering a payment, if capital was above £3,000, could be a matter for further consideration but would make the system more complicated to administer. A lower income limit for entitlement than £13,230 (the level up to which maximum child credit is paid) might be IS applicable amounts for adults plus the child tax credit payable but this would make the test more complicated. Where a person qualifies for maximum child tax credit during the course of a year then it is recommended the payment should be made.

Home Establishment Grant/Secure Homes Grant

This is the largest of the grants proposed here and is intended to allow families to buy all the basic essentials to furnish a home if rehoused. The main aim of this provision is to help those moved out of unsuitable accommodation, those fleeing domestic violence, or those who need new accommodation following a relationship breakdown or loss of home because of a disaster such as a fire[8] or flood. In 2001/02, local authorities accepted responsibility for housing 118,360 homeless households. 34 per cent lost their last home because friends or relations could no longer accommodate them, 22 per cent because of relationship breakdown and 2 per cent because of mortgage arrears.[9] Many of those accepted for rehousing will have insufficient savings, if any at all, to pay for basic furniture and electrical and gas appliances.

The circumstances in which the grant is payable and the income conditions could be listed in regulations as is the case for the Sure Start Maternity Grant. A claim for the payment could be processed by Jobcentre Plus.

Who qualifies   Income qualifications could be set by reference to entitlement to IS/IBJSA, or the total of IS/IBJSA applicable amounts for adults plus the child tax credit payable, or entitlement to maximum child tax credit (£13,230 annual income limit). Further consideration will be needed to the question as to whether capital over £3000 should disqualify the claimant or whether the amount paid should be tapered to reflect capital over £3000. It should also be considered whether a family in work but on low income ought to qualify. The exclusion of low-income workers may also act as a deterrent to working given the high level of expenses involved in this payment. The fact of rehousing rather than the items needed should be the test for the payment. Alternatively, the claimant would have to provide evidence that there was a need for new or additional furniture. The first option would be easier and cheaper to administer.

If the payment is not based on need for individual items, further examination is needed to discover whether the payment should be a fixed amount or related to size of family and/or take into account disability. These would all be matters easily established from existing social security and tax credit records. An alternative would be to cost the items needed, but this increases the administrative load and the cost of processing a claim.

The local authority providing the accommodation could provide the necessary evidence that a grant is required. If however the new accommodation were provided through the private sector more thought should be given to identifying an alternative means of authorising the payment. There should also be further consideration given to whether it would be appropriate to have a halfway house payment where a family were moved into temporary accommodation and then found a permanent home several months later.

Although this need can be met in part by a community care grant (CCG) there is no certainty that one will be paid because of the system of priorities and the budget. Moreover some claimants are awarded budgeting loans instead which merely creates a long-term debt and reduces future weekly income. This is the one grant that arguably should continue to be available to some families even after increases in benefits lift families out of poverty.

Health and Safety or Core Items Grant

This is designed to help families replace key items of furniture and household appliances. Payment would depend on proof of need for the items. The main purpose of the grant is to ensure that families can afford to replace a gas or electrical cooker that is faulty, that beds can be replaced plus any item of furniture considered vital to the child's health and safety. The items of furniture considered necessary should ideally include a fridge so that food and if necessary drugs could be stored safely. Much of the food available at supermarkets should be stored in fridges and few homes have pantries.

The justification for such a grant, lays in the high number of refusals of CCGs under the current scheme and the research that points to the difficulty claimants on benefit have budgeting to save for replacement of expensive items. Repair and replacement of electrical (or gas) appliances (cooker, heater etc) was considered as essential by 85 per cent of the public, and lacked by 12 per cent. Beds and bedding were thought to be essential by 95 per cent of the population and lacked by 12 per cent (Gordon et al, 2000). It was found that a cooker was one of the top five items requested by lone parents (Huby and Dix, 1992).

The level of the grant might be calculated in one of two ways. Firstly, by standard amounts payable for specific items; and secondly, by a round figure approximating to the cost of replacing three main items. There is a need to find a balance between the complexities of meeting actual need and using a more broad-based way of providing support to claimants. Core items might include: for example, heating equipment, fire, cooker, fridge, beds per child.

This is a grant for which evidence would be required to establish need. It is possible that a official other than from the Department for Work and Pensions or the Inland Revenue could provide the necessary evidence. Reform has to take into account the fact that representatives of some professions do not feel it is appropriate for them to police access to financial assistance on the grounds that it may damage relations between them and their clients.

Opportunity Grant

This new grant would bring together the variety of help currently offered to claimants returning to work and would be consistent with the government's welfare to work objectives referred to at the beginning of this Chapter. Currently, there is the £100 Job Grant, payments made under the Adviser Discretion Fund of New Deal, help with some child care costs before a person returns to work, plus the transitional allowances made to help the transition into work (e.g. the lone parents run on and back to work bonus). However an evaluation of New Deal for Lone Parents showed the payments were infrequently used and only a quarter were advised of funds to reimburse travel costs.

There is a need to rationalise these varied and complex payments. The new over-arching role of Jobcentre Plus makes such reform easier to envisage with payments made by personal advisers. Some payments meet one off costs and other payments are for ongoing expenses. Arguably there should be a differentiation between the two so that a person might claim an opportunity grant for the one off payments, and an opportunity allowance to cover the period of transition *into work*. Ideally, this allowance would be treated as IS for the purposes of means testing and passporting. The considerable increase in alignment payments[10] demonstrates the need for a more systematic method of support. The income conditions for qualifying for the opportunity grant could be similar to those for the Child Development Grant. For the ongoing allowance, the normal test for IS/IBJSA should apply.

Conclusion

The government has committed itself to ending child poverty by the year 2019, a long haul! What will society accept as a measure of living above the poverty threshold almost two decades hence? Whether or not this government achieves this objective over that time, families in poverty need additional help in the meanwhile. The proposals for a framework of grants discussed above would provide the additional financial support to families who are still living in poverty and will not escape it until some time between now and 2019.

Notes

1   However, families still have to find 30 per cent of childcare costs from their pay and this help is only available to some people in full time work. There is no guarantee that affordable childcare will be available to a lone parent wishing to work.
2   This would be consistent with the recommendations of the McPherson Report.
3   See *Income Support Quarterly Statistical Enquiry* (DWP), May 2002, Table 12.3.
4   *Ibid*, Table 12.2 and *Jobseekers Allowance Quarterly Statistical Enquiry* (DWP), May 2002, Table 10.2.
5   The fact that 10% of adults have been unable to save £10 a week on a regular basis is a demonstration of the difficulty budgeting for larger items of expenditure even if the need is predictable: see Gordon et al (2000).
6   Mortgage costs continue to be included in the applicable amount of IS and IBJSA.
7   These proposals deal only with the needs of families with children: pensioners, disabled people, the single unemployed and homeless people all need access to a system of grants to supplement weekly income.
8   In the adjournment debate on the social fund Karen Buck M.P. referred to the disproportionate number of domestic fires in multi occupied accommodation. See House of Commons (2002), col. 248WH.
9   Office of the Deputy Prime Minister, *Housing Statistics Postcard*, June 2002, at http://www.housing.odpm.gov.uk/information/keyfigures/#homeless.
10 Alignment payments currently use up 40% of the social fund budget despite the fact that 313,000 are turned down.

Chapter 11

Discretionary Assistance to the Poor: The Case of France

Anne Daguerre and Corinne Nativel

The Changing Face of Social Protection

The post 1945 welfare state was designed to protect individuals against 'old social risks', that is, sickness, old age, unemployment and caring for a dependent such as a child or a frail elderly person (Esping-Andersen, 1999). The four types of welfare regimes (Continental, Southern European, Scandinavian and liberal) identified by Esping-Andersen (1990) and Ferrera (1996) covered the average male production worker against such risks. Changes in the labour market due to the transition to a post-industrial, service-oriented economy led to the apparition of new social risks from the late 1970s onwards. This trend has accelerated ever since and has become a major challenge for contemporary welfare states. The lack of relevant skills in an increasingly selective labour market and long-term unemployment represent these core new social risks. Esping-Andersen's authoritative argument is that the traditional welfare state, regardless of regime differentiation, is ill-equipped to meet the common new challenges of the 21st century. He claims that:

> most European social protection systems were constructed in an era with a very different distribution and intensity of risks and needs than exists today [...]. The post-war model could rely on strong families and well-performing labour markets to furnish the lion's share of welfare for most people, most of their lives. (Esping-Andersen, 2000)

In fact, the founding fathers of the welfare state were committed to a full-employment society, whereby social assistance would become redundant since all individuals would be protected through their participation in the labour market.

The French welfare state was, and to a certain extent still is, based on this model. It rests upon two components: social insurance benefits financed by social contributions on the one hand, and a tax-financed system which includes minimum income, social assistance policies and new social policies, on the other. Due to the Bismarckian design of the French social security system, social insurance was meant to be the main pillar of the French welfare state. The second tax-based component of the French system is referred to as policies of national solidarity and was supposed to disappear with the advent of a full-employment society (for a brief overview of the French social protection system, see also Palier, 1996). This explains why poverty was publicly acknowledged at a relatively late stage by contrast to the British case, although minimum income policies expanded from the 1960s onwards as entire sections of the population did not have access to the social insurance system.

There has been relatively little debate on poverty as such in France: instead, the debate has focused on social exclusion defined as a multi-dimensional phenomenon rather than deprivation alone. Levitas (1998, p.21) notes that 'the origins of social exclusion lay in France, where the opposite of exclusion was insertion'. Indeed, the expression 'social exclusion' was coined by René Lenoir who published the first book on this topic in 1974, *Les Exclus* ('the excluded'). Social exclusion became the dominant paradigm amongst many French policymakers and experts in the 1990s (Paugam, 1996). Social exclusion is directly linked to the emergence of new social risks and brings to the fore forgotten notions such as extreme hardship. Yet social assistance schemes involving regular monthly or weekly payments such as income support and housing benefits are ill-suited to respond to exceptional hardship. Thus, the debates on emergency single payments schemes occur in the context of the rising awareness of the inadequacy of traditional social assistance responses to these new needs (Sykes *et al*, 2001; Taylor-Gooby, 2001). There is indeed a strong rationale for using discretionary payments to meet exceptional hardship. As increasing sections of the population (most notably the long-term unemployed, unskilled workers and single mothers) become exposed to new social risks, another approach to hardship, focused on daily, non-cyclical events is required. It should be noted that this pattern of emergency intervention, which developed in the early 1980s, represents a break with the French tradition of social assistance. During the *Trente Glorieuses* period,[1] social assistance benefits were closely controlled by the central state under the auspices of Republican social solidarity.

This Chapter examines the way in which the challenge of meeting the exceptional needs of the poor has been addressed in France. Drawing on key notions of social solidarity and 'gift-giving', it will provide an account of the evolution and structure of non-contributory, supplementary welfare assistance. The first section explains the principles of the French tradition of social solidarity. The second section explores the main dimensions of the development of social exclusion throughout the 1990s. It then provides a brief overview of the policy responses to this new phenomenon. It will thus examine policy developments in the second pillar of the French social protection system alongside two main dimensions: discretionary payments, i.e. minimum income run by public agencies and 'new' social policies. The third section classifies the major actors and policy instruments which distribute in-kind and in-cash benefits by administrative category: the traditional social security system managed by the central state, the local social assistance system run by local authorities and the voluntary sector, with a special emphasis on the creation of new actors closely linked to the emergence of new social policies and emergency poor relief. The fourth section assesses the extent to which the development of discretionary and emergency payments has changed the way in which the French welfare state addresses the risks of poverty and social exclusion. The conclusion tries to answer the following question: does the development of the voluntary sector and emergency social funds indicate a changing pattern of intervention of the French welfare state, whereby the state encourages rather than counteracts the initiatives of the private/voluntary sector, thus bringing it closer to the English model of a mixed economy of care?

A Tradition of Republican Solidarity which Counteracts the Notion of Discretionary Payments

The solidarity paradigm has prevailed in France since the Second World War. The Preamble of the Constitution of 1946 – then incorporated in the 1958 Fifth Republic Constitution – claims that each individual has a right to social assistance: 'Every person who is not able to work due to his/her age, physical or mental condition, or to the general economic situation, is entitled to receive from society the means to make a decent living.'[2] By contrast to the English tradition, in which individuals were not entitled to social assistance on the grounds of citizenship alone, Republican citizenship imposed an obligation on the State to assist in the inclusion of the excluded at the turn of the 20th century (Lenoir, 1996, p.81; Choffé, 2001, p.228). The Republican tradition is based on the concept of social solidarity which is essential to the fabric of society itself. The centralist tradition derived from the legacy of the French revolution, rejects traditional forms of poverty relief provided by the church or the voluntary sector. The Allarde decree, issued during the Revolution (1791) prohibited associations and was only abolished in 1901. The 1901 law allowed the creation of associations but remained reluctant to fully acknowledge their role in public life. In practice, the French State has tried to limit the role played by the voluntary sector in poverty relief.

Moreover, the founding fathers of the French social security system in 1945, especially the French resistant Pierre Laroque, rejected the notion of emergency poverty relief since it was associated with charity (Palier, 2002, p.70). Likewise, Bouget (2001, p.213) argues that 'until the 1970s, France had sustained the futuristic ideology of a non-poverty society. The conjunction of full employment and social insurance was able to fulfil the dream of universal social protection'. The ideal of Pierre Laroque was to create a social Republic of workers based on social insurance mechanisms. In his view, social assistance would become redundant in a full employment economy. Social assistance benefits, which were already in place since the 1930s, would be maintained on a temporary basis for the people whose earnings did not entitle them to contributory benefits, especially widows and handicapped people. The social security system would deliver these benefits in a bureaucratic fashion in order to avoid stigmatisation and control of the poor. Unfortunately, Laroque's dream never came to fruition. French legislators never managed to completely eradicate arbitrary social aid as they intended to do so in the early stages of the creation of the French welfare state. Alongside the centralised system of means-tested benefits coexisted a system of discretionary social help administered at the local level. The decree adopted in November 1953 reintroduced discretionary social aid for vulnerable citizens. These cash benefits were administered in a discretionary fashion by the boards of social aid (*bureaux de l'aide sociale*, noted BAS) in the French municipalities. Therefore, social assistance was never considered an unconditional entitlement despite the commitment to social solidarity included in the French Constitution. The BAS decided to grant benefits to individuals provided they had a good case for claiming such help, for instance if they had difficulties paying their rent. Although boards of social assistance could in theory provide in-kind benefits such as food vouchers, clothes and gifts, the use of cash benefits was much more common (Lenoir, 1996). This is because French social workers sought to differentiate themselves from charities and religious organisations, whose philanthropic activities they perceived as patronising. By contrast, Anglo-Saxon local authorities have traditionally been more inclined to provide in-kind benefits and non-monetary forms of assistance (Morel, 2000). Cash payments imply a certain level of trust as opposed to in-kind benefits which impose a form of control over welfare recipients. The marginalisation of charities and the greater involvement of public bodies in the distribution of discretionary payments at the end of nineteenth century France meant that loans and in-kind benefits have been relatively uncommon in the French context. In the eyes of the French social workers, gifts are patronising and aggravate the stigmatisation of the poor. Nevertheless, one should bear in mind that the voluntary sector and the Church always played a more significant role than was publicly acknowledged by policymakers in the *Trente Glorieuses* era. Furthermore, the expansion of social exclusion and poverty in the 1970s due to massive long-term unemployment led to the development of discretionary, emergency social assistance to an extent that had not been foreseen by policymakers in the 1950s.

The Development of Social Exclusion throughout the 1980s-1990s and the Policy Responses

The development of social exclusion

In the late 1970s, structural unemployment became a widespread phenomenon. In March 1974, the unemployment rate stood at 2.7 per cent and constantly increased until the mid-1980s. From 1987 to 1991, unemployment declined and reached 9.1 per cent in March 1991. However, due to the economic crisis, it rose again to reach a peak of 12.5 per cent both in March 1994 and in March 1997. Since then, unemployment has decreased steadily and fell below 10 per cent in 2000. In March 2002, unemployment reached 9.1 per cent of the labour force, which represented a slight increase over the previous year.

Although the French labour market is in a much better shape in 2002 than in mid-1990s, the emergence of mass unemployment has unsurprisingly been correlated with higher levels of social exclusion. According to the National Observatory on Poverty and Social Exclusion established in 1999, social exclusion is characterised by three main dimensions (see Loisy, 2000):

- Unemployment and the lack of a job, the chronic or repeated insufficiency of financial means;
- The non-recognition, or lack of use, not only of social rights but also of political and civil rights;
- Isolation and break-up of family ties.

Long-term unemployment and job insecurity have hit relatively 'stable' individuals and households, reflecting a social 'disaffiliation' in the words of Castel (1995), or 'disqualification' according to Paugam (1991). This 'new poverty' particularly affects younger and older people, lone parents as well as those lacking qualifications and skills, who are falling out of the social safety net.

When seeking to measure social exclusion, the French contrast 'monetary' and 'administrative' poverty, the former reflecting final disposable income and the latter corresponding to the total number of individuals in receipt of social minima. In 1997, 14.1 per cent of the French population declared an income below the poverty threshold, which conventionally amounts to less than half of the median level of income. In 1997, the threshold corresponded to 3,500 French Francs for a person living on their own (£335). As Table 1 indicates, welfare redistribution reduced the amount of households living in poverty by half, i.e. to seven per cent.[3] In other words, in 1997, 4.5 million people were living below the poverty threshold. The statistics on administrative poverty indicate that the number of excluded individuals was higher, at 5.5 million (*Observatoire national de la pauvreté et de l'exclusion sociale*, 2002, p.12).

In addition, it was estimated that in 1997, 665,000 people were long-term unemployed, while 50,000 young people left school without any qualifications. Two million individuals lived in poor housing conditions, while another 200,000 were counted as homeless (Delhoume, 2001, p.97).

Table 11.1   Percentage of Households on Low Income, Before and After Social Transfer Payments

Percentages (%)

	All households[a]		Salaried households[b]		Pensioners	
	Low income (declared)	Low income (final)	Low income (declared)	Low income (final)	Low income (final)	Low income (final)
1970	20.3	15.7	9.5	4.0	30.4	27.8
1975	18.3	12.6	9.1	3.9	25.6	18.2
1979	16.5	9.1	10.5	4.9	21.2	10.7
1984	15.4	7.1	10.6	4.7	16.5	7.0
1990	14.5	7.1	12.0	4.9	13.0	5.9
1997	14.1	7.0	13.6	6.6	8.5	4.2

[a] This category includes pensioners and salaried households, as well as independent and in-active households.
[b] This category includes unemployed households with some employment history.

Source: Insee (Institut National de la Statistique et des Etudes Economiques), Fiscal Revenue Surveys, various years.

Some commentators have argued that more attention must be paid to financial exclusion as an indicator of deprivation, stigmatisation and marginalisation of a segment of the population (Servet, 2000; Gloukoziezoff, 2001). At the turn of the century, five million individuals were reported as not holding a bank account, which represents nine per cent of the overall population while 600,000 households had major debts arrears (Le Duigou, 2000).

Policy responses

In the light of the development of social exclusion, it appeared necessary to revise the French system of social assistance which was insufficient to meet new social needs. One should bear in mind, however, that the French social assistance system expanded considerably throughout the 1970s and 1980s. There are at present seven social minima targeted at special vulnerable categories such as the handicapped, widows, single mothers and the long-term unemployed. The expansion of the traditional cash assistance system represents the first policy response to the development of social exclusion. However, it became clear by the late 1980s that an increasing number of individuals were not receiving any kind of social benefit. This required another policy response which took the form of the institution of a generalised minimum income for social and economic integration. The minimum income for adults, the *Revenu Minimum d'Insertion* (RMI) introduced in December 1988 was designed to fill the gaps of the traditional, targeted social assistance programmes and the contributory-based unemployment compensation system. The RMI represented a new policy instrument and its introduction gave rise to an intense political debate. This monthly non-contributory allowance of currently €405,62 (£256) is available to established residents aged over 25.[4] Thus young adults are not entitled to the RMI unless they have a child, which explains why social exclusion affects primarily young people in France. The tax-funded RMI acts as the third and last pillar of the unemployment benefit system, beside the unemployment insurance benefits paid by the ASSEDIC (*Association pour l'Emploi dans l'Industrie et le Commerce*) and the *Allocation Spécifique de Solidarité* (ASS), a categorical minimum income for the unemployed introduced in 1984.[5]

The RMI packages together access to a set of basic rights and is a mechanism for integration. An integration contract links the beneficiary to the public authority but this does not change the unconditional nature of the income. By contrast to the income-based Job Seeker Allowance in the United Kingdom, the recipient of the RMI is not obliged to accept job offers or to participate in training programmes. In fact, French legislators carefully avoid any assimilation to Anglo-Saxon workfare policies (Rees, 2000). In the French context, workfare is seen as an erosion of basic social rights, which would ultimately undermine social solidarity by creating a division between the deserving and the undeserving poor. Thus the receipt of the RMI is not conditional upon participation in a labour market programme, by contrast to the English New Deals for Young People and the Long-Term Unemployed.

The management of the RMI reflects the emphasis on local partnership that has been central to French social assistance policies since the mid-1980s. As Thomas Choffé points out:

> the integration mechanism associated with the RMI is managed at the *département* level under the joint responsibility of the *Préfet*, as representative of the state, and the President of the General Council (*Conseil Général*) of the *département*. Also associated are many organisations or groups brought together at the *département* level in an integration council. (Choffé, 2001, p.226)

In 2001, it was estimated that just over one million individuals received the RMI (2.2 millions if dependants are included), out of which 40 per cent had no qualifications and 56 per cent were claiming housing benefits (Vidana, 2001, p.147). As Table 11.2 indicates, the number of beneficiaries decreased in 2000 and 2001.

Table 11.2   Beneficiaries of the RMI since 1996

					Percentage (%) Change
1996	1997	1998	1999	2000	2001 first half
+7.5	+5.8	+3.8	+2.5	-5.3	-1.7

Source: Observatoire National de la Pauvreté et de l'Exclusion (2002), p.16.

The law of 29th June 1998 concerning the fight against exclusion (*Loi contre les Exclusions*) reinforced the RMI by stressing the importance of several fundamental rights, such as the right to affordable housing. This law represents the cornerstone of the struggle against the various forms of social exclusion. The first article of the law states that 'the struggle against exclusion is a national imperative founded on respect of the equal dignity of all human beings (…). The present law aims to guarantee throughout the country, effective access for all to fundamental rights.' The noteworthy element is the emphasis on universal rights through the implementation of a multi-dimensional policy which aims to address the various aspects of social exclusion. The law comprises 159 articles intended to provide access to housing, health care, education and labour market (see Choffé, 2001, p.215). Another important aspect of this document is that it seeks to mobilise all social partners, including the voluntary sector and local authorities, in the struggle against social exclusion on the basis of local partnerships. In each *département*, a committee for the prevention of and fight against exclusion is presided by the *préfet*, who represents central government, and comprises representatives of local governments and administrations, as well as representatives of the relevant community and voluntary sector organisations. The 1998 law strongly emphasises the local dimension of anti-poverty policies. As such, this law is indicative of a changing pattern of state intervention that emerged in the late 1980s France as a result of the inability of the central state to tackle new social needs.

Many commentators have remarked that throughout the last twenty years, the various reforms to the social insurance system have exacerbated the cleavage between the contributory and non-contributory segments of the workforce by establishing a sharp distinction between insured job seekers whose contribution records entitle them to unemployment insurance benefits and other job seekers who are covered by unemployment assistance. The shift of the French protection system has been described as a shift from horizontal to vertical solidarity and as a liberal move towards residual welfare (Bouget, 2001; Palier, 1997, 2002).

Multiple Forms of Intervention

Whilst an exact equivalent to the British social fund does not exist in France, a range of salient instruments can be mobilised in order to meet exceptional hardship. As demonstrated above, the patterns of voluntary and discretionary intervention are best understood when positioned against the broader statutory framework of social security provision. The frontiers of such assistance are becoming increasingly fluid as France has moved way from the predominance of central government to a more hybrid type of governance, including a greater devolution of power based on notions of proximity and local democracy (de Maillard, 2000). For example, the voluntary and community sector is increasingly called upon to reinforce the role of public agencies, particularly at the local level, where the needs of marginalised individuals are more readily identified. Hence three forms of social assistance provision can be distinguished, depending on the type of actors involved: (1) central state, i.e. the social security system; (2) local authorities which played and increasingly important role since the decentralisation laws of 1983; and (3) the voluntary sector, which is also expanding rapidly although it remains difficult to accurately measure its expansion due to the lack of reliable data.

The social security system

Several public sector administrations, under the joint responsibility of the State and the social partners (employers and employees associations) distribute minimum income payments to people who are not entitled to social insurance benefits.

First, all unemployment compensation is paid through the ASSEDIC. The ASSEDIC is a highly selective and fragmented system which distributes the new unemployment benefit created in 2001, *l'allocation de remplacement pour l'emploi*, and the aforementioned *Allocation Spécifique de Solidarité*. Moreover, the ASSEDIC administers its own social fund which corresponds to a two per cent levy on the unemployment insurance receipts. This fund was originally set up to respond to the exceptional hardship of the unemployed with the possibility of a 48 hours release. Yet further to several conflicts and controversies (see below), the ASSEDIC's social fund is now used parsimoniously, essentially to assist a period of training or retraining.

The second main key actor in the payment of minimum income is the Family Allowance Fund, the *Caisse Nationale des Allocations Familiales* (CNAF). An overarching public body managed on the basis of parity between the social partners and the state, the CNAF can also distribute cash payments to meet emergency social needs. The CNAF is represented throughout the French territory with 125 funds (*caisses d'allocations familiales*, noted CAF) at the local level which deliver twenty-five different family-related benefit. It delivers minimum income schemes such as the isolated parent allowance (*allocation de parent isolé*), the RMI, the widowhood allowance (*allocation veuvage*).

These local branches assess the requests made for means-tested family assistance. For example, the *Allocation de Soutien Familial* (ASF), a family support allowance is paid to single parents if the second parent does not provide adequate child support. Although the ASF is in principle a universal family benefit, in practice it is granted to poor families with dependent children. The CAF can also pay targeted benefits for special needs such as the new-school year allowance (*allocation de rentrée scolaire*) or allowance for mother's help or nannies (*allocation de garde d'enfants à domicile*). But most of its services go to housing benefits such as *the Allocation Personalisée au Logement* (APL) and social housing allowance (*allocation sociale de logement*). Within the housing benefits category the relocation allowance (*Prime de Déménagement*) could be classed as a tool to meet exceptional circumstances, as this is granted to those in need of assistance with the costs of moving home. Most of the beneficiaries tend to be welfare recipients or poor isolated single-parent families, families with more than three children, or students. For example, in 2000, students received seventy per cent of the supplementary assistance provided by the CNAF. A total of €2.4 billion were spent by the CNAF in the year 2000, which represents a 4.9 per cent increase over 1999.[6]

Local authorities

The decentralisation laws of 1982-1983 have transferred the bulk of responsibilities for local social assistance (*aide sociale*) to the *départements*. At this level, social assistance consists of several means-tested benefits:

- social assistance for children (*aide sociale à l'enfance*)
- social assistance for the disabled (*aide aux handicappés*)
- social assistance for old people (*aide sociale aux personnes âgées*)
- social assistance for sick people (*aide médicale*) for people without any social insurance. The universal health coverage law (*couverture maladie universelle* or CMU) effective as of 1 January 2000 has replaced the previous *aide médicale*.

Local social assistance is mostly reserved to people who are not covered by another social protection scheme, including the minimum income payments distributed by the social security system. Whether in-kind or in-cash, local social assistance obeys a discretionary principle since needs are assessed by a local commission at the municipal level, the *Centre Communal d'Action Sociale* (formerly called the *bureau d'aide sociale*). It is administered on the basis of subsidiarity, that is, once all other sources of private or public help have been exhausted. Local social assistance is considered as a last resort safety net. For instance, the *Conseils Généraux* (county councils) can help pay electricity bills or other emergency needs under the budgetary line 'monthly help with child care' (*aides mensuelles de l'aide sociale à l'enfance*). The same possibility exists in Britain under the Children Act 1989.

Within large towns, local social assistance is increasingly linked to the urban *Politique de la Ville*, which was introduced in 1983 and consists of a contracting process between each town, its region and the state in order to provide instruments of social intervention in deprived areas (Jacquier, 2001). New social policies and urban policies are intertwined and characterised by a superimposition of competencies and responsibilities as new needs arise. The result is an extremely fragmented system with numerous overlaps of competencies and interventions. Urban policies have been criticised for their lack of direction and accountability. Local authorities are the centre of these new territorial policies as they seek to take a targeted spatial approach to addressing multiple social needs such as employment, housing and social services. The law against exclusion tries to simplify access to the various services provided under the new urban policies by creating single gateway services, the Emergency Social Action Committees, *Commissions d'Action Sociale d'Urgence* or *CASU* (Choffé, 2001, p.218). The CASU are hybrid organisations trying to respond to urgent social needs as they arise with the help of all actors involved in this field regardless of their administrative status. They are additional to the local authorities' own network of centres open to socially excluded people, the *centres d'hébergement et de réinsertion sociale*. These centres are open to specific sub-groups such as lone mothers or migrant workers and are clearly a response to urgent social needs. Such centres have flourished in large cities, as situations of extreme hardship have become increasingly common at the turn of the last century, requiring an urgent response from the municipalities. For example, in Paris, a centre is open to people who have been evicted from their homes or lost their homes following a damage or accident and who cannot be accommodated by relatives.

In recent years, several French regions and localities have been exposed to industrial and natural disasters, such as the explosion of the AZF plant in Toulouse in September 2001, which have brought a renewed focus on the notion of urgency. For example, following a series of floods in the summer of 2002, the local authorities of the Gard and Vaucluse departments in the South East of France provided emergency support to respond to the urgent needs of the victims. Resident adults were immediately entitled to €150 and children to €65 following a simple request. Of course, public sector emergency relief is understandably different in the case of a national collective urgency. Such events receive high levels of political and media coverage. Some authors have argued that it is precisely because of the lack of collective organisation and representation until the mid-1990s that socially excluded people have suffered from a lack of emergency relief measures in their favour (Demazière, 1996; Salmon, 1998). During the summer 2002 events, concerns were raised that standardised responses did not take into account the unevenness of damage experienced by the victims. Vulnerable families who live in the most deprived areas of the region and rarely had home contents insurance, were most dramatically hit by these events (Henry, 2002). By appealing to public generosity, non-government organisations such as the *Secours Catholique* managed to raise further donations.

These examples show that whether experienced on an individual or collective level, situations of extreme hardship have led to a multiplication of initiatives and partnerships between local authorities and voluntary sector organisations, often on the margins of the institutional system of social protection (compare with Chapter 4 by Roger Smith in this volume).

The growing significance of charitable bodies (associations humanitaires)

A growing number of charitable organisations have sought to fill the space left vacant by the traditional social security system, many of which have a wide-ranging action from helping third world countries to providing proximity services at home (Chappuis, 1999; Salmon, 1998). The size and scope of the community sector has indeed grown tremendously over the past twenty years. The media have notably played an instrumental role in promoting the visibility of its action (Paugam, 1996; Salmon, *op cit*).

Following the decline of religious faith, the more neutral concept of 'solidarity' has tended to replace the religiously connoted notion of charity. It is hence not surprising to find an important link between religious communities and voluntary sector organisations. Whilst the importance of the Protestant ethic in community action has been largely explored by the literature, Catholicism, which is the dominant religion in France, is also at the roots of the voluntary movement based on compassion and charity as Tropman (1993) points out. Therefore charismatic religious leaders established several charitable organisations. The *Secours Catholique* was created in 1946 by Father Rohhain, *Emmaüs* by Bishop Pierre in 1949 and *ATD Quart Monde* by Father Joseph Wresinski in 1957.[7] These organisations seek to fulfil the mission of fighting against the most extreme forms of poverty and to improve social cohesion. Gift giving is at the heart of the catholic benevolent movement by contrast to the secular poverty relief institutions run by the state. By definition, they are more likely than the public sector to provide in kind-benefits such as free meals, clothes and beds.

Alongside the political engagement of religious figures, political or 'humanitarian' movements created other well-known organisations such as the Red Cross and the *Secours Populaire*. Furthermore, many celebrities have drawn attention to problems of social exclusion and have obtained strong media coverage. A notorious example is that of the restaurants of the heart (*Restos du Coeur*), a free *canteen* launched by the French humorist Coluche on 26 September 1985.[8] Coluche originally aimed at providing 20,000 free meals. His accidental death shocked public opinion and mobilised a variety of French celebrities so that Coluche's organisation has grown to now be seen as one of the most important ones in the voluntary sector (Salmon, *op cit*).

An opinion poll carried out on a representative sample of the French population by the Sofres Institute in March 2002 indicated that 85 per cent of the respondents felt that charitable organisations have an important role to play in the fight against poverty. However, a further poll on the social economy in October 2000 showed that only 12 per cent of the French population would be prepared to donate money to charities, while 31 per cent were willing to devote some of their time to charitable action, 39 per cent were willing to donate old goods and items, and 44 per cent would consider purchasing 'ethical' products.[9]

Urgency Funds versus Permanent Irrigation

In France, socially excluded people have not solely gained a voice through high media coverage. France is well known for its strong culture of militant and mass popular protest (Neveu, 1996). Following the example of the workers' and trade union movements, the socially excluded found a new collective representation through several organisations such as *Agir Ensemble Contre le Chômage!*[10] who put mounting pressure on governments through mass street demonstrations on various occasions (see Demazière and Pignoni, 1998; Salmon, 1998). The most significant events occurred in the winters of 1984 and 1997, when the unemployed occupied many of the ASSEDIC's local offices. The 1997 events were triggered by the UNEDIC's attempt to scrap the social fund administered by the ASSEDIC and originated in the Bouches-du-Rhône region where the unemployed demanded the 3,000 French Francs 'Christmas bonus' that had been granted by this particular office for several years. On these occasions, governments responded through the immediate release of exceptional urgency funds in order to appease the social unrest. Thus emergency state support is best described as reactive, ad hoc and sporadic. Yet governments have been far less responsive to a series of similar movements (occupation of churches and hunger strikes) by the so-called *sans-papiers*, i.e. immigrant workers awaiting the delivery of residence permits, which suggests that the demands of the long-term unemployed are ranked more highly, arguably because these possess citizenship, hence a voting right.

The outcomes of the 1984 and 1997 protests were relatively similar in terms of patterns of emergency state support. In 1984, a first special urgency programme (*Plan d'Urgence* contre la *Pauvreté et la Précarité Sociale*) was adopted. Over one billion francs were distributed during the

1984-85 period to charities through the regional authorities (Vidana, 2001, p.145). This sum was raised through a symbolic tax levy of 0.5 per cent on wealth and covered the provision of 7,500 beds and meals for 650,000 people, as well as the first programme of financial assistance towards rent arrears. Similarly, the *Fonds d'Urgence Sociale* (FUS) adopted in early 1998 also amounted to a highly symbolic one billion francs lump sum. On this occasion, the regions administered the fund which benefited 600,000 individuals in 1999. The distribution of monies from the FUS to individual households has been well documented in the literature. For example, an empirical study conducted by (Fassin *et al*, 2000, 2001) explored the norms and criteria applied by local committees when 'splitting the cake', as these had discretionary powers regarding the amount to allocate on a case-by-case basis. According to official application procedures, individual households had to formulate a request for financial assistance in writing. These authors argued that applicants were turned into 'beggars', as they had to make an eloquent and detailed account of their misery in the public arena. This rationalisation of charity could to some extent echo the many sophisticated verbal accounts of their unfortunate trajectories and the lamentations expressed by beggars of the Paris metro, which according to Isambert (1996) has now been turned into a voting space. Moreover, in contrast to the proximity that traditionally characterises charity, the allocation of financial assistance by means of cheques and postal payments is symptomatic of a form of 'donor distancing', which in the case of the FUS resulted in arbitrary decisions and highly unequal outcomes. A distance can also be observed in the action taken by the major French foundation, the *Fondation de France*,[11] whose establishment was largely inspired by the American community trusts model (Pavillon, 1995). The *Fondation de France*'s set mission is to prevent and dampen the social ills caused by the evolution of the industrial society through a donation of monies to smaller grassroots organisations operating in four areas: solidarity, health, culture and the environment.

The changing pattern of emergency state support parallels the new social irrigation role played by civil society. Arguably this growing significance may in fact reflect a new role division between the public and the voluntary sector, with the latter acting as a substitute for the provision of services hitherto provided by the welfare state (see OECD, 2002, forthcoming). Whilst some of the now well-established charitable organisations originally displayed spontaneous action, they have maintained and expanded their activities, beyond their original aims. Indeed, in their annual reports, many organisations report increased levels of donations and new activities. For example, five years after its establishment, the *Restos du Cœur* had trebled its distribution of free meals (Salmon, *op cit*). The organisation currently has 2,000 centres throughout France with 36,000 voluntary workers providing 500,000 free meals on a daily basis. Likewise, the Secours Catholique has 4,200 teams operating from 2,500 local centres, which represents 72,000 volunteer workers. Its 2000 activity report states that it was involved in 750,000 cases of assistance towards poor families throughout France. The Secours Catholique reports that the majority of its action consists in offering personal services, such as help with food shopping, and in some cases, home equipment such as micro-waves and washing machines. It notably provides food vouchers, the distribution of which was established in the 1998 law on social exclusion (article 138), although shop keepers are still reluctant to accept this method of payment.

It remains difficult to undertake an accurate overall evaluation of the socio-economic contribution made by the voluntary sector, since discretionary assistance, particularly in-kind assistance is under-recorded and cannot be statistically captured. Several suggestions have been made regarding the necessity to develop new evaluation tools that would help establish the impact made by this sector (see OECD, *op cit*). Furthermore, kinship and family networks – the significance of which should not be neglected – may also prevent individuals from seeking assistance outside the household and family sphere, which is equally difficult to monitor. Nonetheless, there is general consensus over the fact that the poor are most likely to be excluded from such networks of social capital.

Concluding Remarks

As we have noted earlier in this Chapter, French policymakers have been very reluctant to acknowledge the scope of new poverty which began to emerge in the late 1970s. Until the mid-1980s, they strongly believed that unemployment was a temporary phenomenon which would be solved by adequate demand-side policies. The failure of Keynesian policies in 1982 coupled with the youth revolts in the suburbs of Lyon in 1981 led to a radical paradigm shift in governmental circles (Belorgey, 1988). In particular, a generation of younger civil servants claimed that the central state alone could no longer address the multiple dimensions of the dislocation of the French social fabric. Instead, they argued that the state should encourage the development of private initiatives and local social assistance policies which would empower socially excluded people. Therefore, the expansion of poverty led to a change in the pattern of state intervention. The state was no longer to be the unique provider of cash assistance – although, as we have argued, this had never been the case even in the golden age of the 1960s. Instead, it was felt that the state should promote the development of territorial social policies in partnership with the voluntary sector, which would represent a radical break with the French dirigiste tradition in the field of social policy. This changing pattern of state intervention has been analysed in conjunction with the emergence of an enabling state, the '*Etat animateur*' (see Donzelot and Estebe, 1994). The notion of an enabling state is an ideal-type since the state remains in practice reluctant to delegate some of its powers to civil society, yet it does help understand the changing mindset of the French political élites.

In sum, recent developments in the field of welfare redistribution suggest a changing relationship between statutory and discretionary assistance to the poor, as France has engaged into the path of remodelling its universal social protection system in favour of a residual model of welfare provision. At the same time, French society has witnessed a growing significance of non-state actors in the field of emergency poor relief. In this respect, we would argue that a pattern of convergence between France and Britain is emerging. Three major factors are contributing to this trend: (1) the rise of poverty and inequality since René Lenoir published the first book on social exclusion, (2) the emphasis in recent French political debates on the virtues of the voluntary sector, participative democracy and civic engagement, and (3) the impact of globalisation and external competitive pressures, which have led to a considerable tightening of welfare budgets.

Concerns about social exclusion have – even more so than in the UK – been equated with the battle against long-term unemployment, which is reflected in France's extensive system of publicly funded job creation schemes, such as the *travaux d'utilité collective* (TUC), the *contrats emploi-solidarité* (CES) or more recently, the *Emplois-Jeunes*. However, this emphasis has overshadowed the problem of financial exclusion and the rise of over-indebtedness. While proponents of a basic income and of a negative rate of income tax have, as in Britain, attempted to raise the potential benefits in the fight against poverty (see Aznar *et al*, 1996; Bouget and Nogues, 1996), it is doubtful whether such fiscal instruments will suffice. In this regard, Prime Minister Raffarin's government pledge of reducing the fiscal burden on taxpayers following the May and June 2002 elections, does little to help excluded groups and may further increase the gap between the rich and the poor.

Notes

1   The thirty glorious years between 1945 and 1975, or more precisely, between the liberation of France in 1944 and the oil crisis in 1973.
2   Preamble of the Constitution of the Fourth Republic adopted in October 1946.
3   Table 1 also shows that pensioners have been the major winners. Indeed in the 1970s and 1980s, these formed the poorest social group. Since 1990, they have become the major beneficiaries of social transfer payments.
4   Amount is for single individuals without dependants. The monthly allowance for couple without children or for lone parents with one child €608,43 (£284); couples with a child receive €730,12 (£461).
5   The ASS concerns unemployed workers who have worked five years or more over the last ten years. In 1999, 470,800 individuals were in receipt of the ASS.
6   See http://www.caf.fr.
7   The Secours Catholique is linked to the international ONG Caritas. For more information on these organisations, see http://www.secours-catholique.asso.fr and http://atd-quartmonde.org; See also De Gaulle Anthonioz (2001) for an overview of the history of ATD Quart Monde.
8   See http://www.restosducoeur.org.
9   The March 2002 poll was carried out on behalf of the Secours Catholique, the October 2000 poll was carried out on behalf of Emmaüs and Le Pélerin magazine. Both can be viewed on http://www.sofres.com/archives_soc.htm.
10   See http://www.ac.eu.org.
11   See http://www.fdf.org.

Chapter 12

A Better Deal: The Prospects for Reform

Trevor Buck and Roger S. Smith

Reviewing the Evidence

The evidence discussed in this volume presents an overall picture of the social fund as a system of cash help which has been dislocated from its original objectives to provide targeted discretionary assistance to those in most need of help with lump sum and emergency expenses. The evidence has accumulated since 1988 from a broad range of sources (see Buck, 2000, Chapter 7, 'A Review of the Research'). As noted in Chapter 5 by Smith, the applicants' own experiences of the social fund are among the most important indicators of its overall lack of effectiveness. Empirical evidence of how both the users and producers of its delivery system actually experience the social fund has been examined by Rowe (Chapter 6) and Davidson (Chapter 7). Their conclusions support the view that its substantive flaws are amplified by the selective and discriminatory manner of the fund's administration.

Further compelling evidence of the parlous state of the social fund has appeared in 2002 in a detailed report produced by the National Association of Citizens' Advice Bureaux (Barton, 2002). Their report is especially worthy of comment as it was based upon the returns of 2,042 evidence reports submitted by 494 Citizens' Advice Bureaux (CABx) in the U.K. (during the period January 1999 to July 2002).

> In this Evidence Report we draw attention to the manifest failings of the social fund to meet the needs of people on low incomes. These failings have left some of the poorest and most vulnerable people in society socially excluded and deprived of the necessities for a decent standard of life. It is particularly shocking when the people who are left to suffer in this way include children and people with severe health problems. (Barton, 2002, para. 1.1)

The report itemises the need for the 'extensive reform' of and 'substantial change' in the social fund in order to meet the government's stated aims to defeat poverty and social exclusion. It argues the need for a 'continuing and wider role' for grants and loans in the social fund. The report provides strong evidence of the problems associated with the delivery of social fund payments.

> All applicants deserve to be fairly treated when they approach a social security office or Jobcentre Plus about a Social Fund payment. Our evidence shows that there are far too many cases in which people have, instead, received misleading or unhelpful advice. (Barton, 2002, para. 1.5)

The report identifies the introduction of Jobcentre Plus and personal advisers as an opportunity to improve service delivery, as does Lakhani (Chapter 10).

There are also criticisms of the revised Budgeting Loan (BL) scheme introduced in 1999 and it is recommended that 'there should be a stronger requirement upon Social Fund staff to ensure that applicants are considered for the type of payment most helpful to them.' The report further recommends the extension of eligibility to the fund to improve user access.

> We recommend that, after April 2003, people who qualify for the maximum child credit and/or qualify for Working Tax Credit should be eligible to apply for help from the both the discretionary and the regulated Social Fund. People whose sole income is a contributory benefit such as Incapacity Benefit or Contribution Based Jobseeker's Allowance should also be eligible. (Barton, 2002, para. 1.9)

On the subject of Community Care Grants (CCGs), Barton claims that the CCG scheme has been a failure: '[p]eople in obvious need fail to meet the criteria for help, and even where a grant is paid the amount is often quite inadequate'. NACAB recommends the review of the CCG scheme and its replacement by 'a system of grants for particular life events and needs, available to anyone on a low income'.

In addition, recommendations are made for the abolition of the current 26-week qualification period for BLs, an increase in the current maximum (£1,000) for loans and a review of the BL formula which tends to preclude many applications because of the existence of outstanding debt. NACAB also advocates the revision of the repayment formula to allow a more modest repayment rate.

There are some fundamental criticisms too of the Crisis Loan (CL) scheme.

> The Crisis Loan scheme should not be used to support delays in making decisions on applications for Income Support and other benefits. 36% of current spending goes on 'alignment payments' to people without money who have made a claim for benefit. This money is therefore not available for other people in need of an emergency loan. Benefit applications should of course not be subject to (sometimes lengthy) delays, but

we recommend that there should be a new fast-track scheme to provide interim advance payments to people who appear to have made a valid claim for benefit. (Barton, 2002, para. 1.14)

The report also questions the legitimacy of the qualification rule in Direction 3.[1] Finally, although the report focuses primarily on the discretionary social fund payments, it also recounts substantial amounts of critical evidence relating to funeral payments in the regulated scheme.

Our evidence suggests that decisions on funeral payments do not always follow the DWP guidance and that DWP staff unfairly refuse payments to recently bereaved families, particularly where there exist family members who are not in receipt of qualifying benefits. (Barton, 2002, para. 1.19)

This evidence is consistent with many of the findings reported in previous Chapters, confirming once again that a recurrent pattern of shortcomings has beset the social fund from its inception. Limited reforms put in place by various governments have not solved these underlying deficiencies. In short, there is no lack of authoritative material to show the many failings of the social fund and the way in which it is delivered. Clarifying these issues in more detail will enable us to set out some key principles and directions for effective reform in the future.

The Structural Issues

There are a number of key structural issues which need to be addressed rigorously in order to approach a satisfactory answer to the problem of lump sum and emergency cash help in social security systems. The comparative and international perspectives offered by Davidson (Chapter 7), Herman and Declercq (Chapter 2) and Daguerre and Nativel (Chapter 11) all indicate, in different ways, how the role and function of such exceptional provision will ultimately rely on how we view the state's fundamental role in this field. France is not alone, as Daguerre and Nativel report, in having its social protection system premised on a number of economic and social expectations (e.g. full employment) which either never have actually occurred, or at least have never been fulfilled in the way envisaged. In the British context, the string of post-Beveridge reforms to the social security system will always look like *ad hoc* policy-making at its worst without a proper understanding of how the expected structural conditions of British society underpinning Beveridge turned out in practice. The assumptions of a full employment society, headed by male breadwinners in a long-gone industrial world, became increasingly exposed in the 1970s and 1980s as anachronistic.

In Britain, (and there are indications in other European states too), 'social insurance' has for many years been a residual element of overall social protection and 'social assistance' has become the dominant element (Harris, 2000, p.116); an ironic turnabout given their original positioning in the Beveridge Plan. Yet the social fund (and its equivalents in other European states), originally identified as a 'residual' element of social assistance, and likely to become superfluous if means-tested assistance were to be properly supported with adequate benefit rates, has become a *persistent feature* of the social security landscape. Indeed, whilst an adequate minimum income might resolve many of the problems of poverty which exceptional payment schemes are intended to address, it now appears more certain that there is likely to be a continuing need for some form of reserve provision of this kind to address urgent and substantial financial problems for those with limited means.

Policymakers will no doubt alter the social fund scheme in years to come in certain respects, but few now doubt its long-term existence in some form or another. In fact, as Craig shows (Chapter 1) the origins of such discretionary provision pre-date even the Beveridge reforms and the immediate concerns of policy makers on the introduction of the social fund under the Social Security Act 1986 were based more on a parochial critique of its antecedents (e.g. the single payments scheme) rather than any fundamental consideration of how such cash support *ought* to be located within the overall structure of provision. One problem is that British policymakers too often focus on the balance between the insurance based system and the non-contributory means-tested system as essentially a financial matter divorced from the social realities of poverty.

There is an increasing desire by European states to develop welfare to work programmes underpinned by 'activation' policies (see e.g. Hermans and Declercq, Chapter 2; Davidson, Chapter 7). However, any significant rise or fall in the (real) unemployment figures generates significant structural pressure on social assistance schemes. The way in which states have and will frame their social assistance policies depends crucially upon the nature and position of cycles of macro-economic fortunes. Furthermore, even if welfare to work policies can work without too heavy a price elsewhere, there is the growing recognition of the degradation of people's quality of life *in work*; the result being the creation of a 'work rich'/'work poor' society (Millar and Ridge, 2002, p. 54). Craig notes the general effect of 'immiseration' on social fund applicants (Chapter 3) but this effect may well appear in respect of those in work on low incomes who have hitherto not been recognised as belonging to traditional categories of the 'poor'.

The nature of the problem of lump sum and emergency payment is further compounded by the need to achieve a judicious balance between mainstream means-tested social security benefit rates and support for exceptional needs. Policymakers will often regard generous resourcing of the latter as tending to threaten the integrity of the former. Furthermore, it may sometimes be assumed that significant hikes in the principal means-tested benefit rates will preclude the requirement for resources to meet exceptional needs. However, precisely because these are often unpredictable, it will remain the case that a contingency scheme of some kind will be required as an integral part of the policy framework.

The analysis of British New Labour policies offered by Smith (Chapter 4, this volume) questions the nature of the development of a 'Third Way' in state welfare provision to address these structural issues. On the one hand the 'benign' view is that New Labour is constructively bringing market philosophy and social inclusion together. Thus, the transposition from 'applicant' to 'customer' and the expected adjustments of the social fund as a means to remove barriers to flexible working. On the other hand, it is argued that the underlying structural inequities in the distribution of power will inevitably be reflected in unequal distributions of income which will additionally be reinforced by modern-day versions of 'badging the poor'.[2] The administration which commenced its welfare policy thinking in 1997 with a determination to 'think the unthinkable'[3] may be in danger of doing the unthinkable, i.e. perpetuating policies, albeit in more acceptable garb, which the traditions of the Labour Party have for so long opposed.

Even if the social fund were to be successfully manipulated in order to provide better consistency with welfare to work policy there remains the enduring problem of meeting the needs of people who have little or no chance of engaging in work or who positively wish to contribute to society in alternative ways. The appearance of such permanently marginalized groups on some estimates is increasing and not reducing to residual proportions. New Labour has made little contribution in addressing their needs or examining the nature and depth of their poverty.

Finally, it ought to be remembered that most European states will increasingly face the challenges presented by a rapidly ageing population. Yet there is some evidence that the take-up rates for pensioners of benefits generally and the social fund in particular are already low (see Cohen et al, 1996). The Department for Work and Pensions has commissioned research into pensioner attitudes to, and experiences of, the social fund (see House of Commons, 2002, col.269WH) precisely because this is an area which is poorly understood. Given the combined effects of the erosion of the value of state and occupational pensions for those retiring in 10 or 20 years time and the increase in the 'dependency ratio' (of pensioners to active economic persons), there are prospects in the future of formidable pressures on the social fund or any equivalent replacement.

The Administration of Exceptional Social Assistance

This book has provided some examples of how exceptional social assistance is delivered in Britain, the Netherlands, France and Belgium. In all cases there are tensions involved in striking the right balance between systems employing 'individualised' discretion and establishing legal rights to support social values of certainty, security and human dignity. One of the aims of the social fund in Britain, according to the original blueprint, was certainly to provide the kind of individualisation delivered by the Public Centres for Social Welfare (PCSW) in Belgium (see Hermans and Declercq, Chapter 2) when administering 'social aid'. But some of the criticisms made of the social fund based on arguments about 'territorial injustice' (Ward, 1989) are also applicable in the Belgian context. It seems inevitable that the approach of individualised discretion, though supported by some strong argument in its favour (Titmuss, 1968), will always carry with it the disadvantages of the inequities perceived from one locality to another.

In any case, it should be remembered that the Belgian arrangements are distinguishable from the British social fund: the social fund has in fact become a much more centrally directed, national scheme without the involvement of any significant local element found in the case of PCSWs. A number of differences in the 'area social fund guidance' have been smoothed out over the years. The formula for allocating local budgets has been distilled to an anodyne statistical exercise hardly requiring any consideration of genuinely local assessments of local needs. The *realpolitik* of the social fund has always been and remains the requirement to manage a constrained national budget, which effectively dampens the exposure of need, rather than to provide a policy device that is fully committed to addressing these particularly difficult aspects of poverty. Furthermore, the 'cash and care' mix originally conceived as the one of the policy justifications for the social fund (see Lister, 1989, for example) has long since been largely forgotten. The attempt to join up the efforts of local social services departments and the Department for Social Security (now Department for Work and Pensions) in a more comprehensive social protection strategy has never matured, despite the vague aspirations of government ministers (see Malcolm Wicks, M.P., House of Commons, 2002, col. 271WH, for example). Perhaps the most convincing evidence of that failure was the eventual abandonment of the back up 'money advice' service in 1996.[4]

The role of administrative justice must also not be forgotten in the field of social assistance schemes. In European social protection systems there are familiar systems of appeal to courts or tribunals which will provide authoritative benchmarks for particularly contested discretionary notions; for example, the concept of 'human dignity' was, as Hermans and Declercq note (Chapter 2), clarified as a result of the availability of appeal to a labour court. In Britain, the social security commissioners provide such authoritative interpretations. The commissioners are a second tier appellate authority with an established reputation for impartiality and specialist expertise in relation to the mainstream social security benefits (see Bonner *et al*, 2001). It has been argued that a most effective reform would be to bring the social fund grievance procedures back into the ordinary social security appeal tribunals:

> It is disingenuous to argue, as the Government has, that tribunals are ill-equipped to deal with the kind of discretionary issues raised by the social fund. Social fund officers are in practice constrained by the same type of detailed directions and guidelines that the tribunals are used to coping with in the form of statutory regulations. (Baldwin, Wikeley and Young, 1992, p.210)

However, for reasons discussed by Buck (Chapter 8) the social fund adopted a different model of 'review' that only reluctantly conceded an external element (the inspectors of the Independent Review Service (IRS)) as the Bill was brokered through its Parliamentary stages. Furthermore, IRS had to spend some years in establishing its independence, and in any event the decisions of inspectors are only binding in individual cases. There are significant contradictions to consider here. On the one hand, there are a number of obstacles working against the delivery of quality review work to all but a small minority of applicants; the lack of proper advice and information is cited in Barton (2002). The existence of the review process probably does more to legitimise an inherently flawed system of cash help than the aggregate good it can deliver to individual applicants. On the other hand, there are aspects of the review model which will need further attention when reform proposals are being seriously considered, particularly its merits as a prototype for 'systemic justice'.

Prospects for Reform

The Select Committee on Social Security, as mentioned at several points in this volume, conducted an inquiry into the social fund in 2001 (see House of Commons, 2001). Despite the weight of evidence presented to the Committee and its recommendations for an 'urgent overhaul' the government appeared to have set its face against any recognition that the social fund is not fulfilling the aims of alleviating poverty and social exclusion (see Department for Work and Pensions, 2001). As noted by Lakhani (Chapter 10) the chair of the Select Committee, Archy Kirkwood M.P., continued to press the case in the following adjournment debate (see House of Commons, 2002), that the social fund was inefficient, expensive, unfair and conflicted with other government objectives.

> The main thrust of the Committee's report was to consider five key objectives for the social fund. The first objective was to contain expenditure, which has been achieved. The second was to maintain the efficiency of the income support scheme; the integrity of the income support scheme has been preserved. However, it is more difficult to be confident about the remaining three objectives. The third objective was to concentrate help on those facing the greatest difficulties, the fourth to enable a more variable response to inescapable individual needs, and the fifth to break new ground in community care. Some progress has been made with community care grants and how they are applied, but the Committee contends that, at the very least, a question mark hangs over whether the latter three objectives set out in 1998 have been met in anything but the breach. (House of Commons, 2002, col. 242WH, Archy Kirkwood, M.P.)

Indeed, he went on to argue that some aspects of the social fund could clearly be seen to work against the government's wider policy aims, such as social inclusion and the eradication of child poverty. He also expressed his specific disappointment at the 'cursory nature of the Government's response' to criticisms. He reiterated the need for both substantive improvements in the availability of cash help by way of grants, and for administrative enhancements to ensure that payments are made efficiently and without stigmatising recipients. Mr Kirkwood highlighted, for example, the need for measures to address the possibility of institutional discrimination, rather than operate a 'colour blind' approach.

These arguments were supported by other M.P.s, including representatives of the Labour Party. Karen Buck, M.P., summarised the dual aspects of the problem.

> The fund is flawed in two respects.... Its provision is not adequate to meet needs... and it cannot assist in the right way those who have recourse to it. (House of Commons, 2002, col. 248WH, Karen Buck, M.P.)

In responding on behalf of the government, Malcolm Wicks, M.P., Parliamentary Under-Secretary of State for Work and Pensions, gave some initial cause for optimism. He expressed a desire, for example, to move towards an individualised approach to assessing and meeting the problems of the poor. However, he also reiterated the government's unwillingness to return to a solely grants-based scheme, partly because 'it may be unfair to people in work', and partly, simply on grounds of cost. At the same time, he reemphasised the original rationale for the development of the concept of 'Community Care Grants' (Department of Health and Social Security, 1985b); that is, that the use of such payments should be oriented towards achieving very specific purposes asociated with social care needs, such as resettlement from institutional settings, or the need to move to escape domestic violence. But, in the absence of any significant new funding and in the light of the social fund's failure to meet this expectation since its inception (see, for example, Lister, 1989; Walker et al, 1992), this is hardly encouraging. The only crumb of comfort offered was the minister's claim that:

> We continue to keep the social fund under review. I am not merely using the usual phrase: the drum beats on the social fund in my department, and our thoughts are active on its future. (House of Commons, 2002, col. 273WH, Malcolm Wicks, M.P.)

Principles of Reform

In the absence of any serious commitment to change from government, it remains to us, at this point, to set out some ideas for the reform of the social fund. It should, of course, be acknowledged here that most, if not all, these proposals have already been aired in one form or another elsewhere (see, for example, Craig, 1992; Commission for Social Justice, 1995; Cohen et al, 1996; Barton, 2002; Howard, 2002).

It is important, first, to be clear about the principles which should underpin the structure and operation of any scheme put in place to address the urgent financial problems of those on low incomes, or receiving social assistance. The following, for example, are key characteristics of any such scheme:

- The ability to provide flexible and individualised help in a financial crisis
- Fairness and equity in the allocation and distribution of cash help
- Effective contribution to the alleviation of poverty
- Non-stigmatising administrative procedures for dealing with identified need based on principles of dignity and respect
- Openness and responsiveness to evidence of need

- Properly accountable delivery mechanisms which are open to challenge and redress.

In order to meet these requirements, any effective exceptional needs scheme will have to put in place a number of specific 'building blocks', both in terms of its substantive provision and its administrative systems.

Firstly, and fundamentally, it will be essential to resource the scheme properly; Craig (Chapter 3) estimates that an adequate net budget for the UK social fund would be in the region of £900 million annually. In real terms, this would restore levels of spending to slightly higher levels than those achieved in the final years of the single payments scheme in the 1980s. It would ensure, however, that the scheme would revert to its former, essentially grants based, character. This kind of substantial reinvestment would clearly be necessary in any case if government has any serious intention to extend the range of the social fund's activities to meet 'community care' needs.

At the same time, the emergence of Budgeting Loans as an accessible state-run banking facility for those who are unable to access this service elsewhere would be unaffected by enhancements to the grants budget. It seems to be agreed that this is an important service in its own right (New Policy Institute, 2002a; 2002b), and it should perhaps be allowed to develop as a free-standing policy innovation, perhaps incorporating a more flexible Crisis Loan element as well.

In addition to a substantial boost to the funds available, payment mechanisms could also be restructured to meet needs more equitably. For example, it has been suggested that a system of payments related to 'life events' could ensure much greater consistency of distribution, whilst at the same time removing a great deal of the stigma attached to seeking help (see, for example, Lakhani, Chapter 10). Such 'life events' payments might, indeed, be seen as a logical extension of current provision for maternity and funeral payments; they could include, for example, the start of schooling for children, or the transition to secondary school. Similar mechanisms could ensure the making of additional seasonal payments, such as the provision for 'Christmas bonuses' in parts of France (see Daguerre and Nativel, Chapter 11).

Other planned transitions (those associated with arrangements to provide 'care in the community', for example) could also be provided for in the form of guaranteed one-off payments. In this way, government would be able to achieve a more integrated approach to social care, offering cash help to support wider social inclusion policies (and, perhaps, enhancing assistance for relatively under-provided groups such as the elderly). An enhanced 'enabling' role for the social fund might also, at the same time, contribute to a much more positive culture amongst those directly responsible for administering payments (see Rowe, Chapter 6).

Whereas it is possible to develop a framework for cash help which takes account of 'life events' or 'transitions', there will remain an inevitable requirement to make help available in unpredictable circumstances, when financial and other crises arise. NACAB argues that payments made available in such cases should be in the form of grants, and that restrictions on the rules of eligibility should be relaxed to avoid arbitrary and unfair disqualifications (Barton, 2002).

In terms of delivery mechanisms, the inflexibility and fettered nature of discretion experienced under the centrally administered social fund, renders the kind of localised schemes evident in other countries quite attractive. The Belgian model, for example, appears to bring sensitive forms of assessment and delivery much closer to the communities that are served (Hermans and Declercq, Chapter 2). The Hardship Fund operating in Glasgow might also provide a potential model for a form of provision which is much more closely attuned to local needs (see Smith, Chapter 5). As we have already suggested, changes in the structure of the social fund must be accompanied by a delivery culture based on notions of rights and fairness. This requires, for example, ready access to review procedures and appeal mechanisms, and a more active and purposeful use of such facilities to achieve collective as well as individualised justice (see Buck, Chapter 8).

This brief summary of the potential reform agenda for the social fund is based on the recognition that there are fundamental weaknesses embedded in the fund as it is currently constituted. If it is genuinely to play a part in the arsenal of measures to counter disadvantage and bring poverty to an end, then a programme of substantial and radical reform is essential.

Notes

1 Direction 3 of the Social Fund Guide issued by the Secretary of State imposes implicit restrictions on the circumstances in which social fund payments can be made in the event of an emergency.

> 'Subject to directions 14, 16 and 17 a social fund payment may be awarded to assist an applicant to meet expenses (except those excluded by these directions) –
> (a) in an emergency, or as a consequence of a disaster, provided that the provision of such assistance is the *only* means by which *serious* damage or *serious* risk to the health or safety of that person, or to a member of his family, may be prevented.... [our emphasis]' (*Social Fund Guide*, 2002).

2   'The Old poor law actually stigmatized the poor with moral delinquency in its statutory provisions. The leading example is the Act of 1697 (8 and 9 Will.III, c.30), which obliged all those receiving poor relief to wear the letter "P" on the right shoulder of their uppermost garment (s.2). Badging the poor was applied at the local level and seems to have continued in some areas even after the legislation was repealed in 1810. Critics such as Joseph Townsend argued that badging discouraged "only the ingenuous, the immodest, and the meek... The modest would sooner die than wear it"' (Cranston, 1985, p.35).

3   This phrase is most commonly associated with Frank Field M.P., who was appointed as Minister for Social Security in the incoming 1997 Labour government with a mandate to put a radical programme of reforms in place. His ambitious project quickly foundered in the face of brute reality and political expediency (Dean, 1999).

4   The money advice service offered by social fund officials was ended in April 1996: 'Because it was found that the service that could be provided by Social Fund Officers was very limited, there was a very low customer take up, and other outside bodies such as the Citizens Advice Bureau were able to provide a comprehensive service' (Peter Mathieson, Chief Executive of the Benefits Agency, Written Answers, House of Commons, vol. 276, col. 253, 25th April 1996).

Bibliography

Abramson, L., Garber, J. and Seligman, M. (1980) 'Learned Helplessness in Humans: an attributional analysis' in Garber, J. and Seligman, M. (eds.) *Human Helplessness: theory and applications*, Academic Press, Orlando.

Adler, M. and Asquith, S. (1981) *The politics of discretion*, Heinemann, London.

Adler, M. and Bradley, A. (1975) *Justice, discretion and poverty*, Professional Books, London.

Alcock, P. and Craig, G. (eds.) (2001) *International Social Policy*, Palgrave, Basingstoke, especially Chapter 7, 'The United Kingdom', pp.126-142.

Alcock, P., *et al* (1990) *Advice centres and the Social Fund*, Unpublished mimeo.

Association of Directors of Social Services (1982) *The monitoring of the new Supplementary Benefits scheme*, ADSS, mimeo.

Aznar, G. *et al* (1996) 'Vers un revenu minimum inconditionnel', *Revue du MAUSS*, no.7, 1st Semester 1996, La Découverte/MAUSS, Paris.

Baldwin, J., Wikeley, N. and Young, R. (1992) *Judging Social Security: The Adjudication of Claims for Benefit in Britain*, Clarendon Press, Oxford.

Barnardo's (1990) *Missing the target*, Barnardo's, Ilford.

Barton, A. (2002) *Unfair and underfunded: CAB evidence on what's wrong with the Social Fund*, NACAB, London.

Becker, S. (1989) 'Small change', *Benefits Research*, No. 3, July, pp.9-14.

Becker, S. and Silburn, R. (1990) *The New Poor Clients: Social Work, Poverty and the Social Fund*, Benefits Research Unit, Nottingham.

Belorgey, J.-M. (1988) *La Gauche et les Pauvres*, Syros Alternatives Sociales, Paris.

Beltram, G. (1984a) *Testing the safety net*, Bedford Square Press, London.

Beltram, G. (1984b) 'Seeing it from the other side', *New Society*, 16 August, pp.140-1.

Bennett, F. (1989) 'The Social Fund in Context', in Craig, G. (ed.) *Your Flexible Friend: Voluntary Organisations, Claimants and the Social Fund*, Social Security Consortium, London.

Beresford, P., Green, D., Lister, R. and Woodard, K. (1999) *Poverty first hand: Poor people speak for themselves*, Child Poverty Action Group, London.

Berthoud, R. (1984) *The reform of supplementary benefit*, Policy Studies Institute, London.

Blair, T. (1999) 'Beveridge revisited: a welfare state for the 21st century' (the Beveridge Lecture, Toynbee Hall, 18th March 1999) reproduced in Walker, R. (ed.) *Ending Child Poverty: popular welfare for the 21st century*, Policy Press, Bristol.

Bolderson, H. (1988) 'The Right to Appeal and the Social Fund' *Journal of Law and Society*, Vol 15.3.

Bonner, D., Buck, T. and Sainsbury, R. (2001) 'Researching the Role and Work of the Social Security and Child Support Commissioner', *Journal of Social Security Law*, pp.9-34.

Bouget, D. (2001) 'The movements by the unemployed in France and social protection: the Fonds d'Urgence Sociale Experience' in Andersen, J.G. and Jensen P.H. (eds.) *Changing Labour Markets, Welfare Policies and Citizenship*, Policy Press, Bristol.

Bouget, D. and Nogues, H. (1996) 'Le revenu d'existence' in S. Paugam (ed.) *L'exclusion, l'Etat des Savoirs*, Paris: La Découverte, pp.540-53.

Bradshaw, J. (2001) 'Child Poverty under Labour' in Fimister, G. (ed.) (2001) *An End in Sight? Tackling Child Poverty in the UK*, Child Poverty Action Group, London.

Brundage, A. (2002) *The English Poor Laws, 1700-1930*, Palgrave, Basingstoke.

Buck, T. (1996) *The Social Fund: Law and Practice* (1st ed.), Sweet & Maxwell, London.

Buck, T. (1998) 'Judicial Review and the discretionary Social Fund: The Impact on a Respondent Organization' in Buck, T. (ed.) *Judicial Review and Social Welfare*, Citizenship and Law Series, Pinter, London & Washington.

Buck, T. (2000) *The Social Fund: Law and Practice* (2nd ed.), Sweet & Maxwell, London.

Buck, T. (2001) 'A Model of Independent Review?' in Partington M. (ed.) *The Leggatt Review of Tribunals: Academic Seminar Papers*, Bristol Centre for the Study of Administrative Justice, Working Paper Series No. 3, pp. 127-140.

Cantillon, B. *et al* (2001) *De welvaartsvastheid en adequaatheid van de sociale minima 1970-2001*, Centrum voor Sociaal Beleid, Antwerpen.

Castel, R. (1995) *Les métamorphoses de la question sociale. Une chronique du salariat*, Fayard, Paris.

Chappuis, R. (1999) *La solidarité: L'éthique des relations humaines*, Que sais-je?, Presses Universitaires de France, Paris.

Choffé, T. (2001) 'Social exclusion: Definition, Public Debate and Empirical Evidence in France' in D. Mayes, J. Berghman and R. Salais (eds.) *Social Exclusion and European Policy*, Edward Elgar, Cheltenham, pp.204-29.

Citizens Advice Bureaux - Scotland (2001) *Memorandum of Evidence to the Social Security Committee, Citizens Advice Bureaux - Scotland*, in House of Commons (2001) *op cit*, pp.157-167.

Clarke, J. and Newman, J. (1997) *The Managerial State*, Sage, London.

Clasen, J. (1999) 'Introduction' in Clasen, J. (ed.) (1999) *Comparative Social Policy*. Blackwell, Oxford.

Clements, T. (1989) 'Port Talbot Community Care Grant take-up campaign', *Benefits Research*, No. 4, November, pp.11-12.

Cleveland County Council (1989) *For richer, for poorer?*, Cleveland County Council Welfare Rights Service, Middlesbrough.

Cohen, R., Coxall J., Craig, G. and Sadiq-Sangster, A. (1992) *Hardship Britain: Being Poor in the 1990s*, Child Poverty Action Group, London.

Cohen, R., Ferres, G., Hollins, C., Long, G. and Smith, R. (1996) *Out of Pocket*, The Children's Society, London.

Cohen, R. and Tarpey, M. (1988) *Single payments: the disappearing safety net*, Poverty Pamphlet No. 74, Child Poverty Action Group, London.

Cole, D. and Utting, J. (1962) *The economic circumstances of old people*, Occasional papers in social administration no. 4, Coldicote Press, London.

Commission on Social Justice (1994) *Social Justice: Strategies for National Renewal*, Vintage, London.

Comptroller and Auditor General (1993) *The Social Fund Accounts 1991-1992*, March 8 1993 (HC 542), The Stationery Office, London.

Comptroller and Auditor General (1994) *The Social Fund Accounts 1992-1993*, February 10, 1994 (HC 213), The Stationery Office, London.

Council on Tribunals (1986) *Social Security – Abolition of independent appeals under the proposed Social Fund*, Special Report, Cmnd. 9722.

CPAG (1969) *A policy to establish the rights of low income families*, Child Poverty Action Group, London.

CPAG (1981) *Memorandum of evidence to the Social Security Advisory Committee*, mimeo.

CPAG (1986) *Briefing on the proposed changes to the Single Payments Regulations*, Child Poverty Action Group, London, Mimeo.

CPAG (1987) *Poverty* 67, Summer.

CPAG (2001) *Memorandum of Evidence to the Social Security Committee, Child Poverty Action Group*, in House of Commons (2001) *op cit.*, pp.87-95.

Craig, G. (1988) 'The nightmare lottery of the Social Fund', *Social Work Today*, 24 November, pp.15-7.

Craig, G. (1990) 'Watching the Social Fund', in Manning, N. and Ungerson, C. (eds.), *Social Policy Review 1989-90*, Longman, Harlow.

Craig, G. (1991) 'Life on the social', *Social Work Today*, 28 March, pp.16-17.

Craig, G. (1992) *Replacing the Social Fund: a structure for reform*, Joseph Rowntree Foundation/Social Policy Research Unit, York.

Craig, G. (1992a) 'Managing the poorest' in Jeffs, T., Carter, P. and Smith, J. (eds.), *Changing social work and welfare*, Open University Press, Buckingham.

Craig, G. (1997) 'The privatisation of human misery', *Critical Social Policy*, February, pp.67-91.

Craig, G. (2001) 'Race and New Labour' in Fimister, G. (ed.) (2001) *An End in Sight? Tackling Child Poverty in the UK*, Child Poverty Action Group, London.

Craig, G. and Datta, J. (2000) *Meeting local poverty*, Social Research Paper No. 5, University of Hull, Hull.

Cranston, R. (1985) *Legal Foundations of the Welfare State*, Weidenfeld and Nicolson, London.

Cuypers, D. *et al* (2001) *Het bestaansminimum en de maatschappelijke dienstverlening door de rechtspraak van het jaar 2000*, Ministerie van Sociale Integratie, Brussels.

Dalley, G. and Berthoud, R. (1992) *Challenging Discretion: The Social Fund Review Procedure*, Policy Studies Institute, London.

Dallison, J. and Labstein, T. (1995) *Poor Expectations: poverty and under nourishment in pregnancy*, NCH Action for Children and the Maternity Alliance, London.

Davies, C. (1989) 'Issues for the Claimant' in Craig, G. (ed.) *Your Flexible Friend? Voluntary Organisations, Claimants and the Social Fund*, Social Security Consortium, London.

Davis, J. (1969) *Discretionary justice, a preliminary inquiry*, Urbana, Chicago.

De Gaulle Anthonioz, G. (2001) *Le secret de l'espérance*, Fayard, Paris.

De Lathouwer, L. *et al* (1997) *Jongeren in de bijstand. Een onderzoek naar de groeiende categorie van jonge bestaansminimumtrekkers*, Centrum voor Sociaal Beleid, Antwerpen.

De Maillard, J. (2000) 'Le partenariat en représentations: contributions à l'analyse des nouvelles politiques sociales territorialisées', Politique et Management Public, Vol.18, No.3, pp.21-42.

Dean, H. (1999) 'Citizenship' in Powell, M. (ed.) New Labour, New Welfare State?, Policy Press, Bristol.

Debt on our Doorstep (2001) Memorandum of Evidence to the Social Security Committee, Debt on our Doorstep, in House of Commons (2001) op cit., pp.41-54.

Dehaes, V. *et al* (2000) De bijstandspopulatie in Vlaanderen. Het bestaansminimum, CBGS, Brussels.

Dehaes, V. *et al* (2001) *De bijstandspopulatie in Vlaanderen. De maatschappelijke dienstverlening van financiële aard*, CBGS, Brussels.

Delhoume, B. (2001) 'L'aide sociale générale' in M. de Montalembert (ed.) *La protection sociale en France*, 3rd edition, La Documentation Francaise, Paris, pp.96-100.

Demazière, D. (1996) 'Des chômeurs sans représentation collective: une fatalité?', *Esprit*, No.11, p.12.

Demazière, D. and Pignoni, M. T. (1998) *Chômeurs: du silence à la révolte. Sociologie d'une action collective*, Hachette, Paris.

Department for Work and Pensions (2001) *Report on the Social Fund, Reply by the Government to the Third Report of the Social Security Committee, Session 2000-01 [HC 232]*, Cm 5237, July 2001.

Department for Work and Pensions (2002a) *Measuring Child Poverty*, consultation document, Corporate Document Services, London.

Department for Work and Pensions (2002b) *Households Below Average Income 1994/95 – 2000/01*, The Stationery Office, London.

Department of Health and Social Security (1985a) *Reform of Social Security Vol 1*, Cmnd. 9517, HMSO, London.

Department of Health and Social Security (1985b) *Reform of Social Security Vol 2*, Cmnd. 9518, HMSO, London.

Department of Health and Social Security (1985c) *Reform of Social Security: Programme for action*, 'White paper', *Cmnd. 9691*, HMSO, London.

Department of Health and Social Services (1978) *Social Assistance: A Review of the Supplementary Benefits Scheme in Great Britain*, HMSO, London.

Department of Social Security (1998) *New Ambitions For Our Country: A New Contract for Welfare*, 'Green Paper', Cm 3805, Stationery Office, London.

Department of Social Security (1999) *The revised social fund budgeting loan scheme: a description of the scheme*, Social Fund Policy Branch, London.

Department of Social Security (2000) *Opportunity for all - One year on: making a difference*, Cm 4865, The Stationery Office, London.

Department of Social Security (2001) *Family Resources Survey Statistical Report 1999-2000*, Corporate Document Services, London.

Ditch, J. (1995) 'Comparing discretionary payments within social assistance schemes', in Guillemard, A.M., Lewis, J., Ringen, S. and Salais, R. (eds.) *Comparing Social Welfare Systems in Europe*, Vol. 1, pp.337-367, Oxford Conference Mission Recherche et Experimentation, Paris.

Ditch, J. and Oldfield, N. (1999) 'Social Assistance: Recent Trends and Themes', *Journal of European Social Policy*, 9(1), 65-76.

Ditch, J., Bradshaw, J., Clasen, J., Huby, M. and Moodie, M. (1997) *Comparative social assistance, localisation and discretion*, Ashgate Publishing, Aldershot.

Dobson, B., Kellard, K.V. and Talbot, D. (2000) *A Recipe for Success? An Evaluation of a Community Food Project*, Centre for Research in Social Policy, Loughborough.

Donzelot, J. and Estebe, P. (1994) *L'Etat animateur: essai sur la politique de la ville*, Esprit, Paris.

Dowler, E., Turner, S. and Dobson, B. (2001) *Poverty Bites: Food, health and poor families*, Child Poverty Action Group, London.

Eardley, T., Bradshaw, J., Ditch, J., Gough, I. and Whiteford, P. (1996a) *Social Assistance in OECD Countries, Vol I: Synthesis Report*. Paris: OECD.

Eardley, T., Bradshaw, J., Ditch, J., Gough, I. and Whiteford, P. (1996b) *Social Assistance in OECD Countries, Vol II: Country Reports*. Department of Social Security Research Reports no. 47, HMSO, London.

Esping-Andersen, G. (1990) *Three Worlds of Welfare Capitalism*, Polity Press, Cambridge.

Esping-Andersen, G. (1999) *The Social Foundations of Post-Industrial Economies*, Oxford University Press, Oxford.

Esping-Andersen, G. (2000) 'Challenge to the welfare state in the 21st century', paper presented at the conference *Comparer les systèmes de protection sociale en Europe*, Conference organised by the MIRE, Ministry of Employment and Solidarity, Paris, 8-9 June.

European Commission (1999) *Commission Report on the implementation of the Recommendation 92/441/EEC of 24 June 1992 on common criteria concerning sufficient resources and social assistance in social protection systems (COM(98)774 final)*. http://europa.eu.int/comm/employment_social/soc-prot/social/index_en.htm.

Fassin, D. (2001) 'Charité bien ordonnée. Principes de justice et pratiques de jugement dans l'attribution des aides d'urgences', *Revue Française de Sociologie*, vol.42, no.3, pp.437-475.

Fassin, D., Defossez, A.C. and Thomas, V. (2000) 'Les inégalités des chances dans l'accès au secours d'urgence', *Revue Française des Affaires Sociales*, vol.55, no.1, pp. 121-38.

Ferrera, M. (1996) 'The Southern Model of Welfare in Social Europe', *Journal of European Social Policy*, vol. 6, no. 1, pp.17-37.

Fimister, G. (ed.) (2001) *An End in Sight? Tackling Child Poverty in the UK*, Child Poverty Action Group, London.

Forest, L. (2001) *Oral Evidence to the Social Security Committee, Liz Forest*, in House of Commons (2001) *op cit.*, pp.48-55.

Franks Commission (1957) (Chair O. Franks) *Report of the committee on administrative tribunals and enquiries*, Cmnd. 218, HMSO, London.

Giddens, A. (1999) 'Why the old left is wrong on poverty' in *New Statesman* (25 October).

Gloucoziezoff, G. (2001) *L'exclusion bancaire et financière des particuliers: du droit à l'accès à l'autonomie*, MPhil Dissertation, Université Lumière Lyon II.

Golding, P. and Middleton, S. (1982) *Images of Welfare*, Blackwell and Robertson, Oxford.

Gordon, D., Adelman, A., Ashworth, K., Bradshaw, J., Levitas, R., Middleton, S., Pantazis, C., Patsios, D., Payne, S., Townsend, P. and Williams, J. (2000) *Poverty and Social Exclusion in Britain*, Joseph Rowntree Foundation, York.

Guibentif, P. and Bouget, D. (1997) *Les politiques du revenu minimum dans l'Union Européenne*, Ministère de la Solidarité et de la Sécurité Sociale, Lissabon.

Handler, J.F. (1979) *Protecting the social service client*, Academic Press, New York.

Handler, J.F. and Hasenfeld, Y. (1991) *The moral construction of poverty: Welfare reform in America*, Sage, Newbury Park USA.

Handler, J.F. and Hollingsworth (1971) *'The deserving poor': a study of welfare administration*. Institute for research on poverty monograph series, Academic Press: New York/London.

Harris, N. (2000) *Social Security Law in Context*, Oxford University Press, Oxford.

Hasenfeld, Y. (1999) 'State bureaucratic discretion and the administration of social welfare programs: the case of social security disability', *Journal of Public Administration Research and Theory*, 9 (1), 1-20.

Hasenfeld, Y. and Weaver, D. (1996) 'Enforcement, Compliance, and Disputes in Welfare-to-Work Programs', *Social Sciences Review*, Vol. 70, no. 2, pp.235-256.

Heclo, H. (1974) *Modern Social Politics in Britain and Sweden: from relief to income maintenance*, Yale University Press, New Haven/London.

Henry, M. (2002) 'Inondations : Les oubliés d'Alès', *Libération*, 12 September 2002.

Hewitt, M. (1999) 'New Labour and social security' in Powell, M. (ed.) *New Labour, New Welfare State?* Policy Press, Bristol.

Hill, M. (1969) 'The exercise of discretion in the National Assistance Board', *Public Administration*, Spring, pp.75-80.

Hill, M. (1990) *Social security policy in Britain*, Edward Elgar, Aldershot.

Hill, M. (1993) *Understanding social policy*, Blackwell, Oxford.

Hills, J. (ed.) (1995) *The Commission on Income and Wealth*, Two Volumes, Joseph Rowntree Foundation, York.

HM Treasury (1999) *Access to financial services*. Report of PAT 14, HM Treasury, London.

HM Treasury (1999a) *The modernisation of Britain's tax and benefits system (No 5) Supporting Children through the Tax and Benefit System*, November 1999.

HMSO (1985) *Reform of social security: Programme for change*, 'Green paper', Cmnd. 9517-9, HMSO, London.

HMSO (1986) *Supplementary Benefit Regulations Etc.*, Cmnd. 9836, HMSO, London.

Hodge, H. (1975) 'Discretion in reality' in Adler, M. and Bradley, A. (1975) *Justice, discretion and poverty*, Professional Books, London, pp.65-76.

Hogwood, B. and Gunn, L. (1985) *Policy analysis for the real world*, Oxford University Press, Oxford.

Holman, R. (2001) *Memorandum of Evidence to the Social Security Committee, Dr. Bob Holman*, in House of Commons (2001) *op cit.*, p.55.

Holterman, S. (1995) *All our futures: the impact of public expenditure and fiscal policies on Britain's children and young people*, Barnardo's, Barkingside.

House of Commons (1990) *Low income statistics*, Select Committee on Social Services, Fourth Report, 30 April 1990.

House of Commons (2001) *The Social Fund*, Third Report (HC 232), 4th April 2001, Select Committee on Social Security, The Stationery Office, London.

House of Commons (2002) *Adjournment Debate on Third Report from the Social Security Committee, Session 2000–01, HC 232, and the Government's response thereto*, Cm 5237, *Hansard*, H.C., cols. 239-274WH, 18 April 2002.

Howard, M. (2002) 'Like It or Lump It', Child Poverty Action Group, London.

Howard, M., Garnham, A., Fimister, G. and Veit-Wilson, J. (2001) *Poverty: The facts* (4th ed.), Child Poverty Action Group, London.

Howe, L.E.A. (1985) 'The deserving and the undeserving: practice in an urban local social security office', *Journal of Social Policy*, 14, 1, pp.49-72.

Huby, M. and Dix, G. (1992) *Evaluating the Social Fund*, DSS Research Report Number 9, HMSO, London.

Hupe, P. L. (1990) 'Implementing a Meta-Policy: the case of decentralisation in the Netherlands', *Policy and Politics*, Vol. 18 no. 3, pp.181-191.

Ignatieff, M. (1990) *The Needs of Strangers*, The Hogarth Press, London.

Isambert, F.-A. (1996) 'L'engagement humanitaire et les formes contemporaines de la solidarité' in S. Paugam (ed.) *L'exclusion, l'Etat des Savoirs*, Paris: La Découverte, pp.101-107.

Jacquier, C. (2001) 'Urban Fragmentation and Revitalization Policies in France: A New Urban Governance in the Making' in H.T. Andersen and R. van Kempen (eds.) *Governing European Cities: Social Fragmentation, Social Exclusion and Urban Governance*, Ashgate, Aldershot, pp.321-46.

Johnson, P. and Webb, S. (1990) *Poverty in official statistics: Two reports*, Institute of Fiscal Studies, London.

Jones, C. and Novak, T. (1999) *Poverty, Welfare and the Disciplinary State*, Routledge, London.

Kempson, E. (1996) *Life on a low income*. Policy Press, Bristol.

Kempson, E., Bryson, A. and Rowlingson, K. (1994) *Hard times? How poor families make ends meet*, Policy Studies Institute, London.

Kempson, E., Collard, S. and Taylor, S. (2002) *Exploring Social Fund use among older people*, Corporate Document Services, Leeds.

Kenway, P. and Palmer, G. (2002) 'What Do The Poverty Numbers Really Show?', *Policy Analysis No 3*, New Policy Institute, London.

Lammertyn, F. *et al* (1990) *Armoede en OCMW. Een onderzoek naar de financiële steunverlening door de Vlaamse OCMW's*, SOI, Leuven.

Lane, J.E. (1995) *The public sector: Concepts, models and approaches*, Sage, London.

Le Duigou, J.-C. (2000) *Endettement et surendettement des ménages*, Avis et Rapports du Conseil Economique et Social, Les Editions des Journaux Officiels, Paris.

Legislative notes (1989/90) (21 644) to the Dutch Act of decentralisation of Bijzondere Bijstand. Year of assembly 1989-1990. Lower House of the Dutch Parliament.

Leibfried, S. (2000) 'Towards a European Welfare State?' in Pierson, C. and Castles, F.G. (2000) *The Welfare State Reader*, Polity Press, Oxford.

Leith Rights Forum (1989) *Social Fund monitoring exercise*, Leith Rights Forum, Edinburgh.

Lenoir, D. (1996) 'L'exclusion face au droit', in S. Paugam (ed.), *L'exclusion, l'Etat des Savoirs*, Paris: La Découverte, pp.78-87.

Lenoir, R. (1974) *Les exclus. Un français sur dix*, Le Seuil, Paris.

Levitas, R. (1998) *The Inclusive Society? Social Exclusion and New Labour*, Macmillan, London.

Lipsky, M. (1980) *Street-level Bureaucracy. Dilemmas of the Individual in Public Services*. Russell Sage Foundation, New York.

Lipsky, M. (1981) 'The Welfare State as Workplace', in *Public Welfare*, Summer 1981, Vol.39, pp.22-27.

Lister, R. (1973) 'The report of the committee on abuse of social security benefits', *Poverty*, 26, pp.9-11.

Lister, R. (1989) 'Conclusion: Privatising Need' in Craig, G. (ed.) *Your Flexible Friend? Voluntary Organisations, Claimants and the Social Fund*, Social Security Consortium, London, pp. 58-70.

Lister, R. (1990) *The Exclusive Society: Citizenship and the Poor*, Child Poverty Action Group, London.

Lister, R. and Emmett, T. (1976) *Under the safety net*, Poverty Pamphlet No. 25, Child Poverty Action Group, London.

Local Government Association (2001) *Memorandum of Evidence to the Social Security Committee, Local Government Association*, in House of Commons (2001) *op cit.*, pp.66-78.

Loisy, C. (2000) 'Pauvreté, précarité et exclusion. Définitions et Concepts', Cahier No.1 des Travaux de l'Observatoire national de la pauvreté et de l'exclusion, La Documentation Francaise, Paris.

Luyten, D. (1993) *OCMW en armenzorg. Een sociologische studie naar de sociale grenzen van het recht op bijstand*, Sociologisch Onderzoekscentrum, Leuven.

Mack, J. and Lansley, S. (1992) *Breadline Britain in the 1990s*, Routledge, London.

Mackenzie, L. (2001) *Oral Evidence to the Social Security Committee, LizMcKenzie*, in House of Commons (2001) *op cit.*, pp.48-55.

March, J. and Olson, J. (1989) *Rediscovering Institutions*, The Free Press, New York.

Marshall, R. (1972) *Families receiving supplementary benefit*, HMSO, London.

Mashaw, J.L. (1983) *Bureaucratic Justice: Managing Social Security Disability Claims*, Yale University, New Haven.

Mead, L. M. (1997) (ed.) *The New Paternalism: Supervisory Approaches to Poverty*, The Brookings Institute, Washington D.C.

Millar, J. and Ridge, T. (2001) *Families, Poverty, Work and Care: A review of literature on lone parents and low-income couple families*, Research Report No. 153, Department for Work and Pensions, Corporate Document Services, Leeds.

Ministry for Social Affairs and Employment (1990) *Social Security in the Netherlands*. Kluwer Law and taxation Publishers, Deventer, Boston.

MISSOC (2000) *Social Protection in the Member States of the EU and European Economic Area*, Luxemburg: Office for Official Publication of the European Communities, http://europa.eu.int/comm/employment_social/missoc2000/index_f_en.htm

Morel, S. (2000) *Les logiques de la réciprocité. Les transformations de la relation d'assistance aux Etats-Unis et en France*, Presses Universitaires de France, Paris.

Morley, B. (1990) 'Charities, the Social Fund, and income support', *Benefits Research* No.5, February, pp.10-13.

Muffels, R., Fouarge, D. and Dekker, R. (2000) *Longitudinal poverty and inequality: A comparative panel study for the Netherlands, Germany and the UK*, EPAG Working Paper 1, Tilburg Institute for Social Security Research, Netherlands.

National Association of Citizens' Advice Bureaux (2000) *CAB evidence on the April 1999 changes to the Social Fund scheme: Submission to the Social Fund Commissioner*, NACAB, London.

National Association of Citizens' Advice Bureaux (2001) *Memorandum of Evidence to the Social Security Committee, NACAB*, in House of Commons (2001) *op cit.*, pp.95-106.

National Audit Office (1991) *The Social Fund*, HC 190, National Audit Office, London.

National Statistics (May 2001) *Quarterly Statistical Enquiry: Income Support*, National Statistics, London.

Nelson, M. (2000) 'Childhood nutrition and poverty', Proceedings of the Nutrition Society 2000, 59:1-9.

Neveu, E. (1996) *Sociologie des mouvements sociaux*, La Découverte, Paris.

New Policy Institute (2002) 'Monitoring Poverty and Social Exclusion: Key Facts', NPI website: http://www.poverty.org.uk/summary/key_facts.htm.

New Policy Institute (2002a) *Reforming Social Fund Budgeting Loans*, New Policy Institute, London.

New Policy Institute (2002b) *The Social Fund: Opportunities for Reform*, New Policy Institute, London.

Newman, J. (2001) *Modernising Governance*, Sage, London.

Nicaise, I. (1999) 'Activering van werkloosheidsuitkeringen: van vraag-naar aanbodstrategie', in Van Hoof J., Mevissen, J. (ed.) *In banen geleid. Nieuwe vormen van sturing op de arbeidsmarkt in België en Nederland*, Elsevier, Amsterdam.

Observatoire national de la pauvreté et de l'exclusion sociale (2002) *Rapport 2001/2002*, La Documentation Française, Paris.

OECD (1998) *The battle against exclusion. Social assistance in Belgium, the Czech Republic, the Netherlands and Norway*. OECD, Paris.

OECD (2002, forthcoming) *New Trends in the Non-profit Sector*, Organisation for Economic Cooperation and Development, Paris.

Oldfield, N. and Yu, A.C.S. (1993) *The cost of a child: living standards for the 1990s*, Child Poverty Action Group, London.

Palier, B. (1996) *Glossaire bilingue de la protection sociale*, Mire, Rencontres et Recherches, Paris.

Palier, B. (1997) 'A liberal dynamic in the transformation of French social welfare system' in J. Clasen (ed.) *Social Insurance in Europe*, Policy Press, Bristol, pp.84-106.

Palier, B. (2001) 'Reshaping the Social Policy Making Framework in France' in P. Taylor-Gooby (ed.) *Welfare States Under Pressure*, Sage, London, pp.52-74.

Palier, B. (2002) *Gouverner la Sécurité Sociale*, PUF, Paris.

Parker, H. (ed.) (1998) *Low cost but acceptable - A minimum income standard for the UK: Families with young children*, Policy Press, Bristol.

Paugam, S. (1991) *La disqualification sociale. Essai sur la nouvelle pauvreté*, Presses Universitaires de France, Paris.

Paugam, S. (1999) *L'Europe face à la pauvreté. Les expériences nationales de revenu minimum*, Documentation Française, Paris.

Paugam, S. (ed.) (1996) *L'exclusion, l'Etat des Savoirs*, La Découverte, Paris.

Pavillon, E. (1995) *La Fondation de France, 1969-1994. L'invention d'un mécénat contemporain*, Anthropos Historique, Paris.

Pressman, J.L. and Wildawsky, A. (1984) *Implementation. How great expectations are dashed in Oakland*, University of California Press, Berkeley.

Prosser, T. (1983) *Test Cases for the Poor*, Child Poverty Action Group, London.

Raphel, T. and Roll, J. (1984) *Carrying the can*, Poverty Pamphlet No. 63, Child Poverty Action Group, London.

Rees, A. (2000) 'Citizenship and Work Obligation in Britain and France' in J. Edwards and J.-P. Révauger (eds.) *Employment and Citizenship in Britain and France*, Ashgate, Aldershot, pp.200-26.

Richardson, G. and Sunkin, M. (1996) 'Judicial Review: questions of impact', *Public Law*, pp.79-103.

Roker, D. (1998) *Worth More Than This*, The Children's Society, London.

Rowe, M. (1999) 'Joined Up Accountability: bringing the citizen back', *Public Policy and Administration*, Vol.14, No.2, pp.91-102.

Rowe, M. (2002) 'Discretion and Inconsistency: implementing the Social Fund', *Public Money and Management*, Vol. 22, No.4, pp.19-24.

Rummery, K. and Glendinning, C. (1999) 'Negotiating Needs, Access and Gatekeeping: developments in health and community care policies in the UK and the rights of disabled and older citizens', *Critical Social Policy*, 19:3, pp.335-351.

Sadiq-Sangster, A. (1992) *Life on Income Support – an Asian experience*, Family Service Unit, London.

Salmon, J.M. (1998) *Le désir de société, des restaurants du cœur au mouvement des chômeurs*, La Découverte, Paris.

SBC (1973) *Exceptional needs payments*, Supplementary Benefits Administration Paper No. 4, Supplementary Benefits Commission, HMSO, London.

SBC (1976) *Annual Report of the Supplementary Benefits Commission, 1975*, Cmnd. 6615, HMSO, London.

SBC (1977) *Annual Report of the Supplementary Benefits Commission, 1976*, Cmnd. 6910, HMSO, London.

SBC (1980) *Annual Report of the Supplementary Benefits Commission, 1979*, Cmnd. 8033, HMSO, London.

Scott, J. (1994) *Poverty and Wealth*, Longman, London.

Secretary of State for Social Security (1989) *Annual Report by the Secretary of State for Social Security on the Social Fund 1988/1989*, Cm. 748, HMSO, London.

Secretary of State for Social Security (1992) *Annual Report by the Secretary of State for Social Security on the Social Fund 1991/1992*, Cm. 1992, HMSO, London.

Secretary of State for Work and Pensions (2001) *Annual Report by the Secretary of State for Work and Pensions on the Social Fund 2000/2001*, Cm. 5238, The Stationery Office, London.

Secretary of State for Work and Pensions (2002) *Annual Report by the Secretary of State for Work and Pensions on the Social Fund 2001/02*, Cm. 5492, The Stationery Office, London.

Servet, J.-M. (2000) 'L'exclusion: un paradoxe de la finance', *Revue d'Economie Financière*, no.58, pp.17-28.

Shaw, M., Dorling, D., Gordon, D. and Davey Smith, G. (2001) 'Health and Poverty' in G. Fimister, G. (ed.) (2001) *An End in Sight? Tackling Child Poverty in the UK*, Child Poverty Action Group, London.

Smith, R. (1990) *Under the Breadline*, The Children's Society, London.

Snape, D. and Molloy, D. with Kumar, M. (1999) *Relying on the State, Relying on each Other*, Department of Social Security, London.

Social Exclusion Unit (2000) National Strategy for Neighbourhood Renewal: a framework for consultation, Cabinet Office, London.

Social Fund Commissioner (2002) *Social Fund Commissioner's Annual Report 2001/02*, Corporate Document Services, Leeds.

Social Fund Guide (2002) Department of Work and Pensions, Corporate Document Services, Leeds.

Social Security Consortium (1989) *Your flexible friend?*, SSC, London (ed. G. Craig).

Social Security Research Consortium (1989) *Social Fund cases taken to advice centres*, Sheffield, SSRC, mimeo.

Social Security Research Consortium (1991) *Cash limited: limited cash*, SSRC, Association of Metropolitan Authorities, Lancaster.

Social Services Committee (1985) *Seventh Report: The Government's Green Paper 'Reform of Social Security'* (HC 451) 17th July 1985.

Spies, H. and van Berkel, R. (2001) 'Workfare in the Netherlands – young unemployed people and the Jobseeker's Employment Act. In Lødemel, I. and Trickey, H. (2001) (eds.) *An offer you can't refuse: Workfare in international perspective*, Policy Press, Bristol.

SSAC (1982) *First Report*, Social Security Advisory Committee, HMSO, London.

SSAC (1983) *Second Report*, Social Security Advisory Committee, HMSO, London.

SSAC (1985) *Fourth Report*, Social Security Advisory Committee, HMSO, London.

SSAC (1990) *Seventh Report*, Social Security Advisory Committee, HMSO, London.

SSAC (1992) *The Social Fund: a new structure*, Social Security Advisory Committee, HMSO, London.

Stewart, G. and Robertson, B. (1989) 'A vicious circle', *Community Care*, 16 November, pp.19-20.

Stone, D. (1984) *The Disabled State*, Macmillan, Houndmills.

Sunderland Welfare Rights Service (2001) *Memorandum of Evidence to the Social Security Committee, Sunderland Welfare Rights Service*, in House of Commons (2001) *op cit.*, pp.189-90.

Sunkin, M. and Pick, K. (2002) 'The Changing Impact of Judicial Review: The Independent Review Service of the Social Fund', *Public Law*, pp.736-762.

Sykes, R., Prior, P. and Palier, B. (eds.) (2001) *Globalization and European Welfare States: Challenges and Changes*, Macmillan, London.

Taylor-Gooby, P. (2001) *Welfare States Under Pressure*, Sage, London.

Tester, S. (1987) *Social Loans in the Netherlands*, Policy Studies Institute, London.

Titmuss, R. (1968) *Commitment to welfare*, Allen and Unwin, London.

Townsend, P. (1959) *The family life of old people*, Routledge Kegan Paul, London.

Tropman, J.E. (1993) 'The Catholic Ethic and Charitable Orientation in Transmitting the Tradition of a Caring Society to Future Generations', *Working Papers from Independent Sector's Spring Research Forum*, March, San Antonio, Texas, pp.379-92.

Van der Veen, R. (1993) 'Matthew effects in policy implementation', in Berghman, J. and Cantillon, B. (eds.), *The European face of social security*, Avebury, Aldershot, pp.153-171.

Van Oorschot, W. (1998) *The reconstruction of the Dutch social security system 1980-2000: retrenchment and modernisation*. CCWS Working paper no. 3/1998.

Van Oorschot, W. (2000) 'Who should get what and why? On deservingness criteria and the conditionallity of solidarity among the public.' In *Policy and Politics*, Vol.28, no. 1: pp. 38-48.

Van Oorschot, W. (2002) Miracle or Nightmare? A Critical Review of Dutch Activation Policies and their Outcomes, *Journal of Social Policy*, Vol. 31, 3, pp. 399-420.

Van Oorschot, W. and Smolenaars, E. (1993) *Local income assistance policies. The Dutch case and a European impression*. Work and Organization Research Centre (WORC) paper, 93.07.011/2B.

Veit-Wilson, J. (1998) *Setting Adequacy Standards: How governments define minimum incomes*, Policy Press, Bristol.

Vidana, J.-L. (2001) 'La lutte contre la pauvreté et l'exclusion' in M. de Montalembert (ed.) *La protection sociale en France*, 3rd edition, La Documentation Francaise, Paris, pp.144-54.

Vranken, J., Geldof, D., Van Menxel, G. and Van Ouytsel, J. (eds.) (2001) *Armoede en sociale uitsluiting. Jaarboek 2001*, Acco, Leuven.

Walker, C. (1983) *Changing social policy*, Bedford Square Press, London.

Walker, R., Dix, G. and Huby, M. (1992) *Working the Social Fund*, DSS Research Report No. 8, HMSO, London.

Ward, S. (1989) 'Efficient and Effective?' in Craig, G. (ed.) *Your Flexible Friend? Voluntary Organisations, Claimants and the Social Fund*, Social Security Consortium, London, pp. 11-23.

Webb, A. (1975) 'The abolition of national assistance' in Hall, P. (ed.), *Change, choice and conflict in social policy*, Heinemann, London, pp.410-471.

West, A., Pennell, H., West, R. and Travers, T. (1999) The financing of school based education: end of award report to the ESRC: main findings, Centre for Educational Research, London.

Whitehead, M. (1988) *Inequalities in Health - The Black Report - The Health Divide*, Penguin Books, London.

Whyley, C., Collard, S. and Kempson, E. (2000) *Saving and Borrowing: Use of the Social Fund Budgeting Loan scheme and Community Credit Unions*. DSS Research Report Number 125, Corporate Document Services, Leeds.

Wright, S. (2001) 'Activating the Unemployed: the street-level implementation of UK policy' in Clasen, J. (ed.) *What Future for Social Security? Debates and Reforms in National and Cross-National Perspective*, Kluwer Law International, The Hague.

Index